THE MARZANO SYNTHESIS

A Collected Guide to What Works in K–12 Education

JULIA A. SIMMS

Foreword by Robert J. Marzano

MARZANO Resources

555 North Morton Street
Bloomington, IN 47404
888.849.0851
FAX: 866.801.1447

email: info@MarzanoResources.com
MarzanoResources.com

Printed in the United States of America

FSC
www.fsc.org
MIX
Paper | Supporting responsible forestry
FSC® C008955

Library of Congress Cataloging-in-Publication Data

Names: Simms, Julia A., author.

Title: The Marzano synthesis : a collected guide to what works in K-12 education / Julia A. Simms.

Description: Bloomington, IN : Marzano Resources, 2024. | Includes bibliographical references and index.

Identifiers: LCCN 2023043618 (print) | LCCN 2023043619 (ebook) | ISBN 9781943360840 (paperback) | ISBN 9781943360857 (ebook)

Subjects: LCSH: Effective teaching. | Learning. | Marzano, Robert J.

Classification: LCC LB1025.3 .S558 2024 (print) | LCC LB1025.3 (ebook) | DDC 371.102--dc23/eng/20231024

LC record available at https://lccn.loc.gov/2023043618

LC ebook record available at https://lccn.loc.gov/2023043619

Production Team
President and Publisher: Douglas M. Rife
Associate Publishers: Todd Brakke and Kendra Slayton
Editorial Director: Laurel Hecker
Art Director: Rian Anderson
Copy Chief: Jessi Finn
Developmental Editor: Laurel Hecker
Copy Editor: Mark Hain
Proofreader: Charlotte Jones
Text and Cover Designer: Kelsey Hoover
Acquisitions Editor: Hilary Goff
Assistant Acquisitions Editor: Elijah Oates
Content Development Specialist: Amy Rubenstein
Associate Editor: Sarah Ludwig
Editorial Assistant: Anne Marie Watkins

To Bob and Jeff,
thank you.

TABLE OF CONTENTS

ABOUT THE AUTHOR

Julia A. Simms is vice president of Marzano Resources. A former classroom teacher, she heads a team that develops research-based resources and provides support to educators as they implement them. Her areas of expertise include effective instruction, learning progressions and proficiency scales, assessment and grading, argumentation and reasoning skills, and literacy development. She has coauthored ten books, including *A Handbook for High Reliability Schools*, *Coaching Classroom Instruction*, *Questioning Sequences in the Classroom*, *Teaching Argumentation*, *Teaching Reasoning*, and *The New Art and Science of Teaching Reading*.

Julia received a bachelor's degree from Wheaton College and master's degrees in educational administration and K–12 literacy from Colorado State University and the University of Northern Colorado.

FOREWORD

By Robert J. Marzano

I started teaching at the high school level in 1968 and began to seriously examine the research and theory on education in 1974 after receiving a PhD from the University of Washington. Some fifty years later, that endeavor has produced a great many works, all developed with the purpose of translating the research and theory into valid and useful programs and practices for educators. When someone gets to the last phases of such a career, their fondest wish is that their work will be improved on and passed on to others. This book does just that. Authored by Julia A. Simms, my colleague of over a decade, the book summarizes and critiques the major topics I have had the pleasure of exploring.

Occasionally, I have been asked, "How do you find topics to write about?" The first time this question was posed to me, I remember finding it odd that someone would have to "find new topics." It seemed to me that topics about which to write were always there and always obvious. On further reflection, I came to the conclusion that this is a byproduct of delving deeply into a specific issue, a discipline I learned from great professors at the University of Washington.

When you delve deeply into a topic, you eventually find its border and come to the realization that you must cross that border to understand it further. My first experience of that was a dissertation that put together the still-developing statistical field of exploratory and confirmatory factor analysis with the still-developing linguistics field of deep structure theory. That work provided me with baseline models for further statistical analyses and further examinations of how knowledge is processed, stored, retrieved, and utilized. This led to examinations of the processes of reading comprehension and writing which, in turn, led to examinations of thinking and reasoning skills which, in turn, led to examinations of effective teaching strategies, and so on.

Probably the most important generalization one should take away from Julia's synthesis is that education is a highly complex and highly integrated field. This implies that to improve the system, one must think well beyond a single intervention. While it is reasonable to identify and implement a single intervention, it is not reasonable to think that the identified intervention will have a robust effect on the entire system. Rather, one must consider how that intervention affects and is affected by the various aspects of the system that Julia articulates for us: instruction, curriculum, measurement, leadership, and so on. In effect, the more one is aware of the various components that interact with the K–12 system of schooling, the better the chances one has to make substantive improvements.

While Julia does an excellent job summarizing what I have written about the various components and updating the research and theory on those components, I believe there are burgeoning new awarenesses that are in need of immediate attention. Here I briefly comment on three such areas.

THE SELF-SYSTEM

If you go back to the 1990s, it is hard to find much discussion of the importance of the self-system in the day-to-day workings of schooling. In the 2020s, the self-system is directly and indirectly acknowledged as critical to many aspects of human motivation and how human beings interact with their environment. The new frontier in this domain is the awareness that the self-system creates a theory of the world regarding what has happened in the past, what is happening in the present, and what will happen in the future. In some writings, I have referred to this as the "theory of the world in one's mind," which I first read about in Frank Smith's 1971 book, *Understanding Reading*. He highlighted the importance of this theory as the vehicle by which we make sense of the world. What is new now is the understanding that these theories are personal and unique constructions of every human being. The implications for this are far reaching in many fields, not the least of which is education. If every student has their own unique theory of the world and their place in it, what does that imply for educators who are dealing with as many theories of the world as there are students in the school?

THE METACOGNITIVE AND COGNITIVE SYSTEMS

The metacognitive and cognitive systems have been discussed in education since the 1980s, during which time educators were developing K–12 curriculums to teach the knowledge and skills associated with these systems. At that time, the endeavor was referred to as "teaching thinking skills." Unfortunately, these curriculums faded away when the movement for high-stakes testing ramped up in the 1990s as a result of the standards movement. Luckily for educators, these skills are now back on the radar of K–12 educators and have been implicitly and explicitly recommended in state standards. But the curricular problem of the 1980s has also been reborn: How are these skills to be taught and assessed in the classroom?

THE TAUGHT CURRICULUM AND THE ASSESSED CURRICULUM

One of the more salient awarenesses that comes from an examination of the research and theory on curriculum and assessment is that what is tested must be taught if we are to be fair to the students we serve. Research and theory have demonstrated that there are many aspects of testing that are not taught to students but are a critical part of how well they perform on a test. The field that addresses this issue is referred to as *construct irrelevant variability* (CIV). While this might sound esoteric and unimportant to practitioners, unless CIV is addressed, the scores students receive on large-scale interim and end-of-year assessments will remain not only imprecise but also unfair, particularly for those students who do not have access to out-of-school support for learning the content tested on large-scale assessments.

This book by Julia A. Simms supplies the reader with a succinct summary of selected components of my theory of the world regarding K–12 education and brings them up to date on the research and theory that I did not cover relevant to that theory of the world. In the epilogue, Julia's parting recommendation to readers is for educators to take it on themselves to translate research and theory into actions they take in their classrooms and study the results of their actions to form their own well-designed theories of the world relative to education as opposed to waiting for researchers and theorists to provide it for them. I wholeheartedly agree with this suggestion.

—Robert J. Marzano

Reference

Smith, F. (1971). *Understanding reading: A psycholinguistic analysis of reading and learning to read.* New York: Holt, Rinehart, & Winston.

INTRODUCTION

Sometimes, the profession of education feels like guesswork. There is no shortage of specific guidance, from John Hattie's rank-ordered lists of educational factors (2009, 2012, 2015, 2023) to Bob Marzano's instructional strategies (2001, 2007, 2017, 2019a). Educators have a myriad of options when choosing professional learning topics, including curriculum, instruction, assessment, grading and reporting, school culture, educator wellness, school reform, and a host of content-specific (mathematics, English language arts, science, social studies) topics. But do we have a comprehensive picture of how all the pieces fit together?

The profession of education has suffered from a lack of organizing structures, and that absence threatens our professionalism as educators. Think of the medical field: at its core is an understanding of human body systems and how they interact with each other. Can you imagine if medical doctors didn't have the framework of the skeletal system, muscular system, circulatory system, pulmonary system, neurological system, endocrine system, and so on to help them diagnose and treat patients? It would be unthinkable and reduce medicine to conjecture. In education, the systems of curriculum, instruction, assessment, and so on are analogous to the systems of a human body; educational systems help the different *structures* of the educational body work together effectively. If the structures of the educational body are students, teachers, and principals, they could be thought of as the head, torso, and limbs of a human body. Students (as the head) are the reason for education. The rest of the educational body exists to promote students' learning in the same way that the rest of the human body exists to support the head (that is, the brain). Teachers are analogous to the torso because without the vital organs in the torso, the brain cannot function. In the same way, without effective teachers, student learning does not happen. And finally, principals are analogous to limbs because effective principals allow students and teachers to function in a fully abled manner (as limbs support the function of the rest of the body).

Dealing with human subjects (such as patients or students) is messy and requires moment-by-moment decision making. I would assert that education is more difficult even than medicine, simply because educators are not often allowed adequate time or data to make important decisions. We must make decisions (that often have large implications) quickly and often only with the data currently available (which can be sparse). Education is what Laura Fries, Ji Son, Karen Givvin, and James Stigler (2021) called a "wicked domain"—one "marked by changing contexts and inconsistent or ambiguous feedback (Epstein 2019)" (p. 742). Given these challenges, it is our responsibility as education professionals to identify the education systems that cause "healthy" learners to thrive and allow us to provide systematic care if students are striving to overcome learning obstacles.

The good news is that this is possible. Since the early 19th century in the United States (and in many countries around the world), formal educational and psychological research have been investigating the systems of the educational body. However, simply because researchers have been investigating these topics does not necessarily mean that their research is always accessible or available to inform the "boots on the ground" practice of educators in schools and classrooms.

This brings me to one of my favorite subjects, the work of Robert J. Marzano. He prefers to be called Bob, and I will refer to him that way throughout this text. I met Bob after five years of teaching. As an alternatively certified teacher, I was deeply frustrated by how helpless I sometimes felt to help my students learn. I had amazing colleagues who shared all they knew, but a lot of that was strategies, tips, tricks, and little bits of their accumulated expertise that they thought would help me. They were giving me fish (and I appreciated it very much!), but I needed someone to teach me how to fish. To feel like I was succeeding—like I belonged in the profession and had something to offer—I needed the big picture. As Fries and colleagues (2021) wrote, "Experts do not see their domains in terms of bits; they see the underlying structure of the domain that makes their knowledge flexible and transferable" (p. 740). In short, I longed for the structural knowledge that would allow me to develop expertise.

Bob's work offers those frameworks, structures, and the strategies that fit into them—all of it supported by the accumulated research and theory of the past hundred years. The thrill of learning about "what works in K–12 education" has kept me working with Bob ever since. But as I learned about Bob's work and realized how many different educational areas it spanned, I also longed to figure out how all the pieces related to and interacted with each other. The advent of High Reliability Schools (HRS) in 2014 was a huge step in that direction; as an organizational structure and measurement process, I've never encountered anything more useful for school leaders. But in my heart, I'm a teacher. For several years, I've endeavored to integrate the frameworks, strategies, and topics Bob has written about over the past fifty years into a comprehensive framework that allows teachers to sort any educational issue into its proper category, associate it with relevant research and theory, and make an informed decision about the best way forward. I wanted to take all Bob's work and put it together with teachers as the primary audience. This book is that endeavor.

BOB'S WORK AND JULIA'S SYNTHESIS

When I was in college, a professor suggested selecting one author and reading everything that person had ever written. Bob is that author for me. To perform the synthesis that produced this book, I collected the sixty-four books that Bob has written as primary author or editor. I also included two important books for which he was a coauthor or coeditor. Table I.1 lists these works.

TABLE I.1: Books Analyzed for *The Marzano Synthesis*

Decade	Title
1970s	*DiComp: A Diagnostic Approach to Teaching Written Composition* (Marzano & DiStefano, 1977)
1980s	*The Writing Process* (Marzano & DiStefano, 1981)
	Reading Diagnosis and Instruction (Marzano, Hagerty, Valencia, & DiStefano, 1987)
	Tactics for Thinking: Teacher's Manual (Marzano & Arredondo, 1987)
	A Cluster Approach to Elementary Vocabulary Instruction (Marzano & Marzano, 1988)
	Dimensions of Thinking (Marzano et al., 1988)

Decade	Title
1990s	*Cultivating Thinking in English and the Language Arts* (Marzano, 1991) *A Different Kind of Classroom* (Marzano, 1992) *Assessing Student Outcomes* (Marzano, Pickering, & McTighe, 1993) *New Approaches to Literacy* (Marzano & Paynter, 1994) *A Comprehensive Guide to Designing Standards-Based Districts, Schools, and Classrooms* (Marzano & Kendall, 1996) *Dimensions of Learning: Teacher's Manual* (Marzano & Pickering, 1997) *Implementing Standards-Based Education* (Marzano & Kendall, 1998) *Essential Knowledge* (Marzano & Kendall, 1999)
2000s	*Transforming Classroom Grading* (Marzano, 2000) *Designing a New Taxonomy of Educational Objectives* (Marzano, 2001) *A Handbook for Classroom Instruction That Works* (Marzano, Norford, Paynter, Pickering, & Gaddy, 2001) *Classroom Instruction That Works* (Marzano, Pickering, & Pollock, 2001) *Classroom Management That Works* (Marzano, 2003a) *The Pathfinder Project: Teacher's Manual* (Marzano, Paynter, & Doty, 2003) *What Works in Schools* (Marzano, 2003b) *Building Background Knowledge for Academic Achievement* (Marzano, 2004) *Building Academic Vocabulary: Teacher's Manual* (Marzano & Pickering, 2005) *A Handbook for Classroom Management That Works* (Marzano, Gaddy, Foseid, Foseid, & Marzano, 2005) *School Leadership That Works* (Marzano, Waters, & McNulty, 2005) *Classroom Assessment and Grading That Work* (Marzano, 2006) *The Art and Science of Teaching* (Marzano, 2007) *The New Taxonomy of Educational Objectives* (Marzano & Kendall, 2007) *Designing and Assessing Educational Objectives* (Marzano & Kendall, 2008) *Making Standards Useful in the Classroom* (Marzano & Haystead, 2008) *Designing and Teaching Learning Goals and Objectives* (Marzano, 2009a) *District Leadership That Works* (Marzano & Waters, 2009) *A Handbook for the Art and Science of Teaching* (Marzano & Brown, 2009)
2010s	*Formative Assessment and Standards-Based Grading* (Marzano, 2010a) *On Excellence in Teaching* (Marzano, 2010b) *Teaching Basic and Advanced Vocabulary* (Marzano, 2010c) *Effective Supervision* (Marzano, Frontier, & Livingston, 2011) *The Highly Engaged Classroom* (Marzano & Pickering, 2011) *Leaders of Learning* (DuFour & Marzano, 2011) *Becoming a Reflective Teacher* (Marzano, 2012) *Teaching and Assessing 21st Century Skills* (Marzano & Heflebower, 2012) *Building Basic Vocabulary: Teacher's Guide* (Marzano, 2013) *Coaching Classroom Instruction* (Marzano & Simms, 2013a) *Teacher Evaluation That Makes a Difference* (Marzano & Toth, 2013) *Using Common Core Standards to Enhance Classroom Instruction and Assessment* (Marzano, Yanoski, Hoegh, & Simms, 2013)

continued →

Decade	Title
2010s	*Vocabulary for the Common Core* (Marzano & Simms, 2013b) *Handbook for High Reliability Schools* (Marzano, Warrick, & Simms, 2014) *Questioning Sequences in the Classroom* (Marzano & Simms, 2014) *Managing the Inner World of Teaching* (Marzano & Marzano, 2015) *Vocabulary for the New Science Standards* (Marzano, Rogers, & Simms, 2015) *Collaborative Teams That Transform Schools* (Marzano, Heflebower, Hoegh, Warrick, & Grift, 2016) *Proficiency Scales for the New Science Standards* (Marzano & Yanoski, 2016) *A Handbook for Personalized Competency-Based Education* (Marzano, Norford, Finn, & Finn, 2017) *Motivating and Inspiring Students* (Marzano, Scott, Boogren, & Newcomb 2017) *The New Art and Science of Teaching* (Marzano, 2017) *Leading a High Reliability School* (Marzano, Warrick, Rains, & DuFour, 2018) *Making Classroom Assessments Reliable and Valid* (Marzano, 2018) *The Handbook for The New Art and Science of Teaching* (Marzano, 2019a) *The New Art and Science of Classroom Assessment* (Marzano, Norford, & Ruyle, 2019) *Understanding Rigor in the Classroom* (Marzano, 2019b)
2020s	*Professional Learning Communities at Work and High Reliability Schools* (Eaker & Marzano, 2020) *Teaching Basic, Advanced, and Academic Vocabulary* (Marzano, 2020) *Improving Teacher Development and Evaluation* (Marzano, Rains, & Warrick, 2021) *Ethical Test Preparation in the Classroom* (Marzano, Dodson, Simms, & Wipf, 2022) *Leading a Competency-Based Elementary School* (Marzano & Kosena, 2022) *Teaching in a Competency-Based Elementary School* (Marzano & Abbott, 2022)

I summarized the content of these books and combined them with recent research. Specifically, I compiled all the articles published between January 2020 and June 2022 in the following scholarly education journals.

- *American Educational Research Journal*
- *Cognition and Instruction*
- *Computers and Education*
- *Contemporary Educational Psychology*
- *Educational Evaluation and Policy Analysis*
- *Educational Measurement*
- *Educational Psychologist*
- *Educational Psychology Review*
- *Educational Research Review*
- *Educational Researcher*
- *International Journal of Computer-Supported Collaborative Learning*
- *Journal of Educational Measurement*
- *Journal of Educational Psychology*
- *Journal of Research on Educational Effectiveness*
- *Journal of the Learning Sciences*
- *Learning and Instruction*
- *Review of Educational Research*
- *Review of Research in Education*

I reviewed the abstracts of these articles, excluded those which were not applicable to my analysis (typically those applying solely to higher education, early childhood, or other non-K–12 contexts), and summarized the contents of each remaining article.

To create the outline for this book, I did not bring a preconceived structure to the material. One of the most important lessons that Bob has taught me about thinking and translating research into practice is to allow the content to dictate the structure of the work (and not try to fit content into a predetermined structure). Therefore, the structure that emerged from my synthesis of Bob's work and research from the previously described date range is the structure of this book.

Given the volume of material I was working with, I inevitably had to draw lines about what to include and what to leave out. In addition to excluding non-K–12 research, I also decided to preserve breadth while limiting depth. First, I chose not to analyze content-specific topics. For example, there are no sections in this book specific to teaching mathematics, science, English language arts (ELA), social studies, or any other specific content area. While I value the content areas highly, and there is fascinating research related to them, the aim of this book is to synthesize topics and research for a broad K–12 educator audience, regardless of which specific content areas they might teach.

Second, the description of my synthesis in this book brings together a wide range of education topics and shows how they relate to and interact with each other by placing them within an organizing structure. By necessity, it does not provide in-depth discussions of individual topics. There may be cases where you are left thinking, "I want to know more about that!" or "Why didn't she go into more detail?" I have assiduously cited the sources of all the material in this book; please use those citations to deepen your understanding of specific topics.

RESEARCH INTO PRACTICE

The subtitle of this book was almost *A Collected Guide to What Might Work in K–12 Education*. Even though research seems definite, it's not. As Xu Qin, Stephanie Wormington, Alberto Guzman-Alvarez, and Ming-Te Wang (2021) succinctly stated, "Context matters" (p. 638). Bob emphasized this in *The Art and Science of Teaching*:

> Research will never be able to identify instructional strategies that work with every student in every class. The best research can do is tell us which strategies have a good chance (i.e., high probability) of working well with students. Individual classroom teachers must determine which strategies to employ with the right students at the right time. (Marzano, 2007, p. 5)

Writing about evidence-based reform in education, Robert Slavin (2020) explained:

> The problem is that it is almost never practically possible to sample experimental and control groups from within an entire population of interest, so there is always a possibility that a treatment that worked in one set of schools will not work in another. . . . For example, a large program evaluation that took place in Chicago and Baltimore might not generalize to Los Angeles or Phoenix, much less to suburban or rural locations. (p. 26)

In their meta-analysis of the effects of writing-to-learn programs on student achievement (effect size = 0.30), Steve Graham, Sharlene Kiuhara, and Meade MacKay (2020) cautioned:

> Teachers should not automatically assume that writing activities that were effective in the research studies reviewed here will automatically be effective in their classrooms. The conditions that exist in a research study and a teacher's class will not be identical. When using writing-to-learn activities, we encourage teachers to monitor if writing activities achieve the desired goals, and to make necessary adjustments if this is not the case. (p. 218)

In addition to the vagaries of context, all research studies contain error. Bob described this in *What Works in Schools*:

> It is almost impossible to control all the error that might creep into a study. This is why researchers assign a probability statement to their findings. When researchers report that their findings are significant at the .05 level, they are saying that there is a very small chance—less than 5 chances in 100—that their findings are a function of the uncontrolled error in the study. . . . By combining the results of many studies, we can say with far more certainty than we can with a single study that certain strategies work or do not work. (Marzano, 2003a, p. 7)

And that phrase—"combining the results of many studies"—is a key to making educational research more reliable and more generalizable. Specifically, when the results of many studies are combined, we call it a meta-analysis.

Meta-Analysis

A researcher named Gene Glass coined the term *meta-analysis* in his 1976 presidential address to the American Educational Research Association. Terri Pigott and Joshua Polanin (2020) explained that a "meta-analysis summarizes the results of several studies" (p. 25). In *School Leadership That Works*, Bob, Timothy Waters, and Brian A. McNulty (2005) described how a meta-analysis can mitigate the error inherent in any one study:

> Meta-analysis helps control for this error by examining findings across many studies. Doing this tends to cancel out much of that uncontrolled error. Whereas the findings in one study might be influenced positively by the background of teachers, let's say, another study might be influenced negatively by the same factor. Across many studies the effect of this factor tends to cancel out. (p. 8)

The metric commonly used to summarize results across studies is *effect size*. As Bob, Debra Pickering, and Jane E. Pollock (2001) explained in *Classroom Instruction That Works*, "an effect size expresses the increase or decrease in achievement of the experimental group (the group of students who are exposed to a specific instructional technique) in standard deviation units" (p. 4). But effect sizes are not as straightforward as you'd expect.

Effect Sizes and Their Drawbacks

Effect size, a statistical measure of an intervention's impact, can be impacted by a lot of things that have nothing to do with the actual intervention being studied. In the book *What Works in Schools*, Bob reported effect sizes for school-level factors (such as curriculum, goals, feedback, parent involvement, collegiality, and so on) and for teacher-level factors (such as instructional strategies and classroom management). He also articulated a qualifier:

> The average effect sizes [for teacher-level factors] look quite large if you contrast these effect sizes with those commonly reported for the school-level factors. . . . Why would the smallest effect size for the instructional strategies reported [0.59 for questions, cues, and advance organizers] . . . be greater than the largest effect size reported for the school level factors [0.39 for time]? It is because the studies from which the effect sizes [for teacher-level factors] were computed generally employed assessments specific to the content being taught while a particular instructional strategy was being used. . . . We might call such assessments "curriculum sensitive." The studies on school-level factors generally employ standardized tests that are more general in nature than such curriculum-sensitive assessments. When general tests are used as opposed to curriculum-sensitive tests, effect sizes by definition will be much smaller. (Marzano, 2003b, p. 81)

And it's not just assessments that impact effect sizes. Robert Slavin and Dewi Smith (2009) found a generally negative relationship between sample size and effect size in their review of 185 studies from elementary and secondary mathematics classrooms. That is, as sample sizes increased, effect sizes decreased. Essentially, the more students you have in the study, the harder it can be to show large effects.

Similarly, Mark Lipsey and colleagues (2012) found that individual or small-group interventions tended to have larger effect sizes (0.40 for individual and 0.26 for small-group) compared to classroom or school interventions (0.18 for classroom and 0.10 for school). And Rebecca Wolf, Jennifer Morrison, Amanda Inns, Robert Slavin, and Kelsey Risman (2020), in their analysis of 169 studies from the What Works Clearinghouse (IES), found that the average effect sizes in studies commissioned by program developers (who have a vested interest in positive outcomes) were 1.8 times larger than the average effect sizes in independent studies. Given that the Institute of Education Sciences (part of the U.S. Department of Education) commissioned the What Works Clearinghouse in 2002 to provide "a central and trusted source of scientific evidence of what works in education" (What Works Clearinghouse, 2017, p. 1), this evidence of bias is particularly disturbing.

To address these issues with effect sizes, some experts have suggested that we use alternative metrics to report the impact of interventions to educators. For example, Hugues Lortie-Forgues, Ut Na Sio, and Matthew Inglis (2021) compiled a list of non-effect-size metrics frequently used to report intervention impact, as shown in table I.2.

On one hand, Lortie-Forgues and colleagues found that teachers have strong preferences about certain metrics: months of progress and threshold metrics were rated as "more informative" than the other metrics. On the other hand, they found that certain metrics "induce different perceptions of an intervention's effectiveness" (Lortie-Forgues et al., 2021, p. 351). When researchers reported the impact of an intervention using "months of progress," teachers perceived it as more effective than when researchers reported the same information using a "test score." Lortie-Forgues and colleagues (2021) explained that:

> Research communicators can, in effect, manipulate the perceived effectiveness of the interventions they study by using different effect size metrics. Reporting effects in terms of months of progress is likely to lead to higher perceptions of effectiveness, whereas using the other metrics examined, particularly Test Score units, are likely to result in lower perceptions of efficacy. Crucially, our findings reveal an important, but as yet undocumented, implication of the various effect size metrics used in education: their potential to mislead teachers. (p. 352)

With public school spending in the United States exceeding $730 billion (according to Bill Hussar and colleagues, 2020), the stakes are high, and research communicators (especially research communicators commissioned or employed by intervention developers)

TABLE I.2: Vignettes Describing Intervention Impact by Metric

Metric	Description	Vignette Used in the Study
Months of Progress	Additional gain reported in a unit of months, based on an estimate of yearly growth	The intervention had an average impact of two additional months' progress. In other words, the pupils receiving the intervention made, on average, two months more progress than the pupils not receiving the intervention.
Percentile Gain	Expected change in percentile rank an average student would have made had the student received the intervention	The intervention had an average impact of 6 percentile points. In other words, an average student (percentile 50) in the group not receiving the intervention would have scored 6 percentile points higher on the test (percentile 56) had the student received the intervention.
Cohen's U3	Percentage of students in the intervention group scoring above the mean of the control group (Cohen, 1988)	Fifty-six percent of the students in the group that received the intervention scored above the mean score of the group that did not receive the intervention.
Threshold	Proportion of students reaching a certain threshold (such as passing a test)	In the group that did not receive the intervention, 79 percent of students received a passing grade on the test, while in the group receiving the intervention. 83.2 percent of students received a passing grade on the test.
Test Score	Impact of the intervention in the outcome's units	In the group that did not receive the intervention, the average standard score on the KS2 Math test was 105.0 out of 120, while in the group receiving the intervention, the average standard score was 106.1 out of 120.

Source: Lortie-Forgues et al., 2021, p. 347.

might be tempted to use certain metrics to influence educator perceptions. So for now, effect sizes are probably the safest metric to use.

Given such a situation, it behooves educators to learn to interpret effect sizes. Matthew Kraft (2020) provided guidance. First, he explained that Cohen's 1969 guidelines for interpreting effect sizes are somewhat outdated:

> The default approach to evaluating the magnitude of effect sizes is to apply a set of thresholds proposed by Jacob Cohen over a half century ago (0.2 = small, 0.5 = medium, 0.8 = large; Cohen, 1969). Cohen's standards are based on a handful of small, tightly controlled lab experiments in social psychology from the 1960s performed largely on undergraduates. Recent meta-analyses of well-designed field experiments have found that education interventions often result in no effect or effects characterized as small by Cohen's standards (Cheung & Slavin, 2016; Fryer, 2017; Lortie-Forgues & Inglis, 2019). Cohen (1988) himself advised that his benchmarks were "recommended for use only when no better basis for estimating the [effect size] index is available" (p. 25). We now have ample evidence to form a better basis. (Kraft, 2020, p. 241)

Many educators rely on John Hattie's (2009) 0.40 "hinge point" to interpret effect sizes. But Kraft (2020) also calls this into question:

> Early meta-analyses of education studies appeared to affirm the appropriateness of Cohen's benchmarks for interpreting effect sizes in education research. A review of over 300 meta-analyses by Lipsey and Wilson (1993) found a mean effect size of precisely 0.50 *SD*. However, many of the research studies included in these meta-analyses used small samples, weak research designs, and proximal outcomes highly aligned to the interventions—all of which result in systematically larger effects (Cheung & Slavin, 2016). Influential reviews by Hattie (2009) continued to incorporate these dated studies and ignored the importance of research design and other study features, further propagating outsized expectations for effect sizes in education research. (p. 242)

Kraft explains that these outsized expectations for effect sizes may be causing educators to ignore interventions that have potential. Therefore, he suggested that educators set appropriate expectations when evaluating effect sizes. This can be done using the questions and guidelines in table I.3.

In light of all these findings, educators are advised to select the best strategies and interventions they can identify, implement those strategies and interventions, and—most importantly—collect data to analyze the effectiveness of the strategy or intervention in their particular classroom, school, or district. The process of implementation, data collection, and analysis is *action research*.

Action Research

As Bob and his colleagues Tammy Heflebower, Jan K. Hoegh, Phil Warrick, and Gavin Grift (2016) explained, *action research* is a process wherein:

> Teachers select an instructional strategy . . . and implement the strategy with one group of students but not with the other. The same pretest and posttest are administered to both groups. The only difference between how instruction manifests is that one group receives the instructional strategy and the other does not. Both groups should be instructed by the same teacher and be similar in beginning knowledge status and other factors. (p. 98)

This is similar to an approach used extensively in the business world and adapted for education: continuous improvement (CI). As Susan Bush-Mecenas (2022) explained, "CI involves iterative, structured cycles of data analysis to solve problems and test new solutions" (p. 462). Maxwell Yurkofsky, Amelia Peterson, Jal Mehta, Rebecca Horwitz-Willis, and Kim Frumin (2020) describe education's adoption of continuous improvement as:

> An exciting shift in education research and practice. As a result of increasing frustration with the dominant "What Works" paradigm of large-scale research-based

TABLE I.3: Questions and Guidelines for Interpreting Effect Sizes

Questions	Appropriate Effect Size Expectations
What outcomes are being studied?	If the outcome is something that is easy to change, expect larger effect sizes. If the outcome is something that can be observed soon after the intervention, expect larger effect sizes.
When are outcomes being measured?	If the outcome is measured soon after the intervention, expect larger effect sizes. If the outcome is measured months or years after the intervention, expect smaller effect sizes.
How are outcomes being measured?	If outcomes are measured using specialized assessments closely aligned to the content that was targeted in the intervention, expect larger effect sizes. If outcomes are measured using standardized tests or other large-scale assessments, expect smaller effect sizes. If the reliability (quality and consistency) of the assessment(s) used to measure the outcome is low, expect smaller effect sizes.
Who is participating in the study?	If participants are from a targeted subgroup, expect larger effect sizes. If participants are a diverse and representative sample, expect smaller effect sizes.
What resources and services (beyond the intervention) did the treatment group have access to?	If the treatment group had access to resources and services (beyond the intervention) that the control group did not have access to, expect larger effect sizes. If the treatment and control groups have access to the same resources and services (except for the intervention), expect smaller effect sizes.
Does the effect size refer to a correlational or causal relationship?	If the effect size refers to a correlational relationship, expect it to be larger. If the effect size refers to a causal relationship, expect it to be smaller.
Does this intervention differentially impact high- and low-achieving students?	If the effect size is higher for high-achieving students than for low-achieving students, it will likely widen achievement gaps (known as the Matthew Effect). If the effect size is higher for low-achieving students than for high-achieving students, it will likely help to close achievement gaps.
How much does the intervention cost?	If the intervention is low-cost, its effect size is more impressive. If the intervention is high-cost, its effect size is less impressive.
How difficult is it to scale the intervention?	If the intervention… · Is only effective with a narrow population · Entails substantial behavioral changes · Requires a skill level greater than that of typical educators · Will face considerable opposition from the public or educators · Depends on the charisma of a single person or small corps of highly trained and dedicated individuals …then its effect size is less impressive.

Source: Adapted from Kraft, 2020; Kuo et al., 2021.

> improvement (Bryk et al., 2015; Penuel et al., 2011), practitioners, researchers, foundations, and policymakers are beginning to favor good practice over best practice, local proofs over experimental evidence, adaptation over faithful implementation, and a focus on practitioners' problems over researchers' solutions. (pp. 403–404)

As Bob and Timothy Waters (2009) explained, action research can be informal or formal:

> Teacher action research can be quite informal or formal. At an informal level, teachers might simply try strategies in their classrooms and then record their impressions of how well the strategies worked. . . . At a more formal and rigorous level, teachers can design and carry out studies involving experimental classes . . . and control classes. (p. 58)

A formal approach would involve comparing the growth of the experimental class to the growth of the control class. If the experimental class exhibited a greater growth rate—compared to the control class—when the strategy or intervention was used, then it is likely effective in your classroom or school context and should be used with the control group as well (to help them catch up). In chapters 5, 7, and 11, we'll detail how to set up a system that makes measuring student growth straightforward, clear, and accurate.

HOW TO USE THIS BOOK

The preceding sections on Bob's work and my synthesis and translation of research into practice help explain why this book is not a catalog of strategies (far from it, in fact): there are already lots of strategies out there with a high probability of positively impacting teaching and learning. Educators need the systems knowledge to determine what problem they need to address, select a strategy that is likely to address it, and measure student outcomes to see if it worked. Therefore, I have organized this book into three parts: (1) students, (2) teachers, and (3) principals. Within each part, we'll address the structures and systems most relevant to the effective functioning of each entity in the educational system.

Part 1 explores students and what they should learn in school. First, we must consider the systems at work in students' brains as they learn. Chapter 1 explains the self-system, chapter 2 the metacognitive system, chapter 3 the knowledge system, and chapter 4 the cognitive system. Traditionally, schools have only been concerned about the knowledge system; in fact, all these systems are essential to students' education. In chapter 5, I explain how teachers might pare down academic standards to make room for these crucial nonacademic skills and then articulate a guaranteed and viable curriculum.

Part 2 discusses teachers and what they do in the classroom. Foremost, teachers are human beings, so chapter 6 covers self-regulation through the lenses of expectations, emotions, and enthusiasm. Chapter 7 delves into measurement, including large-scale assessments, classroom assessments, and grading and reporting. Chapter 8 synthesizes topics related to instruction.

Part 3 considers the roles of principals. Chapter 9 explores the role of the principal as an organizational leader and discusses the High Reliability Schools framework as a tool for organizational management. Chapter 10 reviews principals as culture builders and how teachers can partner with them to support and grow the people in schools. Chapter 11 focuses on instructional leadership and discusses how principals and teachers can partner to promote productive teacher evaluation, professional learning, and data-driven improvement.

My hope is that the organizational structure and educational knowledge I offer in this book will allow all educators to move past routine expertise and into adaptive expertise. As Fries and colleagues (2021) explained:

> *Routine experts* have a lot of knowledge, both declarative and procedural, which they have mastered well enough to perform with fluency up to some standard in familiar circumstances. In contrast, *adaptive experts* stand out for their ability to flexibly apply their knowledge in a wide range of contexts, both familiar and novel. (p. 742)

The key to adaptive expertise is how knowledge is organized:

> In general, research on the nature of expert understanding paints a consistent picture: adaptive experts' knowledge is organized in a different way. . . . Adaptive experts' knowledge organization is more coherent, interconnected, and reflective of the relational structure of the domain. . . . The building blocks of this transferable knowledge, sometimes referred to as schemas, emphasize the connections between abstract relations (such as hierarchies, embedded categories, and functional systems) rather than lists of discrete facts and procedures. (Fries et al., 2021, p. 743)

This highly organized knowledge allows adaptive experts to perform the quick decision-making that is essential to being an educator:

> Because their knowledge is highly organized and interconnected, adaptive experts perceive the world differently than routine experts or novices. They easily and quickly identify and attend to the relevant structural information critical to understanding the situation at hand, filtering out the irrelevant features of a problem to home in on a solution path. . . . They anticipate how modifications to a system will influence outcomes and can explain why and how concepts from one scenario may apply to another. (Fries et al., 2021, p. 743)

Therefore, I hope that this book will allow you to increase the coherence and interconnectedness of your educational knowledge. Where appropriate, I hope that you will reorganize your knowledge and add additional details, generalizations, and processes to it. More than anything else, I hope this book serves you as you educate students. Thank you for all you do.

PART I

STUDENTS

In part I, we explore key topics from Bob's research and writing related to students and what they should learn. First, we'll learn about four systems that make up students' thinking and learning processes, and then discover how they work together with traditional academic content in the context of a curriculum. The ways that students think and interact with content are often defined by educational taxonomies. In 2007, Bob and John Kendall published *The New Taxonomy of Educational Objectives*. In it, they presented a model of thinking processes, which figure P.1 (page 14) depicts.

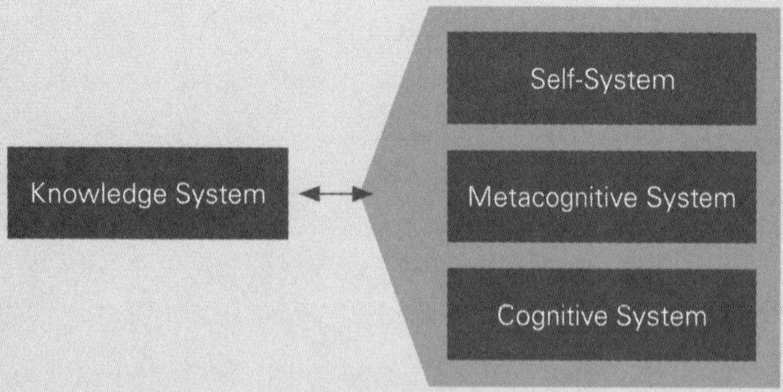

Source: Adapted from Marzano & Kendall, 2007.

Figure P.1: The New Taxonomy.

Notice that the knowledge system is distinct from the cognitive, metacognitive, and self-system hierarchy. Essentially, the knowledge system acts on and is acted on by the other systems, but it is not a part of the hierarchy. Bob explains that one of the defining features of "the New Taxonomy is that the New Taxonomy separates various types of knowledge from the mental processes that operate on them" (Marzano & Kendall, 2007, p. 21).

The hierarchy of mental processes—self-system, metacognitive system, and cognitive system—is ordered in terms of control. As Bob and Kendall (2007) explained, "Some processes exercise control over the operation of other processes" (p. 11). To conceptualize how this works, imagine a student has been presented with a new task. The first system to activate is the self-system. The self-system decides whether or not to engage in the new task; if the self-system decides not to engage in the new task, the student will likely continue their current task or behavior. But if the self-system does decide to engage, the metacognitive system is activated. The metacognitive system is responsible for planning, managing, and monitoring the task; it then activates the cognitive system to do the thinking necessary for the task.

Bob and Kendall (2007) provided a detailed explanation of each of the systems in the New Taxonomy.

- The **self-system** is a network of beliefs and goals that a person uses to decide whether to engage in a new task. It also plays a major role in motivation to complete a task. If the person believes that a task is important, that they have a good chance of success, and that they will enjoy the process, they are more likely to be motivated to engage in the task. However, if they believe that the task is unimportant, that they have a low chance of success, and that they will not enjoy the process, they are less likely to be motivated to engage in the task. In other words, the self-system acts as a kind of filter that determines whether someone is motivated to engage in a new task.
- When a person starts working on a new task, the **metacognitive system** kicks in. This system is responsible for helping someone think about their thinking. One of the first things it does is help them set goals for the task. Once they have goals, the metacognitive system helps them design strategies for achieving them. In other words, the metacognitive system helps people to plan and execute tasks effectively—identify what they need to do to achieve goals and break down the task into manageable steps. It also helps monitor progress and make adjustments as needed.
- The **cognitive system** is responsible for processing the information needed to complete a task. It does this by performing analytic operations such as making inferences, comparing, and classifying.
- The more **knowledge** someone has about a task, the more likely they are to succeed at it. This is because knowledge creates a better understanding of the task and helps develop effective strategies for completing it. Knowledge also helps anticipate and avoid problems. Knowledge is essential for success in any new task.

We will take the next four chapters to explore these systems and research concerning them. We'll explore how the systems can become part of the academic curriculum in chapter 5 (page 69).

CHAPTER 1

THE SELF-SYSTEM

The self-system is the set of knowledge and skills that we use to interact with ourselves and with others. The self-system is malleable and can grow and change; it is not fixed. Teaching students (1) that the self-system exists and (2) that they can control and regulate it might be the single most life-changing lesson that the K–12 education system can impart. As Bob and Kendall (2007) explained:

> The self-system determines whether an individual will engage in or disengage in a given task; it also determines how much energy the individual will bring to the task. Once the self-system has determined what will be attended to, the functioning of all other elements of thought (i.e., the metacognitive system, the cognitive system, and the knowledge domains) are, to a certain extent, dedicated or determined. (p. 55)

Talking about the self-system is complicated by considerable conceptual confusion in the research literature. Specifically, there are several overlapping concepts and theories, often with different names for the same things and combining different elements of the self-system in different ways. To illustrate this point, table 1.1 (page 16) summarizes the different ways that research from the past three years and Bob's past and current work describe just one of these elements: engagement.

Many experts say engagement is important, but if they don't all define it the same way, it may not provide much practical help to educators. For example, Christine Bae, Morgan Les DeBusk-Lane, and Ashlee Lester (2020) observed:

> Findings from a large number of studies, across grade levels and subject areas, show that higher engagement, in its many forms (e.g., on-task behaviors, excitement during an activity), significantly and positively predicts students' success in school (e.g., Lee, Hayes, Seitz, DiStefano, & O'Connor, 2016; Skinner, Pitzer, & Steele, 2016; Wang & Holcombe, 2010; Wigfield, Eccles, Schiefele, Roeser, & Davis-Kean, 2006). (p. 1)

But if we don't have clarity on what engagement is, then what exactly is predicting students' success in

TABLE 1.1: Varied Definitions of Engagement

Citation	Description of Engagement
Marzano, 2007	"By engagement I refer to students **attending to the instructional activities occurring in class**" (p. 99).
Marzano & Pickering, 2011	"Where attention applies to a specific event in class, engagement **goes well beyond a single activity and event beyond a single class period**. When students are engaged, they tend to think about the topic frequently and in-depth" (p. 87).
Marzano, 2017	"Engagement is possibly the **gatekeeper to mental readiness**. . . . Engagement is divided into four components: (1) paying attention, (2) being energized, (3) being intrigued, and (4) being inspired" (p. 65).
Bae, DeBusk-Lane, & Lester, 2020	"Engagement in the classroom or school refers to **students' connection to learning activities** in educational settings" (p. 2).
Bergdahl, Nouri, Fors, & Knutsson, 2020	"Engagement often refers to **students' level of involvement with and effort in learning**" (p. 2).
Engels, Spilt, Denies, & Verschueren, 2021	"School engagement is the **quality of students' involvement with the endeavor of schooling** and is seen as a necessary condition for learning and achievement" (p. 2).
Gaspard & Lauermann, 2021	"Engagement refers to the quality of a student's **involvement with school-related activities, goals, and people**. . . . It can also be considered 'the outward manifestation of a motivated student' (Skinner et al., 2009, p. 494)" (p. 3).
Goldberg et al., 2021	"Engagement is defined as a **multidimensional meta-construct** and represents one of the key elements for learning and academic success" (p. 29).
Olivier, Galand, Morin, & Hospel, 2021	"Engagement refers to students' **involvement in their learning activities** and typically encompasses the behavioral, emotional, and cognitive dimensions" (p. 2).
Widlund, Tuominen, & Korhonen, 2021	"School engagement is . . . defined as **a positive, fulfilling, study-related state of mind** comprising three components: energy, dedication, and absorption" (p. 2).
Marzano & Abbott, 2022	"When we say students in a class are engaged, we mean they are **paying attention to and making sense out of what is occurring in the classroom**" (p. 104).
Sun et al., 2022	"Engagement refers to students' **attitude towards school** and their **participation in school and classroom activities**" (p. 2).
Wong & Liem, 2022	"Learning engagement refers to **students' psychological state of activity** that affords them to feel activated, exert effort, and be absorbed during learning activities" (p. 120). "School engagement refers to **students' state of connection with the school community**" (p. 125).

Emphases added.

school? And how can educators leverage "engagement" in the classroom if we can't really pin down what it is? A number of popular terms in education suffer from the same "conceptual haziness" (Wong & Liem, 2022, p. 107), including the following.

- Agency (Bandura, 2001)
- Flow (Csikszentmihalyi, Abuhamdeh, & Nakamura, 2014)
- Grit (Duckworth, Taxer, Eskreis-Winkler, Galla, & Gross, 2019)

While this confusion is frustrating, there is a wonderful term to describe the problem: *jingle-jangle fallacies*. The jingle fallacy refers to the assumption that one label is always associated with one meaning, and the jangle fallacy refers to the assumption that if there are two different labels, they refer to two different things (Reschly & Christenson, 2012). In reality, one label like *engagement* actually refers to lots of different things. And terms like *grit* and *perseverance* may or may not refer to two different things (the research is equivocal; see Morell et al., 2021). Jingle-jangle fallacies plague educational communication (along with our alphabet soup of acronyms), and I urge educators to guard against it. The simplest way to avoid it is to always ask, "What do you mean by ______________?"

All that said, there are several theories and models in educational psychology that *are* well-defined and are therefore useful to educators, and it is those that we will focus on during our discussions of the self-, metacognitive, and cognitive systems. Let's begin by considering self-determination theory.

SELF-DETERMINATION THEORY

Self-determination theory (Ryan & Deci, 2000, 2017, 2020) states that for "healthy development," people need three things (Ryan & Deci, 2020, p. 1).

- **Autonomy:** Ownership of one's actions
- **Competence:** Ability to succeed and grow
- **Relatedness:** Sense of belonging and connection

As the theory goes, if these needs are met, a person will likely be *intrinsically motivated* to engage in tasks. Richard Ryan and Edward Deci (2020) explained, "Intrinsic motivation is based in *interest and enjoyment*—people do these behaviors because they find them engaging or even fun" (p. 3). Other bases of motivation typically result in *extrinsic motivation*.

Here are some simple descriptions of various types of extrinsic motivation:

> *External regulation* refers to behaviour that is motivated by outside forces such as external rewards or punishment, whereas *introjected regulation* is driven by a need to foster self-worth or to avoid guilt, anxiety, or shame. . . . *Identified regulation* occurs when individuals willingly engage in and value an activity for the benefits it procures even when it is not experienced as interesting or enjoyable. . . . *Integrated regulation* occurs when extrinsic pursuits are both personally valued and align with core beliefs and interests. (Gill, Trask-Kerr, & Vella-Brodrick, 2021, p. 1555)

As you can see, not all forms of extrinsic motivation are undesirable. Identified and integrated regulation both involve a lot of *volition*, or willingness; of the four, those two have the most autonomy in them. Often, educators aim for identified and integrated regulation (while hopefully avoiding the more negative external and introjected regulation); students need to learn things in school that they may not find personally interesting and enjoyable. Identified and integrated regulation are "based on a sense of *value*—people view the activities as worthwhile, even if not enjoyable" (Ryan & Deci, 2020, p. 3). However, intrinsic motivation is the gold standard of self-determination theory, and to the greatest extent possible, we want to promote intrinsic motivation in students as they engage in learning tasks at school.

Self-determination theory also helps us divide the self-system into two categories. Autonomy and competence are products of a student's interactions with themselves: To what extent do they take ownership of their actions? Do they believe in their ability to succeed and grow? Relatedness is a product of a student's interactions with others: How strong is their sense of belonging and connectedness? The remainder of this chapter addresses self-determination theory by examining how students interact with themselves (autonomy and competence) and how students interact with others (relatedness).

INTERACTIONS WITH SELF

Self-regulation is the ability to regulate one's thoughts, emotions, and behaviors. (Note that this concept is different from *self-regulated learning*, a synonym for metacognition; see chapter 2, page 33). Martin R. West and colleagues (2020), citing the Collaborative for Academic, Social, and Emotional Learning (CASEL, 2005), included "managing stress, delaying gratification, motivating oneself, and setting and working toward personal and academic goals" (p. 282) as skills related to self-regulation. Bob actually used a stronger term, *control*, to discuss self-regulation—"Students should be given the message that they are responsible for their own behavior and that they should be provided with strategies and training to realize that control" (Marzano, 2003a, p. 77)—but I'm going to stick with *regulate*, for the simple reason that this discussion includes emotions, which can be regulated but not controlled.

Students' interactions with themselves involve three parts.

1. **Attention:** What am I thinking about?
2. **Emotions:** How do I feel?
3. **Beliefs:** Can I? Do I want to?

The heart of this discussion—and the part that connects directly to self-determination theory—is beliefs, but we're going to discuss attention and emotions first because they have such a large and often involuntary impact on beliefs. If students understand how their attention and emotions influence their beliefs, they'll have a much easier time regulating their beliefs (and therefore their behaviors).

Attention

Working memory is center stage for the educational endeavor. I cannot overstate its importance. Let's start with a picture; see figure 1.1. Working memory receives a constant stream of information from two sources: sensory memory and long-term memory. *Sensory memory* is a brief store of sensory information, such as sights, sounds, and smells. *Long-term memory* is a more-or-less permanent store of information, such as knowledge, skills, and experiences. Working memory processes and organizes the information it receives from these two sources. It also integrates this information with existing knowledge and goals to guide thoughts and actions. If we need to remember the information for later use, we can transfer it from working memory to long-term memory.

Joni Holmes and colleagues (2021) described *working memory* as the cognitive system that "combines short-term storage with the attentional capacity to integrate temporary representations of recently processed information with sources of long-term knowledge" (p. 1456). Let's break that down.

- **Short-term storage:** You can only hold information in working memory for about fifteen to thirty seconds unless you employ a specific strategy to keep it there longer (like saying it out loud repeatedly).
- **Attentional capacity:** Whatever is in working memory is what you are paying attention to at that moment.
- **Integrate temporary representations:** The only way to get something into long-term memory is to pass it through working memory (represented by the arrow pointing from working memory to long-term memory in figure 1.1).
- **Recently processed information:** Sensory memory entails all the stimuli that constantly bombard us from both our inner world (like emotions) and the outer world (like visual or auditory input).
- **Sources of long-term knowledge:** Working memory also receives input from long-term memory (represented by the arrow pointing from long-term memory to working memory).

Students' working memory is the currency of education, as information from sensory memory and long-term memory meet, mix, and mingle in working memory. As Martin and colleagues (2021) explained, "Learning takes place when information is successfully 'moved' from working memory and encoded in long-term memory in a way that the learner can successfully retrieve this information later" (p. 1128). Like any good currency, working memory is in demand, and educators have to work for it:

> Whatever is in the student's working memory at any point in time is what that student is paying attention to. The battle for students' attention . . . [requires the teacher] to determine at any moment in time what type of activity will most probably capture students' interest powerfully enough to override possible distractions. (Marzano & Abbott, 2022, p. 104)

Source: Adapted from Marzano & Pickering, 2011.

Figure 1.1: Interaction between types of memory.

Also like any good currency, supply is limited. Working memory is not just limited by how long-information stays there unassisted (fifteen to twenty seconds). There's also a capacity restriction; it can hold only so much information. There has been much debate about *just how much* information working memory can hold, but the consensus continues to hold around George Miller's 1956 estimate that we can hold about seven (plus or minus two) chunks of information in working memory (as cited in Rau, 2020). This brings me to cognitive load theory.

John Sweller and Marvin Levine originally proposed cognitive load theory in 1982, and Sweller has continued to refine it ever since. Sweller, Jeroen van Merriënboer, and Fred Paas (2019) described cognitive load theory's basic premise as follows.

> Human cognitive processing is heavily constrained by our limited working memory which can only process a limited number of information elements at a time. Cognitive load is increased when unnecessary demands are imposed on the cognitive system. If cognitive load becomes too high, it hampers learning and transfer. (p. 262)

At its core, cognitive load theory turns learning—relative to working memory capacity—into a mathematical relationship of sorts. To conceptualize this relationship, consider three concepts that Sweller, van Merriënboer, and Paas introduced to the theory in 1998.

- **Intrinsic load:** How much working memory capacity a task requires; the complexity of a task
- **Extraneous load:** Working memory capacity that is being used in an unproductive way (that won't lead to learning); distractions
- **Germane load:** Working memory capacity that is being used in a productive way (that will lead to learning); on-task attention

Essentially, working memory capacity is taken up by the germane load plus the extraneous load. If the intrinsic load of a task is less than or equal to the germane load, learning is likely to occur. But if the intrinsic load of a task is greater than the germane load, learning is not likely to occur. Extraneous load influences capacity by detracting from the amount of germane load students can dedicate to a task. Teachers can increase germane load by reducing extraneous load.

Let's use a few examples to solidify this theory. Imagine a learning task that is, by its nature, complex—that is, it has a high intrinsic load. For a middle schooler, this might mean constructing a function to model a linear relationship between two quantities. As a teacher, you want the student to dedicate as much germane load as possible to the task. To reduce the extraneous load associated with this task, you might do the following.

- Ensure that the student's working environment is free from distractions (irrelevant noise, social stimuli).
- Ensure that the student is physiologically comfortable (temperature, hunger, movement).
- Remove distracting elements of learning materials (unnecessary pictures, colors, patterns, text).
- Utilize effective instructional strategies (chunking, processing, recording, comparing).
- Prompt students to close their eyes or avert their gaze to "[free] cognitive resources that would otherwise have been involved in monitoring the environment" (Wang, Ginns, & Mockler, 2022, p. 426).

To illustrate cognitive load theory with numbers (which I made up to show the impact of adjusting one on the others; there is no significance to the numbers beyond their relative values), assume that the middle schooler's constructing a function task has an intrinsic load of six and that the middle schooler's working memory has a capacity of six. Each time you reduce the extraneous load, you free up more germane load for the task, as shown in figure 1.2.

Intrinsic load		Germane load		Extraneous load
6		4	+	2
6		5	+	1
6		6	+	0

Figure 1.2: Effect of reducing extraneous load on working memory capacity.

You might not be able to get the extraneous load down to zero—schools are not perfect environments all the time, for reasons teachers often can't control. So, if you can't completely reduce extraneous load, you might also need to reduce intrinsic load. This means, essentially, making a complex task easier or simpler. The best way to do this is to ensure that students learn foundational concepts before more complex concepts.

As students become more familiar with content, there is a natural reduction in the intrinsic load associated with that content. As Michael Noetel and colleagues (2022) explained, each time the brain draws information from long-term memory into working memory (recall figure 1.1, page 18) and adds new knowledge to it, the representation of that information gets refined, extended, and sharpened. The next time that particular bundle of information gets drawn into working memory, it's easier to work with, leading to lower intrinsic load.

For example, if you were teaching about the lymphatic system and found that the intrinsic load was too high for a task, you could shift focus to one aspect of that system—the spleen—help students understand the spleen more fully and then return to the larger lymphatic system. Noetel and colleagues (2022) elaborated:

> Increasing the learner's knowledge reduces the amount of intrinsic load placed on the learner, because each "element" becomes more complex (Kalyuga, 2011; Sweller, 2010). Once learners have easily accessible internal models of each component in a system (e.g., complex models of a spleen and of lymph nodes) they can then more easily handle the interactions between each element. (p. 415)

This is the principle behind a spiral curriculum; students build toward highly complex concepts by gradually acquiring foundational concepts. That way, when they get to the highly complex concept, the intrinsic load doesn't overwhelm their working memory (as it would if they were unfamiliar with the foundational concepts).

Let's return to our middle schooler constructing a function. The teacher decides to reduce intrinsic load by ensuring that students understand foundational concepts (plotting points on a coordinate plane, concepts of slope and intercept, function notation) before constructing the function. The intrinsic load falls, as shown in figure 1.3.

Intrinsic load		Germane load		Extraneous load
6		5	+	1
5		5	+	1
4		5	+	1

Figure 1.3: Effect of reducing intrinsic load on working memory capacity.

One final scenario related to extraneous load: sometimes students suffer from negative (or even traumatic) circumstances that can be powerful distractors. Think about a student who didn't sleep enough the night before. Or who suffers from social anxiety. Or whose parents are going through a divorce. Or worse. Heartbreakingly, educators can't erase or even mitigate these sources of extraneous load, and they may need to reduce intrinsic load even further. To do this for the function-constructing task, a teacher might do the following.

- Provide a visual of the points plotted on a coordinate plane.
- Label the independent and dependent variables using the words "input" and "output."
- Provide a list of steps for constructing the function (1. determine slope, 2. determine y-intercept, 3. write function).
- Provide the slope intercept formula ($y = mx + b$).

As shown in figure 1.4, these accommodations reduce the intrinsic load to a point where the student can be successful despite the high extraneous load.

Intrinsic load		Germane load		Extraneous load
4		3	+	3
3		3	+	3
2		3	+	3

Figure 1.4: Accommodating high extraneous load with reduced intrinsic load.

I acknowledge that reducing the intrinsic load of a task in this way may mean that a student is not necessarily meeting the requirements of the standard for that task. But in situations where excessive extraneous load cannot be reduced or mitigated, reducing intrinsic load through accommodations is a good option for helping a student move forward with their learning. As we'll discuss in sections of chapters 5 (proficiency scales), 7 (grading and reporting) and 11 (data-driven improvement), systems that allow teachers to clearly measure and track students' status and growth create space to accommodate students' real-life circumstances while maintaining a high level of accountability around mastery of the standards.

We will return to cognitive load theory several times throughout this book, but in the context of interacting with oneself, it presents a very practical way for teachers to help students understand the role of working memory and attention in their learning.

Emotions

Have you ever been "so angry you can't think"? Or "so sad you don't know what to do"? That's why we're talking about emotions before beliefs: if not regulated, they are powerful enough to override our beliefs. Or as Bob said, "Emotions are primary motivators that often override an individual's system of values and beliefs relative to their influence on human behavior" (Marzano, 2003b, p. 147).

It's important to understand that we don't choose our emotions. Recall the distinction between control and regulation—we can influence our emotions, we can respond to them, we can succumb to them, but we do not choose them. Nikki Lobczowski (2020) described emotions as:

> A type of affect, which includes other phenomena such as preferences, attitudes, dispositions, moods (Scherer, 2005), reflexes, stress responses (Gross, 2015) and physiological drives (e.g., hunger; Smith & Lazarus, 1990). Specifically, emotions are dynamic processes in which an event triggers a response from an individual (Scherer, 2005; Smith & Lazarus, 1990). (p. 55)

Note words like *phenomena*, *trigger*, *reflexes*, *stress responses*, *hunger*—all things that happen *to* us that we cannot control. To go a step further and delve into the physiological aspects of emotions, in 2012, Bob and Tammy Heflebower described the "amygdala hijack" triggered by emotions:

> When people experience strong emotions, they think very differently from when they are calm. . . . The thalamus (the part of the brain that processes sensory input) sends signals to various areas of the brain in order to prepare the body to respond. One signal is sent to the amygdala, the part of the brain that triggers emotional responses, and another signal is sent to the prefrontal cortex, which helps a person decide on a smart course of action. The signal sent to the amygdala arrives about a fraction of a second before the signal sent to the prefrontal cortex reaches its destination. This results in precognitive emotion, meaning that the body's emotional reaction is triggered before the situation is processed cognitively. The amygdala releases a burst of adrenaline, filling the body with energy and making it difficult to control one's actions. (Marzano & Heflebower, 2012, pp. 27–28)

"Precognitive emotion"—emotions happen, and then we think about them; not the other way around. I'll emphasize the physiological nature of emotions with one more long quote about the response of the nervous system to stress:

> In response to stress, the autonomic nervous system reacts by making the body ready for action, including increased heart rate and vasodilation. However, it should be noted that different emotions (e.g., anxiety and excitement) can have the same physiological signatures and, since the autonomic nervous system serves a general purpose, its activity is not exclusively a function of emotional responding, but rather encompasses a wide variety of other functions, such as homeostasis (i.e., keeping the body's internal environment in balance) and digestion (Cacioppo et al. 2000). (Roos et al., 2021, p. x)

My goal with these examples is to illustrate that emotions happen to us involuntarily, and humans (including students) should not be judged for the emotions they experience. However, we should be held responsible for appropriately regulating and responding to those emotions.

Though our primary focus in this section is on interactions with self, emotions can muck up interactions with others. As Sebastian Gerbeth, Elena Stamouli, and Regina H. Mulder (2022) noted, "Emotions . . . have an interpersonal effect" (p. 2). Lobczowski (2020) elaborated, "Emotions are inherently social . . . and within a social context, attempts at intrapersonal regulation can have social influences and impacts (e.g., controlling emotions to improve or maintain their social status at school or work)" (p. 56). School is a primary social context for both students and educators, and every aspect of the educational endeavor is entangled with emotions. Students and educators need to understand them, be aware of them, and be able to regulate them to have a chance of achieving their goals. To understand how emotions can affect interactions with both oneself and others, the following sections will discuss the nature of emotions and the importance of cultivating positive emotions in the educational setting.

Defining Emotions

The research literature typically characterizes emotions along two dimensions: valence and activation (Di Leo & Muis, 2020; Shuman & Scherer, 2014). Figure 1.5 illustrates the plane of emotions according to these characteristics.

As you can see, the upper right quadrant contains positive activating emotions such as enjoyment and pride. The lower right has negative activating emotions like anxiety and anger. The lower left features negative deactivating emotions such as boredom and sadness, and the upper left has positive deactivating emotions exemplified by relief and serenity. Interestingly, Iris Mauss and Michael Robinson (2009) characterized surprise as neutral in valence (sitting right on the horizontal axis of the grid) since "it can elicit positive or negative arousal depending on the context" (p. 2).

While there are innumerable shades of emotions, most can be categorized under a few basic feelings. In his work in the 2000s, Bob has typically kept lists of emotions simple. In 2007, he highlighted a short list of emotions, saying that "for instructional purposes students can be presented with the simple model that there are four basic emotions: glad, sad, mad, and afraid" (Marzano & Kendall, 2007, p. 164). He added two more in 2012—*ashamed* and *surprised* (Marzano & Heflebower, 2012, p. 141)—for a total of six.

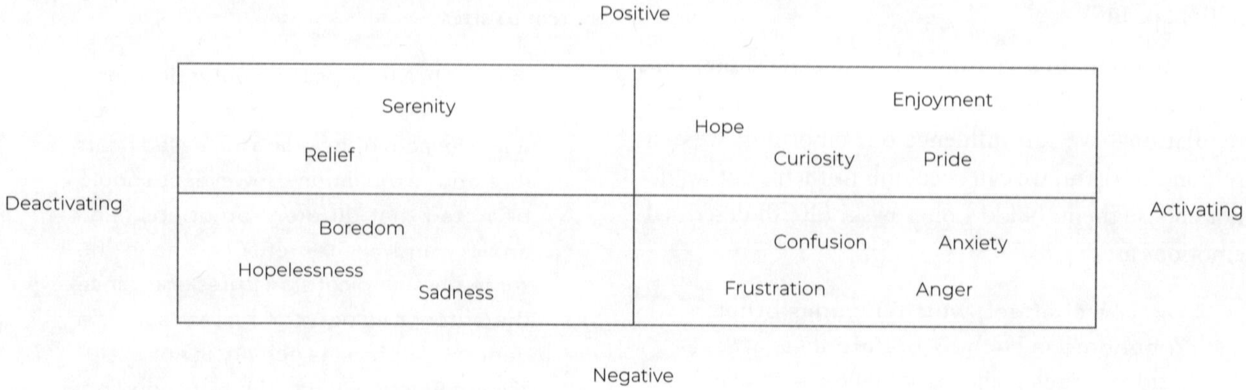

Figure 1.5: Quadrants of valence and activation for emotions.

Cultivating Positive Emotions

So what are the roles of emotions in schools? Jesús Camacho-Morles and colleagues (2021) quantitatively synthesized (this is just a fancy way of saying "meta-analysis") sixty-eight studies and computed effect sizes for the relationships between four emotions (enjoyment, anger, frustration, boredom) and academic achievement. Table 1.2 shows their findings. These results are not terribly surprising, but they do reinforce the importance of cultivating positive emotions for students in school contexts. As illustrated here by enjoyment, feeling good helps students learn better.

TABLE 1.2: Effect Sizes of Emotions on Student Achievement

Emotion	Number of studies	Number of participants	Mean observed correlation (r)
Enjoyment	57	31,868	.23
Anger	25	11,153	-.31
Frustration	9	1418	-.02
Boredom	66	28,410	-.22

Emotions in school are highly influenced by the extent to which students' physiological, safety, belonging, and esteem needs are met. Those of you familiar with the work of Abraham Maslow (1943, 1954, 1969, 1970) will recognize these needs as representing the first four levels of his hierarchy of needs and goals (shown in figure 1.6).

The first four levels all have to do with feelings.

- Level 1 Physiology—Do I feel comfortable?
- Level 2 Safety—Do I feel safe?
- Level 3 Belonging—Do I feel like I belong here?
- Level 4 Esteem—Do I feel like I am valued here?

If students' needs at the first four levels of the hierarchy are not being met, it is highly probable that they will be so distracted by negative emotions that they may be unable to learn.

Here, we'll take the first two levels of Maslow's hierarchy together (physiology and safety) in a brief snapshot of classroom management. Then, we'll look at levels three and four (belonging and esteem) in a short discussion of teacher-student relationships. We will discuss the top two levels of the hierarchy when we get to beliefs. My treatment of Maslow's hierarchy will be general and somewhat cursory. If you'd like to explore this topic and the specific strategies that teachers can use to support students at each level in depth, please consult Bob and colleagues' very fine work in *Motivating and Inspiring Students* (Marzano, Scott, et al., 2017).

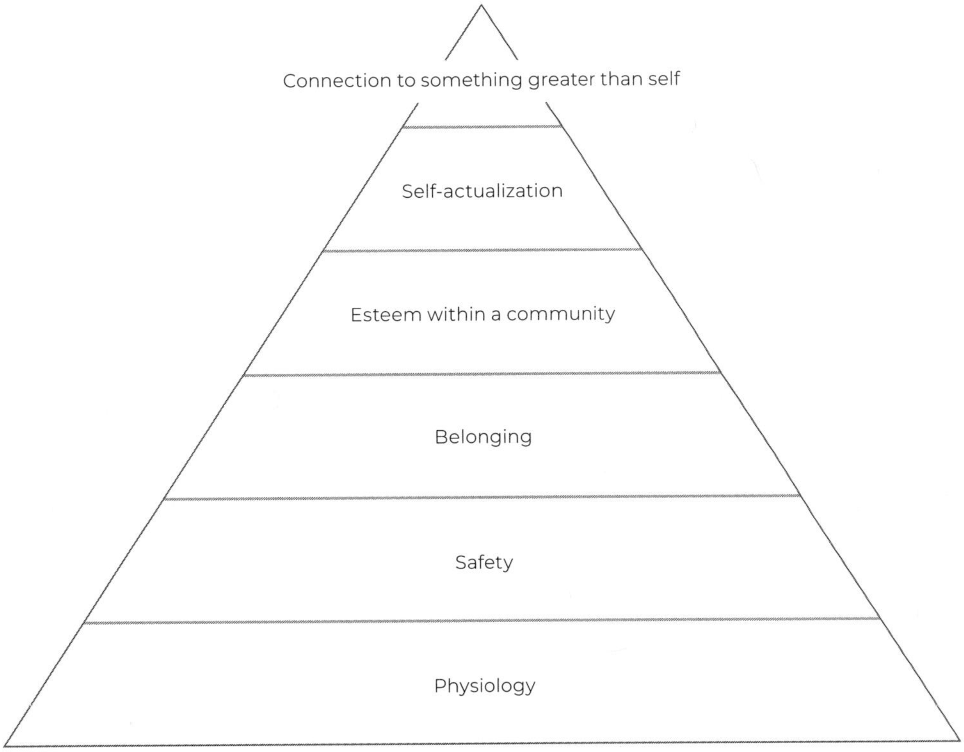

Source: Marzano, Scott, et al., 2017, p. 3.

Figure 1.6: Maslow's hierarchy of needs and goals.

CLASSROOM MANAGEMENT

Classroom management is directly tied to the self-system. As Keith Herman, Wendy Reinke, Nianbo Dong, and Catherine Bradshaw (2022) noted, "students will not learn if they are not paying attention or are distracted by disruptive behaviors of other students" (p. 144). Therefore, we're going to discuss four general moves you can make to create a safe and comfortable classroom environment.

1. **Set up your classroom in a way that allows you to see and move easily to all areas of the classroom.** If you're a novice teacher, this is even more important, because novice teachers take longer to notice potential disruptions and students that need help (Seidel, Schnitzler, Kosel, Stürmer, & Holzberger, 2021). Creating clear pathways for you to move around will help you get quickly to needy or disruptive students once you do notice them. As Bob, Barbara Gaddy, Maria Foseid, Mark Foseid, and Jana Marzano (2005) said, "The overriding principle for classroom organization is to create a set of physical conditions that are an advantage to you as a teacher. Studies show that one of the most effective deterrents to off-task behavior is teacher proximity" (p. 135). If possible, try to make sure every student is three to four steps from where you physically spend most of your instructional time.
2. **Work with your students to create classroom rules expressed either as procedural lists or flowcharts** (Marzano, Norford, et al., 2017). When students are involved in creating the rules, they are more likely to understand and follow them, which can lead to a more positive and productive learning environment. Additionally, co-created rules can foster a sense of community and belonging in the classroom, which can also support student learning. You might supply one rule as an example (such as, "What to do if I need to leave the classroom") so that you're ready for that first bathroom request on day one, but set aside time on day one to facilitate students articulating the other rules. It's best to limit classroom rules to no more than eight (Marzano, 2007).
3. **Monitor the classroom; when rules aren't being followed, notice and respond appropriately.** This is much easier said than done, especially for novice teachers. Eye-tracking studies have found that expert teachers "distribute their attention evenly across the classroom, while novices tend to remain on individual aspects and possibly overlook other important events" (Wyss, Rosenberger, & Bührer, 2021, p. 94). When you notice issues, try to identify the action you can take "in order to sustain learning" (Wolff, Jarodzka, & Boshuizen, 2021, p. 135). This educator disposition of noticing and taking action is called *withitness* (coined by Jacob Kounin in 1983, as cited in Marzano, 2017).
4. **Clearly articulate the approach you will take when rules are not followed, and follow through.** This creates a reliably safe classroom and is especially important for rules about interpersonal interactions. Hinke Endedijk and colleagues (2022) describe the teacher as a "safe haven for the student . . . and available for comfort whenever the student feels threatened, for example, in interaction with peers" (p. 373). In 1992, Bob described this dynamic as follows: "Students must believe that they won't be victimized by other students in direct or indirect ways, and that if they are, teachers will immediately intervene" (Marzano, 1992, p. 24). In 2017, Bob pointed out that "student compliance is not the goal of rules and procedures," but instead, "the goal is for students to perceive the classroom as safe and orderly" (Marzano, 2017, p. 81).

That last point provides the perfect segue into our discussion of teacher-student relationships. Although a comprehensive review of the research on this topic would be too long for this book, there is a clear consensus—not surprisingly—that teacher-student relationships are critical to educational success. Bob calls them the "keystone of effective management and perhaps even the entirety of teaching" (Marzano, 2007, p. 149).

TEACHER-STUDENT RELATIONSHIPS

Research shows that the most important thing that teachers can do relative to teacher-student relationships is *not have bad relationships with students*. In their meta-analysis of the association between teacher-student relationships and student-peer relationships (more about those when we talk about interacting with others), Endedijk and colleagues (2022) found that negative teacher-student relationships (such as those characterized by high conflict) had a much larger negative impact on peer relationships than positive teacher-student relationships. Apparently, when peers witness conflict between the teacher and a student, that student's peer relationships are likely to suffer. Because of the teacher's important role in the classroom community,

> the teacher's behavioral cues also affect how peers evaluate a student who interacts with the teacher, with more positive teacher-student behavior or feedback resulting in better peer relationships and more negative teacher-student interactions resulting in lower quality peer relationships. (Endedijk et al., 2022, p. 374)

Therefore, Endedijk and colleagues (2022) recommended proactive classroom management strategies to avoid the need for "negative teacher-student interactions such as corrective teacher feedback or punishment" (p. 401).

To achieve this "proactively avoid bad, let good exist" dynamic, research recommends that teachers assume a *warm demander* attitude. Leigh McLean, Nicole Sparapani, Carol McDonald Connor, and Stephanie Day (2020) described this attitude as "an ability to secure and maintain student attention, proactively address student behavior, effectively and respectfully redirect students, utilize encouraging and respectful talk, engage all students in learning opportunities, and encourage positive peer interactions" (p. 3). Bob described this as the interaction between two dimensions: dominance and cooperation. He explained, "Dominance is characterized by clarity of purpose and strong guidance," while cooperation "involves demonstrating concern for each student and building a sense of community within the classroom" (Marzano, 2007, pp. 150–152).

Teachers should carefully avoid communicating rejection to students in any way; even if students don't seem affected by it, rejection hurts them. One of the most interesting (to me, at least) findings related to relationships is that when people experience rejection, their primary reaction is emotional numbness; they are hurt but they don't show it. Emeritus professor Roy Baumeister—who was a pioneer in the study of the human need for belonging—shared his findings related to rejection in an interview:

> I spent many years . . . studying social rejection. . . . My initial theory was that this would produce emotional distress. . . . Yet, in study after study, we found . . . no reports of emotional distress.
>
> The absence of distress after lab rejections (also confirmed by a meta-analysis of a couple hundred lab studies of rejection) puzzled me for years until we came across MacDonald and Leary's (2005) great review of evidence showing a lack of pain sensitivity among rejected or excluded animals. . . .
>
> Many animals have a kind of shock reaction of physical numbness right after injury. This presumably evolved to enable an injured or wounded animal to escape from a dangerous situation without being hampered by intense pain. It seems social injuries such as rejection produce the same kind of shock reaction. (Allen, Gray, Baumeister, & Leary, 2022, pp. 1140–1141)

This awareness can be transformative for educators' interactions with students. While social rejection from teachers may not cause immediate pain or obvious behavioral responses, it does harm students. In fact, it is so painful that the body numbs the emotions to allow the rejected person to carry on; otherwise the emotional pain might be overwhelming. Given these findings, teachers should be proactive in demonstrating their acceptance of and care for students—it can be as simple as asking a student, "How are you doing?"—and extremely careful about doing anything that might communicate rejection to a student.

My final point about relationships relates to the work of Geoffrey Borman. In 2019, Borman, along with

Christopher Rozek, Jaymes Pyne, and Paul Hanselman, tested an intervention with 1,304 sixth-grade students who were transitioning to middle school (and therefore facing some possible belonging-related challenges) in the Madison Metropolitan School District in Madison, Wisconsin. The intervention was simple: once in September and once in early November of their first year in the new school, students read a vignette written from the perspective of another student recalling their first year in middle school, how they worried about the challenges of fitting in socially, and how eventually they reappraised those challenges and overcame their worry. Then, the students completed a written reflection on the vignette. The intervention took place in students' homeroom classes and lasted only fifteen minutes. As described by Jaymes Pyne and Geoffrey Borman (2020), the researchers found:

> Compared to control group students, following the administration of the two exercises those in the intervention group experienced increases in grade point average, attendance, trust in adults at school, social belonging among peers, and identification with the goals of schooling—and decreases in the number of failing grades they received, disciplinary infractions, and anxiety over being evaluated by others. This equates to an 18% reduction in failing grades, a 34% reduction in disciplinary involvement, and a 12% reduction in absences across the district as a result of implementing the interventions. The effect size of the influence on GPA is d = 0.09, and on failing grades is d = 0.11. (p. 655)

Those are small effect sizes, but the return for such a small investment (thirty minutes and a few pieces of paper) is significant! And better yet, Pyne and Borman (2020) replicated the study with 2,171 rising seventh graders. They found, again, that "on average, intervention group students see a modest increase in their GPA and corresponding decrease in failing grades following implementation, compared to control group peers" (p. 666). It's the modesty of this intervention and the repeated positive outcomes that make Geoffrey Borman one of my favorite educational researchers (and his research will inform our discussion of beliefs in the next section, too).

To transition from our discussion of emotions to our discussion of beliefs, I'll introduce the control-value theory of achievement emotions. First articulated by Reinhard Pekrun in 2006 (and updated in 2018 and 2021), the theory asserts that there are specific emotions that occur frequently during educational activities and in response to educational outcomes. The achievement emotions related to *activities* include the enjoyment that might arise from learning a topic of interest and the boredom that might arise from classroom instruction perceived as irrelevant to a student's interests or concerns. The emotions related to *outcomes* include forward-looking ones like hoping for success or fearing failure on a test, and backward-looking ones such as pride or shame after receiving feedback about performance. The crux of the theory is Pekrun's assertion that students' beliefs, in large part, determine the emotions they feel in the classroom, and those emotions influence their academic achievement. So let's delve into those beliefs.

Beliefs

Control-value theory (Pekrun, 2006, 2018, 2021) says that there are two kinds of beliefs that determine students' achievement emotions: control beliefs ("Can I do this?") and value beliefs ("Do I want to?"). As shown by the Camacho-Morles and colleagues (2021) meta-analysis—and also demonstrated in meta-analyses by Virginia Tze, Lia Daniels, and Robert Klassen (2016) and Kristina Loderer, Reinhard Pekrun, and James Lester (2020)—there is a correlation between specific achievement emotions (enjoyment, boredom, anger, frustration) and academic achievement. Further, students' control and value beliefs influence their achievement emotions and, therefore, their academic achievement.

Table 1.3 shows the correlations that Lara Forsblom, Reinhard Pekrun, Kristina Loderer, and Francisco Peixoto (2022) found between control beliefs, value beliefs, achievement emotions (enjoyment, anger, boredom), and mathematics achievement. They explained, "students' perceived control and perceived value were positively related to their enjoyment and negatively related to their anger and boredom. . . . Students' enjoyment correlated positively with their math achievement; anger and boredom correlated

TABLE 1.3: Correlations Between Beliefs and Emotions

	Enjoyment	Anger	Boredom	Mathematics Achievement
Perceived control	.36 to .67	-.56 to -.33	-.57 to -.33	.53 to .68
Perceived value	.40 to .82	-.58 to -.32	-.71 to -.32	.25 to .42
Enjoyment				.26 to .46
Anger				-.45 to -.31
Boredom				-.40 to -.28

negatively with achievement" (p. 356). In short, it is likely worthwhile for educators to instill and reinforce positive control and value beliefs in students.

Control Beliefs and Self-Efficacy

Control beliefs answer the question, "Can I do this?" The primary determiner of how students answer is their level of self-efficacy. As Bob explained, *self-efficacy* is "the extent to which an individual believes he or she has the ability, power or necessary resources to gain competence relative to a specific knowledge component" (Marzano & Kendall, 2008, p. 23). West and colleagues (2020) described it as "the belief in one's ability to succeed in achieving an outcome or reaching a goal" (p. 282).

Interestingly, in their study of burnout in students, Daniel Madigan and Thomas Curran (2021) found that reduced self-efficacy had the largest negative correlation with academic achievement. This stands in sharp contrast to studies of burnout in adults (for example, Taris, 2006), where exhaustion is typically the largest negative correlate with performance. These findings suggest that, whereas burned out adults are so tired they can't go on, burned out students have lost their belief that they can succeed.

There are many ways for educators to encourage positive self-efficacy beliefs in students. Teaching about growth and fixed mindsets (Dweck, 2006; Yeager & Dweck, 2012) and helping them cultivate a growth mindset is a well-known one. As Qin and colleagues (2021) explained:

> Recent studies have indicated that cultivating a growth mindset about learning may help students better cope with adversity and, as a result, achieve academic success. In contrast to a fixed mindset (i.e., an entity belief of intelligence), a growth mindset enables students to view intelligence as mutable and responsive to internal forces, such as effort and differential strategy use (Dweck, 2006; Dweck & Leggett, 1988). Compelling correlational and experimental evidence has suggested that adopting a growth mindset is positively associated with adaptive outcomes such as grades and persistence, particularly for students with a history of low achievement (e.g., Paunesku et al., 2015; Yeager et al., 2016). (p. 619)

But I'd like to return to Geoffrey Borman, and consider the power of self-affirmations. In the context of another study in the Madison (Wisconsin) Metropolitan School District, Geoffrey Borman, Jaymes Pyne, Christopher Rozek, and Alex Schmidt (2022) explained, "when one's self-competence is threatened, it helps to have opportunities to reflect on sources of self-worth (e.g., being a family member, enjoying sports, being creative, or having a sense of humor" (pp. 285–286). Therefore, they designed an intervention that used self-affirmation to reduce the gap in suspension rates between Black and White students.

Two successive cohorts of seventh graders (2,328 students) at eleven middle schools across the district participated in the study. The treatment group completed a self-affirmation exercise; the control group completed a similar but non-affirming exercise. In the treatment group exercise, the first page contained a list of values, such as friends, family, sports, creativity, and so on, and asked the student to choose three of the listed values that were most important to them. On the second page, students were asked to write about why the values they selected were personally important to them. This was repeated three more times over the course of the school year. Each instance took fifteen to twenty minutes, and students wrote about seventy words each time, on average. The results are staggering. This one-hour intervention reduced the average gap in suspension rates between Black and White students by 67 percent over the last two years of middle school.

Geoffrey Borman, Yeseul Choi, and Garret Hall (2021) followed these students (who received the intervention during seventh grade) through high school and examined the impact of the intervention on Black and Latino students' GPAs and high school graduation rates. They classified Black and Latino students as "those who are potentially subject to stereotype threat" (p. 608). Not only did they find that the intervention narrowed the GPA achievement gap between potentially threatened and nonthreatened students by over 40 percent, but they also found that it halved the achievement gap for on-time graduation rates, reducing it from 18.35 percentage points to 8.99 in the treatment group.

Borman and colleagues (2022) acknowledged the limitations of this practice but emphasized its minimal demand on resources:

> Self-affirmation is not a panacea, and it is not likely to solve all . . . inequities in U.S. schools. However, the opportunity costs for using self-affirmation interventions, as opposed to engaging in a similar alternative intervention or creative writing activity, are negligible. Because students already engage in numerous writing activities over the course of the school year in their classes, teachers could integrate . . . the 45 to 60 minutes of self-affirmation exercises during the school year in ways that are unlikely to noticeably interfere with typical class routines. (p. 309)

The gains demonstrated by Borman for all students, especially for students who are vulnerable to stereotype threat, represent massive educational returns on a very small investment. I strongly urge educators to consider using these interventions to strengthen students' self-efficacy and control beliefs.

Value Beliefs and Expectancy-Value Theory

Value beliefs answer the question, "Do I want to do this?" Jacquelynne Eccles and Allan Wigfield's (2020) expectancy-value theory (which they've been refining since Eccles and colleagues proposed it in 1983) provides an excellent structure to explore students' value beliefs. Essentially, it categorizes value beliefs into four reasons a student might value a task.

- **Intrinsic value:** The enjoyment or pleasure one gains from doing a task.
- **Relative cost:** What one has to give up to do a task (and any negative consequences of a task).
- **Utility value:** The extent to which a task furthers one toward future plans and goals.
- **Attainment value:** The importance of a task in terms of one's life goals and identity.

Here, we briefly consider each of the four types of value beliefs, along with how educators might encourage positive value beliefs for academic tasks.

Intrinsic value has to do with the positive emotions you expect (and actually get) from a task. It is closely related to the concepts of situational and individual interest. *Individual interest* is just what it sounds like: a long-term predisposition toward particular domains, objects, or topics. Connecting back to our discussion of working memory, students typically choose to bestow their attention (space in working memory) on things they are interested in. When academic topics and tasks align with student interests, intrinsic value is high. *Situational interest,* on the other hand, is caused by a stimulus in the environment. Rather than students bestowing their attention for internal reasons, an external pressure captures their attention. This act of capturing students' attention is called *triggered situational interest.* Holding it over time is called *maintained situational interest* (Schiefele, 2009, as cited in Marzano & Pickering, 2011). Educators can trigger situational interest in many ways; one of the simplest is to present content with pieces missing. The human brain cannot resist a mystery or a puzzle—a principle called *cloz-entropy*—and missing information typically grabs our attention (Marzano, 2007). When students sense that a task has intrinsic value, they are more likely to be motivated to engage in it.

Relative cost has to do with resource allocation. If students are going to give their attention to a task, they will be giving up the opportunity to focus their attention on other tasks. This value belief has implications for the idea of multitasking. Multitasking is largely a myth and is only really possible in situations where one of the tasks is automatic (like running on a treadmill or riding a stationary bike; Dönmez & Akbulut, 2021). Onur Dönmez and Yavuz Akbulut (2021) explained the connection between multitasking and working memory:

> Learning requires intensive cognitive effort. . . . Cognitive Load Theory (Sweller, 2011, pp. 37–76) asserts that our working memory capacity is limited and new tasks for the working memory induce an additive cognitive load. Learning is not possible if the total cognitive load exceeds the working memory capacity. When both tasks within a multitasking scenario cause an unmanageable cognitive load, this should result in poorer learning performance. This claim was supported through a series of research findings (Courage et al., 2015; Junco & Cotten, 2011; Mayer & Moreno, 2003). (p. 2)

Bob and Heflebower (2012) agreed: "Multitasking . . . is not something that should be encouraged in students" (p. 19). Students need to understand that, for tasks that require focused attention (as is the case with most school tasks), there is a cost involved. They need to decide whether they will dedicate their attention to the task at hand, or continue to give their attention to other pursuits (which might include socializing or exploring individual interests). Educators can help students in relative cost situations by explaining the value of the educational task at hand. If students see that the value of an educational task is higher than the value of other tasks they might wish to engage in, they are more likely to choose to engage in the educational task.

At first glance, utility value and attainment value look similar, but they are different. A task with high utility value gets one closer to a goal; a student might strive to do well in a mathematics class because she has the goal of graduating from high school. A task with high attainment value is aligned with one's current or desired identity; a student might tutor younger students because he sees himself as a teacher and mentor. Fascinatingly, high attainment value can compensate for low intrinsic value. Sven Rieger and colleagues (2022) found that students who scored high in "conscientiousness" but low in "math interest" exerted the same amount of effort as other students who scored high in "math interest." In other words, the conscientiousness aspect of these students' identities was compensating for any lack of interest they might have felt toward mathematics topics. If educators help students tap into critical characteristics of their identities and their aspirations, those factors have the potential to carry them successfully through learning situations that may lack intrinsic value for them.

Utility value and attainment value are both addressed by one of my favorite strategies. The possible selves activity—originally proposed by Hazel Markus and Paula Nurius in 1986—involves asking students to visualize and then write or speak about their future selves. These mental pictures might include their career aspirations or life goals, or might simply articulate "how they want to behave with other people, how hard they want to work, and so on" (Marzano & Abbott, 2022, p. 133). Additionally, students can envision negative possible selves, which can function as deterrents and help them achieve clarity about paths they don't want to pursue. Possible selves activities are culturally responsive, as students will likely include culturally important values in their possible selves. Johnmarshall Reeve and Sung Hyeon Cheon (2021) warned that this approach requires "a great deal of teacher perspective taking, adaptation, and accommodation" but that it is a worthwhile endeavor as it can help teachers cultivate "a deep appreciation and respect for their students' values, goals, perspective, worldview, obstacles, and preferred instructional methods" (p. 70). When students believe that a task will propel them toward their future goals and identities, they are more likely to be motivated to engage in it.

As we transition to our discussion of interacting with others, I'll remind you of Ryan and Deci's (2020) self-determination theory and the three things needed for healthy development: autonomy, competence, and relatedness. In our discussion of interacting with self, we've addressed autonomy and competence, and touched on relatedness. To finish this chapter, we'll dive deeper into relatedness by addressing the knowledge and skills students need to effectively interact with others.

INTERACTIONS WITH OTHERS

A sense of belonging and connection to others (relatedness) is a basic psychological need, and satisfying it requires students to interact with others. Here, we focus on three categories of social skills that educators and students can leverage to this end: awareness, communication, and collaboration.

Awareness

West and colleagues (2020; citing CASEL, 2005) defined *social awareness* as "the ability to take the perspective of and empathize with others from diverse backgrounds and cultures, to understand social and ethical norms for behavior, and to recognize family, school, and community resources and supports" (p. 282). We'll discuss perspective taking in the next chapter because it is often needed for specific tasks (that is, it is a metacognitive skill). In this chapter, we focus on awareness of others' emotions, in the same way that we talked about helping students become aware of and regulate their own emotions earlier in this chapter. But instead of regulating others' emotions, students aim to understand them and then regulate their own behavior appropriately in light of their understanding (this category of abilities is sometimes called *conative skills*; Marzano & Heflebower, 2012).

As an example of the positive power of awareness, Jessica McManus, Donald Saucier, and Jane Reid (2021) meta-analyzed fifty-nine studies of intervention programs designed to raise students' awareness of their peers with intellectual disabilities (N = 7,724 students). They found that *regardless of the design of the intervention program*, students who participated had "more positive attitudes toward their peers with intellectual disabilities" (p. 13). The overall effect size was $d = 0.44$. They interpreted this optimistically:

> For those interested in reducing biases toward children with intellectual disabilities . . . nearly any intervention effort will be successful. With very few exceptions, no matter what researchers chose to do during the intervention, the intervention was effective. . . . The results of this meta-analysis suggest that most strategies are successful, and that doing something is better than doing nothing. (p. 13)

Kalina Gjicali, Bridgid Finn, and Delano Hebert (2020) offered another example of the transformative power of simple awareness, albeit with adults. To study the impact of awareness on cross-cultural competence ("a person's ability to engage effectively with people from different cultures" [p. 2]), participants played an online game where they interacted with characters from a fictional culture (the Ustradian people) characterized by hierarchy and collectivism. The intervention group was prompted to articulate their beliefs about the Ustradian culture several times while playing the game; the control group simply played the game. Those prompted to articulate their beliefs throughout performed better on a quiz about the Ustradian culture and demonstrated more culturally-appropriate actions during their game play.

Finally, fairly extensive research has shown that "facial emotion recognition ability is associated with better academic outcomes" (White, Russell, Qualter, Owens, & Psychogiou, 2021, p. 1). For example, table 1.4 shows three such studies. For older students, White and colleagues reported:

> Numerous studies . . . of ability to identify emotions expressed in faces, have found associations with better academic outcomes among adolescents (Qualter, Gardner, Pope, Hutchinson, & Whiteley, 2012), and higher grade point average among college and undergraduate students (Lanciano & Curci, 2014; MacCann, Fogarty, Zeidner, & Roberts, 2011). (White et al., 2021, p. 2)

Given the associations between facial emotion recognition and positive academic and social outcomes, it seems reasonable to suggest that activities that help students practice this recognition and raise their awareness of others' facial expressions would be worth educators' consideration.

Communication

When it comes to classroom talk, quality matters. Lauren Resnick, Christa Asterhan, and Sherice Clarke (2015) found that students who engaged in effective classroom communication—a set of practices they labeled Accountable Talk—demonstrated improved academic performance not only in the subjects they talked about but in other subjects too. In a

TABLE 1.4: Research on Facial Emotion Recognition and Academic Outcomes

Study	Sample	Intervention	Outcome
Agnoli et al., 2012	352 eight- to eleven-year-old children	Children identified emotions shown in pictures (anger, sadness, happiness, fear, disgust, neutral).	Facial emotion recognition was positively associated with grades in mathematics and language.
Goodfellow & Nowicki, 2009	840 seven-year-old children	Children identified happy, sad, angry, and fearful expressions in pictures.	Facial emotion recognition was negatively associated with learning problems and poor social relationships.
Izard et al., 2001	72 children from low-economic backgrounds	Children pointed to the picture that showed the emotion cued by the researcher.	Ability to recognize emotions at age five predicted academic competence and social behavior at age nine.

Source: Adapted from White et al., 2021.

meta-analysis, Karen Murphy, Ian Wilkinson, Anna Soter, Maeghan Hennessey, and John Alexander (2009) found similar results. Simply increasing the amount of student talk did not impact achievement; instead, the kind of talk students engaged in was what mattered. Using data from over seventy classrooms, Christine Howe, Sara Hennessy, Neil Mercer, Maria Vrikki, and Lisa Wheatley (2019) showed positive associations between high-quality classroom talk and student learning. Resnick and colleagues (2018) identified four specific effects on student learning that result from productive classroom talk:

- Increased learning of the subject matter under study (better initial learning)
- Learning gains that endured longer (learning retention)
- Better learning in other subject matter that had not been taught through discussion (far transfer)
- Better performance on tests of reasoning skills (general intelligence)

All these findings lead to the question, What constitutes productive classroom talk? Fortunately, Lauren Resnick and Sarah Michaels have defined it. Their academically productive talk (APT) framework articulates four goals for student talk (Michaels, O'Connor, & Resnick, 2008; Resnick, Michaels, & O'Connor, 2010).

1. **Elaborating:** Share your own ideas.
2. **Reasoning:** Deepen your reasoning.
3. **Listening:** Listen carefully to one another.
4. **Thinking with others:** Engage with others' ideas.

For each goal, teachers can specifically prompt students to talk productively. To elicit elaborating talk, ask students to "say more about that" and revoice students' thinking through paraphrasing. To encourage reasoning talk, ask for explanations and evidence or challenge students' reasoning with questions such as, "Does it always work that way?" To prompt listening, ask students to revoice their peers' thinking through paraphrasing. And to push students toward thinking with others during talk, ask them to agree or disagree with what was said, to add to what was said, or to explain why a peer may have made a specific statement.

High-quality classroom talk (both in-person and online) allows students to practice and refine their communication skills as they engage in learning tasks.

Collaboration

Collaboration is costly in terms of working memory but often valuable in terms of academic gains. When students work together, they must expend effort to coordinate and communicate with each other; this is effort that might otherwise be expended on learning. As described by Stephan Mende, Antje Proske, and Susanne Narciss (2021), the culprit for this extraneous cognitive load seems to be an act called *referencing*, which involves "paying attention to and taking up content-relevant information externalized by co-learners" (p. 30). Referencing, in turn, leads to the *collaborative inhibition* effect.

In research by Stéphanie Marion and Craig Thorley (2016), collaborative groups frequently performed worse on academic measures than nominal groups (who work in proximity to each other but not interdependently).

The best empirically supported explanation for this is that, as collaborative group members share information, they disrupt each other's retrieval strategies. Remember the diagram of sensory, working, and long-term memory in figure 1.1 (page 18)? The two arrows between working memory and long-term memory represent the ongoing process of retrieval and storage during learning. Evidently, students "develop individual retrieval strategies while encoding to-be-learned information. . . . [Therefore] group members will retrieve the to-be-learned information in different orders. When retrieving information together, they thus disrupt each other's retrieval strategies" (Mende et al., 2021, p. 31).

This does not mean that collaboration is detrimental. On the contrary, collaboration has many benefits associated with it, including improved understanding of academic content (as in Resnick's research) and improved collaboration skills, which are essential for most 21st century life pathways. And the good news is that, as collaborative groups work together over time and get to know each other, they develop a *transactive memory system* (Wegner, 1987), which means that they develop shared knowledge "regarding other group members' knowledge, ideas, and perspectives as well as how far there is a shared understanding among the group members" (p. 33) and the potential for extraneous cognitive load decreases. All of this means that, as Bob, Pickering, and Pollock put it in 2001, "cooperative learning should be applied consistently and systematically, but not overused" (p. 88). And educators should provide structures that allow students to move through collaborative inhibition to transactive memory as quickly as possible. One very promising approach involves providing scripts.

Jessica Vandenberg and colleagues (2021) found that simply handing students sticky notes with prompts on them during collaboration and asking the student to read the prompt aloud increased the quality of their collaboration. Instead of just telling each other what they were doing and thinking as they worked side by side (as students in the control group did), students in the sticky-note intervention "more frequently asked *questions* of each other, proposed *alternative ideas*, and *justified* their thinking" (Vandenberg et al., 2021, p. 360). Sticky note prompts could include the following.

- **Challenging with questions:** Ask your partner why they think their idea is a good one.
- **Sharing alternative ideas:** Tell your partner about your best idea.
- **Justifying thinking:** Use the word "because" to tell your partner why your idea is a good one.

While some might question whether scripts threaten student autonomy, a meta-analysis by Anika Radkowitsch, Freydis Vogel, and Frank Fischer (2020) found absolutely no evidence of scripts negatively affecting motivation. And, at the risk of sounding repetitive, the return on this investment (just the cost of sticky notes and the time it takes to write prompts on them) has the potential to be quite high.

SUMMARY

In this chapter, we discussed the self-system and its critical role in student motivation. We began by discussing how the self-system functions when students interact with themselves relative to their working memory and attentional resources, their emotions, and their beliefs. Then we discussed how the self-system functions when students interact with others relative to their awareness of others, their communication with others, and their collaboration with others.

As we conclude our discussion of the self-system and its associated self-oriented constructs (attention, emotions, beliefs) and others-oriented constructs (awareness, communication, collaboration), I will emphasize again the central importance of the self-system. It is not an add-on to the curriculum. Rather, unless students understand their self-systems and have some level of skill with regulation, it is doubtful that we will be able to achieve our educative goal of success for all students. But self-system prowess isn't all they need. In addition to being able to regulate themselves and interact with others, students need to understand how to regulate their learning. For that, we turn to the metacognitive system.

CHAPTER 2

THE METACOGNITIVE SYSTEM

The defining characteristic of the metacognitive system is that we use it to regulate our performance *on specific tasks*. The self-system decides to do a task; the metacognitive system is in charge of getting it done. Metacognitive skills go by various names and descriptions, including the following.

- **Conscious control of one's own cognitive actions** (Marzano et al., 1987)
- **Ability to monitor or judge the quality of one's thinking** (Marzano et al., 1987)
- **Awareness and control of our own thinking** (Marzano et al., 1988)
- **Being aware of our thinking as we perform specific tasks and then using this awareness to control what we are doing** (Marzano et al., 1988)
- **Executive control over one's actions** (Marzano & Kendall, 2007; Marzano & Kendall, 2008; Marzano, Norford, et al., 2017)
- **Self-regulated learning** (Cragg & Gilmore, 2014; Dignath & Veenman, 2021; Di Leo & Muis, 2020; Schunk & Zimmerman, 1997; Wang, Mayer, Zhou, & Lin, 2021)
- **Thinking about one's thinking** (Kuhn, 2022; Marzano & Kosena, 2022)

At their core, metacognitive skills are the skills students use to approach, complete, and evaluate their performance on specific learning tasks.

Ernesto Panadero (2017) reviewed six different metacognitive models and synthesized their components into three major phases relative to a specific task: the preparatory phase, the performance phase, and the appraisal phase. Table 2.1 summarizes Panadero's review, including the source for each model, how many times other educational researchers and theorists have cited it (which is a fairly good way to determine its influence), and how the phases from each model fit into his overarching phases.

As with collaborative learning, it is important to remember that self-regulated learning (especially when students are learning how to do it) carries a cognitive load (van Gog, Hoogerheide, & van Harsel, 2020). Students must dedicate working memory to metacognition about the task they're working on. However, unlike the cognitive load ramifications of collaborative learning—where "group thinking" creates extraneous load that can distract from the task and impede performance—metacognition just adds to the intrinsic load of a task. That is, it's costly but worth it: when students regulate their own learning, they learn more. This is a bold claim, so let's review the meta-analytic evidence to support it. The effect sizes reported in table 2.2 represent the effects on academic achievement of teaching students to use metacognitive skills.

TABLE 2.1: Three Main Phases of Metacognition and Their Components

Source	Average Number of Citations per Year Since Publication	Preparatory Phase Components	Performance Phase Components	Appraisal Phase Components
Boekaerts & Corno, 2005	84.25	Identification, interpretation, primary and secondary appraisal, goal setting	Goal striving	Performance feedback
Efklides, 2011	41.83	Task representation	Cognitive processing, performance	
Hadwin, Järvelä, & Miller, 2011	32.67	Planning	Monitoring, control	Regulating
Pintrich, 2000	200.94	Forethought, planning, activation	Monitoring, control	Reaction and reflection
Winne & Hadwin, 1998	54.58	Task definition, goal setting and planning	Applying tactics and strategies	Adapting metacognition
Zimmerman, 2000	245.24	Forethought (task analysis, self-motivation)	Performance (self-control, self-observation)	Self-reflection (self-judgment, self-reaction)

TABLE 2.2: Meta-Analytic Evidence in Support of Student Self-Regulation

Meta-Analysis	Levels	Mean Effect Size	Context
Dignath, Buettner, & Langfeldt, 2008	K–5	0.73	Classroom and school context
Dignath & Büttner, 2008	K–5 (forty-nine studies) 6–12 (thirty-five studies)	0.69	Classroom and school context
Xu, Zhao, Zhang, Liew, & Kogut, 2022	K–5 (seven studies) 6–12 (twenty-three studies) Higher ed (sixty studies)	K–5: 2.21 6–12: 0.43 Higher ed: 0.58	Online or blended learning environments
Zheng, 2016	K–16	0.44	Computer-based learning environments

Although I recommend caution when looking at the 2.21 effect size for K–5 in the Zhihong Xu, Yingying Zhao, Bingsheng Zhang, Jeffrey Liew, and Ashlynn Kogut (2022) study because it's only based on seven studies, the rest of the effect sizes (while lower) are compelling. Metacognitive skills are worth teaching to students, and self-regulated learning is worth using. When asking students to self-regulate their learning, teachers must recognize that they may have to reduce the difficulty of the learning tasks to free up the working memory resources needed to support students' metacognition.

So, how do you teach students to use metacognitive skills? There are two parts to this answer, summed up best by the expression, "You can lead a horse to water, but you can't make him drink." You can teach metacognitive skills to students, but you can't make them use them. They must choose to use them. That is why metacognitive skills have frequently been presented as *dispositions*, *habits of mind*, or *mental habits* (Costa & Kallick, 2009; Marzano & Kendall, 2008) rather than as skills. As Deanna Kuhn (2022) expressed it:

> The applied, and particularly educational, significance of metacognition is in large part as a disposition rather than competence. One may have the competence to exercise metacognition but it will count for little if one lacks the disposition to do so. (p. 73)

Logan Fiorella (2020) expanded on this idea:

> Knowing effective study strategies or being motivated to complete an assignment is different from the general habit of studying or the habit of using study strategies in specific contexts. This distinction is important because it can help explain situations in which students fail to use effective strategies, and it yields unique instructional implications. (p. 612)

Note Fiorella's use of the word *habit* in the first paragraph of the quote. Later in his article (titled "The Science of Habit and Its Implications for Student Learning and Well-being"), he cites research by Judith Ouellette and Wendy Wood (1998) which found that "prior habits predict future performance better than current intentions" (p. 613). Thus, we want metacognitive skills to become habitual behavior for students. For this reason, we begin our discussion of metacognitive skills with the science of habit.

HABITS

Fiorella (2020) defines *habits* as behavioral tendencies tied to specific contexts or cues. For example, we might do the same thing every time we wake up in the morning (time-of-day cue), every time we arrive home (location cue), every time we see a good friend (person cue), every time we brush our teeth (action cue), or every time we feel sad (mood cue). And habits are durable; despite all your best intentions, willpower, and motivation, unless you disrupt their cues, they will continue. According to Fiorella (2020), chances of successful habit modification increase if you:

- **Disrupt the cue for an undesirable habit (*creating friction*):** The goal is to "get in your own way" when you try to automatically enact an undesirable habit. If you can disrupt your automatic response, you create space to choose something different. For example:
    - If you want to focus more while you are studying, put your phone in a different room.
    - If you want to go to sleep earlier, take your television or computer out of your bedroom.
    - If you want to eat healthier food, do not go to restaurants that serve unhealthy food.
    - If you want to stop being distracted during class, don't sit near friends who like to talk.
- **Amplify cues associated with the desired behavior (*reducing friction*):** The goal is to make the desired behavior as easy as possible. For example:
    - If you want to eat more vegetables, buy frozen ones that are easy to cook and keep them in the most visible place in your freezer.
    - If you want to take more time to reflect, buy a journal and pen you like writing

with and put it next to your favorite place to sit at home.

  - If you want to generate more ideas before deciding on a course of action, hang out regularly with friends who love to think creatively and brainstorm.
  - If you want to get more exercise, join a gym that is close to your house and keep clean exercise clothes packed in a duffel.
- **Link the desired behavior to existing habits (*stacking*):** The goal is to "stack" or add desired behaviors to existing positive habits. For example:
  - If you want to start flossing, keep the floss next to your toothbrush.
  - If you want to start tracking your goals, add a goal-tracking app or doc to the home screen of your phone.
  - If you want to address confusion when it occurs, journal about that specific topic during your regular journaling time each day.
  - If you want to identify incremental steps for a project, add a box for that information to the template you use to plan a project.
- **Make the desired behavior rewarding (*rewards*):** The goal is to help your brain associate pleasure with the desired behavior. For example:
  - If you want to exercise more, make that the only time you allow yourself to listen to a certain podcast or read a book that you love.
  - If you want to set goals more often, give yourself a treat every time you set a goal.
  - If you want to increase the quantity of your effort, allow yourself ten minutes of leisure for every ten minutes that you press on past the point of being tired with a task.
  - If you want to increase the quality of your effort, buy yourself a gift every time you consider two strategies for a task and choose the one you think is most productive.

Once students are empowered to turn metacognitive skills into habits, educators can teach them explicit metacognitive skills.

SKILLS

Experts have articulated many metacognitive skills. Here, we focus on a few research-based examples, using Panadero's (2017) organizational phases (preparatory, performance, appraisal).

Preparatory Phase

The preparatory phase involves any metacognitive activity that students benefit from performing before they begin a learning task. This includes goal setting, identifying incremental steps and milestones, making plans, and accessing resources, among others. Here we focus on goal setting with a particular emphasis on Tim Urdan and Avi Kaplan's (2020) achievement goal theory.

Achievement goal theory stretches back to the late 1970s, and includes prominent names such as Carole Ames, Carol Dweck, Martin Maehr, and John Nicholls. In 2020, Urdan and Kaplan summarized the history and main ideas of achievement goal theory, which proposes that when students set goals, they assume one of three possible *goal orientations*:

- **Mastery approach:** I'm trying to do better than I've done in the past.
- **Performance approach:** I'm trying to do better than my peers.
- **Performance avoidance:** I'm trying to avoid doing worse than my peers.

Which of the three do you want to see in your students and in your classroom? Research has shown that both mastery-approach and performance-approach goal orientations are associated with improved student achievement; in fact, performance-approach goals "predict academic achievement more reliably than do mastery goals" (Senko, 2016, p. 5). However, mastery-approach goals have some very important benefits, as demonstrated in a meta-analysis by Megan Krou, Carlton Fong, and Meagan Hoff (2021), and shown in table 2.3. They studied the effects of mastery-approach goals and goal structures on academic dishonesty. Keep in mind that a negative effect size (in this context) means that a factor leads to less academic dishonesty.

The effects of the third approach, performance avoidance, are not as positive. As Urdan and Kaplan (2020) explained, "Performance-avoidance goals—engaging in the task with the goal of avoiding demonstrating low ability . . . are generally associated with negative emotions, disengagement following obstacles, and low achievement" (p. 3). Thus, while educators should be careful about potentially harmful outcomes of students comparing themselves to each other, educators should also be aware of the potentially powerful motivational effects of both performance-approach and mastery-approach goal orientations.

TABLE 2.3: Effect of Mastery Goals on Academic Dishonesty

Factor	Description of Factor	Number of Studies	Number of Effect Sizes	Effect Size (*r*) on Academic Dishonesty
Mastery-approach goal	Goals focused on developing competence and mastery of a task	30	55	−.17
Mastery goal structure	Perception of classroom or school goals focused on learning and mastering course content	11	16	−.21

Performance Phase

Relative to the performance phase of metacognition—which can potentially involve many individual skills—we focus on two that are supported by research conducted since 2016: taking perspectives and resolving confusion.

Taking Perspectives

In 2018, Ha Yeon Kim and colleagues articulated two levels of perspective taking.

1. **Articulation:** "Making an explicit statement that refers to the thoughts, feelings, preferences, and orientations to the actions of another person" (Kim et al., 2018, p. 26).
2. **Positioning:** "Explicitly situating, and usually interpreting, the point of view attributed to another person in the contextualization of knowledge about that person" (Kim et al., 2018, p. 26).

Positioning is obviously more complex, but it can't happen without articulation happening first: you must become aware of others' perspectives before you can interpret them.

To consider the perspective of another, students must "bracket" their own perspective. According to Keith Stanovich (2016), *bracketing* is a metacognitive function in which students parcel out a specific segment of their thinking and pay attention to it, while blocking out other aspects of their thinking. The concept of bracketing here helps counter the misconception that one's own perspective is dormant during the process of perspective taking. Rather, when one's own perspective is bracketed, and another's perspective has been articulated, "both remain accessible, making it possible to compare and contrast their points of similarity and difference, seeking to coordinate and possibly reconcile them" (Kuhn, 2022, p. 77). And while perspective taking is very often performed with another person physically present, it is just as feasible with a nonpresent person (like the author of a text) or with an imagined person (Zavala & Kuhn, 2017).

The positioning phase of perspective taking requires students to be aware of errors that can occur during the process and work to counteract those errors. Gideon Dishon and Yasmin Kafai (2020) provided the following examples of perspective-taking errors.

- **Overestimation of the similarities** between one's own perspective and the perspective of others
- **Relying on stereotypes** to fill in gaps between one's own perspective and the perspective of another person from a particular group
- **Mistaking a partial understanding** of another's perspective **for a complete understanding** of another's perspective
- **Reluctance to fully understand** a perspective different from one's own

In most cases, these errors can be avoided or corrected through questioning and clarification. When the other person is concretely present, this would require the self-system skills associated with communication and collaboration (as articulated in chapter 1, page 15). When the other person is a nonpresent or imagined other, it might involve research or investigation (for details, see chapter 4, page 47).

Resolving Confusion

As you may recall from our discussion of emotions in chapter 1 (page 15), confusion is typically considered a negative emotion. However, in learning contexts, Sidney D'Mello and Art Graesser (2012) found that it is neutral—a kind of articulation point from which a student can move forward to positive emotions (if the confusion is resolved and learning continues) or negative emotions (if the confusion persists and leads to frustration). Several studies have illustrated this "fork in the road" nature of confusion with K–12 students, including Ivana Di Leo, Krista Muis, Cara Singh, and Cynthia Psaradellis (2019) and Krista Muis, Cynthia Psaradellis, Susanne Lajoie, Ivana Di Leo, and Marianne Chevrier (2015). As Ivana Di Leo and Krista Muis (2020) explained, confusion "can be related to optimal achievement outcomes when students appropriately implement learning strategies to resolve the confusion" (p. 13).

Given these findings, Di Leo and Muis (2020) designed and tested an intervention with fifth-grade mathematics students to empower them to resolve confusion when it occurs. Their goal was to "normalize the experience of confusion and to model to students what learning strategies they could implement to resolve it" (p. 15). For example, when students encounter confusion during learning, they might use a process such as the following.

1. Pause to calm down. Take a deep breath.
2. Say what I am feeling right now. What emotions am I experiencing?
3. Say what I am thinking right now. What is the problem I am experiencing?
4. Affirm myself. Tell myself out loud that I can solve this problem.
5. Think of strategies to solve the problem. Write down or say at least three strategies.
6. Pick a strategy and try it out. Did it help to solve the problem?
7. Figure out what to do next. If the strategy worked, keep on learning. If it didn't, go back to step 1 and try again.

In addition to a process, Di Leo and Muis (2020) provided students with possible strategies for solving learning problems (in case they couldn't think of any on their own), including the following.

- Reread the question
- Highlight important information
- Summarize important information
- Summarize what I need to do to solve the problem
- Summarize what I need to do to move on
- Check and review my work
- Check and review my final answer

They found that, of the students in the intervention group (those who used process and strategies documents) who experienced confusion, only 18.75 percent expressed frustration following their confusion; the rest moved forward to more positive emotions. In contrast, of the students in the control group who experienced confusion, 66.67 percent expressed frustration following their confusion.

I do not offer this example of an intervention with the intention that educators should copy it (although they may; it "worked" well in this particular study). Instead—and like the previous interventions designed by Geoffrey Borman—it illustrates the power of simple processes and supports to help students use self-system and metacognitive skills. Designing a process for any metacognitive skill is fairly straightforward, and artificial intelligence tools can assist teachers by suggesting a set of steps to use as a starting point. The more frequently educators encourage students to enact metacognitive processes in appropriate situations, the more likely these crucial skills are to become habits.

Appraisal Phase

In the appraisal phase, we focus on the powerful metacognitive skill of reflection. As Bob and Seth Abbott (2022) explained, reflection is critical to metacognition because "if students are not aware of their perceptions, interpretations, and actions, self-regulation is difficult—if not impossible" (p. 138). In 2009, Bob and John Brown recommended the following questions to stimulate reflection on a specific learning task:

> - What were you right and wrong about?
> - How confident are you about what you have learned?
> - What did you do well during your learning experience and what could you have done better? (p. 78)

Cheryl Travers, Dominique Morisano, and Edwin Locke (2015) found that students keeping records of their reflections enhanced their goal setting and academic striving, as well as provided an increased awareness of how their teachers supported their learning. Bob (2007) referred to this type of record as a *reflection journal* and pointed out that such activity "not only enhances their learning but also provides the teacher with valuable diagnostic information" (p. 39). Additionally, reflection journals open up new possibilities in terms of teacher-student conferences. As far back as 1991, Bob recommended reflective conferences: the student brings their reflection journal to the conference and selects the information that they would like to share with the teacher about their use of metacognitive strategies. To respond, the teacher might ask students to:

- Restate what they wrote in their journal in a more general or specific form
- Tell the story of how their use of the strategy has developed over time
- Predict how continued use of the strategy will affect their future academic performance
- Make a plan for continued use of the strategy

We'll discuss grading, scoring, and record keeping in depth in chapter 7 (page 103), but for now, suffice it to say that reflection conferences also provide seamless opportunities for teachers to assign formative scores to students for specific metacognitive and self-system skills.

Reflection journals can focus on as many different topics as there are metacognitive skills. However, one topic that teachers may want to ask students to focus on, given its increasing importance as technology becomes more ubiquitous, is academic integrity. In the high-tech, information-rich, artificial intelligence-enabled world, students have many temptations toward academic dishonesty. Krou and colleagues (2021) defined academic dishonesty in terms of eight specific behaviors:

> (a) copying sentences of material without footnoting the reference; (b) bibliography padding or including sources that were not used throughout the project; (c) plagiarizing from public sources; (d) turning in a paper completed entirely or partly by another; (e) receiving questions or answers from another who had already taken the exam; (f) collaborating with peers on an assignment without the teacher's permission; (g) copying off others during an exam; (h) taking unauthorized material into an exam. (pp. 428–429)

In their meta-analysis of the peer cheating effect (that is, students are more likely to cheat if they see their peers cheating; effect size = 0.37), Li Zhao and colleagues (2022) cited research showing:

> Neutralizing ones' moral concerns [justifying your own cheating because you see a

> peer do it] does not necessarily mean that individuals are disengaging from moral principles about honesty and integrity. . . . After using neutralization to justify their own cheating, most students still evaluate their past cheating behaviors negatively. (p. 2)

While it might seem counterintuitive (and possibly fruitless) to encourage students to reflect on their past cheating behavior, reflecting on those choices might also help to discourage such behavior in the future, especially if teachers build positive *error climates* in their classrooms.

As Annalisa Soncini, Emilio Paolo Visintin, Maria Cristina Matteucci, Carlo Tomasetto, and Fabrizio Butera (2022) explained, error climate is composed of three dimensions.

1. The attitudes teachers display about errors
   - The extent to which they tolerate errors
   - Whether errors are considered relevant for assessment
   - Support shown to students when they make an error
   - Avoidance of negative responses to student errors
2. The attitudes and behaviors of other students
   - Students do not react negatively to their classmates' errors
   - Students publicly take the risk of making an error
3. The ways teachers productively use errors for instruction
   - Lessons that include error analysis
   - Explanations that allow students to learn from errors

Robert Grassinger, Annette Scheunpflug, Horst Zeinz, and Markus Dresel (2018) have shown that there is a relationship between students' perceptions of an error-friendly environment and higher student achievement. In a highly error-friendly classroom, students who have made academically dishonest choices in the past might feel free to reflect on those choices, identify the errors they made, and set goals to choose academic integrity in the future.

We close our discussion of metacognition with error climate for a very important reason: metacognition is a powerful construct because it puts students in control of their learning and growth processes. It involves "maintaining control of the evolution of one's beliefs as new experiences, ideas and influences are encountered" (Kuhn, 2022, p. 82). As student grow, educators need to expect that they may change their minds about past, current, and future choices, approaches, strategy use, and so on. These adjustments should be well thought out and defensible. They should occur strategically rather than frequently. As Kuhn (2022) explains, "changing one's mind very rarely or very often are both suggestive of poor metacognitive management" (p. 82). The extent to which students feel free to change their minds depends in large part on their perceptions of a positive error climate in their classrooms and schools.

SUMMARY

In this chapter, we discussed the double-edged sword of metacognitive skills. Students not only need to know what the skills are and how to perform them, but they also must develop the habit of using them. Teachers can help students do this by prompting them to use appropriate skills during the preparatory, performance, and appraisal phases of the learning process. As with self-system skills, metacognitive skills are not an optional addition to the curriculum. Rather, metacognitive skills are essential for students to become independent and successful learners. They help students understand how they learn best, monitor their progress, and make adjustments as needed. They allow students to exercise control over the cognitive system as they learn new knowledge and skills. However, in the next chapter, before proceeding to the cognitive system, we pause to consider the knowledge system. Specifically, we focus on the crucial distinction between declarative and procedural knowledge.

CHAPTER 3

THE NATURE OF KNOWLEDGE AND THE KNOWLEDGE SYSTEM

This chapter is a bit of a time-out. Given the function of each system, we'd usually proceed from the self-system and metacognitive system directly to the cognitive system.

- **Self-system:** Interacting with *self and others*
- **Metacognitive system:** Interacting with *learning tasks*
- **Cognitive system:** Interacting with *knowledge*

But we must pause and consider the knowledge system before the cognitive system because there are two different kinds of knowledge, and the cognitive system interacts with each of them in a different way. It is impossible to understand the cognitive system if you do not grasp the distinction between declarative and procedural knowledge.

Declarative knowledge is stuff you know. *Procedural knowledge* is stuff you do. That is an unsophisticated way of saying it, but sometimes to make educational research accessible, you just need to be unsophisticated. The main reason educators *must* make a distinction here is because declarative knowledge develops differently from procedural knowledge. As Bob and Debra Pickering explained in 1997, declarative knowledge is learned in three phases.

1. Constructing meaning
2. Organizing
3. Storing

Declarative knowledge involves content in the form of pieces of information. They might be small pieces (like vocabulary terms), medium-sized pieces (like facts), or big pieces (like principles and generalizations).

Think about the difference between the word *exercise* and the phrase *people who exercise regularly tend to have better overall health than those who lead sedentary lifestyles*. Both are examples of declarative knowledge, but the first is a little piece (vocabulary term), and the second is a big piece (generalization).

Procedural knowledge is learned in three entirely different phases.

1. Modeling
2. Shaping
3. Internalizing

Procedural knowledge involves processes, or things you do. These processes are usually defined by a set of steps or actions, which may or may not need to be performed in a specific order. Think of the process of long division contrasted with the process of reading a map. Long division steps must be performed in a specific order; the steps for reading a map do not. Both are examples of procedural knowledge.

The declarative learning phases are cyclical; as you develop declarative knowledge, you loop through the phases over and over again. The procedural phases are linear; as you develop procedural knowledge, you progress from lower stages to higher stages (and do not move backward). Figure 3.1 illustrates this difference.

As this chapter proceeds, you may notice that there is very little up-to-date research cited. That is because I was unable to find much research done after 2010 on the distinction between declarative and procedural knowledge, at least in the education field. Almost everything that I know about declarative and procedural knowledge I have learned from Bob. In his work, he cites researchers such as John Anderson (1982, 1983, 1995; Anderson, Reder, & Simon, 1996), who wrote extensively about the nature of knowledge in the context of his work with artificial intelligence. If you want to know more about the history of and research on this distinction, see *A Different Kind of Classroom* (Marzano, 1992) and *Classroom Assessment and Grading That Work* (Marzano, 2006). In this chapter, my goal is to provide practical information that allows educators to leverage this distinction for greater clarity and curriculum organization in K–12 education.

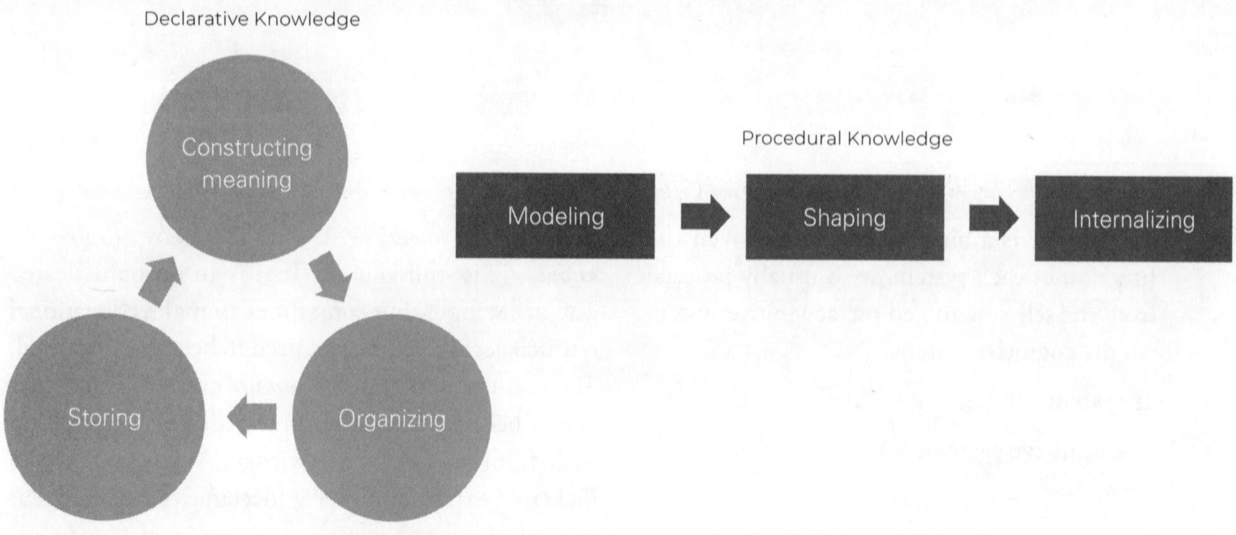

Figure 3.1: Phases of learning declarative and procedural knowledge.

DECLARATIVE KNOWLEDGE

As hinted at previously, different types of declarative knowledge are differentiated by chunk size. Following Bob and Kendall's (2007) lead, I'll call small and medium pieces of declarative knowledge (such as vocabulary terms and facts) *details* and larger pieces (such as generalizations and principles) *organizing ideas*.

As I also mentioned, the phases for learning declarative knowledge are nonlinear, and students cycle through them during learning.

Imagine that a student is learning about the distinction between physical and chemical changes in science. This new learning involves two vocabulary terms (*physical changes* and *chemical changes*) and one generalization ("all changes in matter are either physical changes or chemical changes"). In order to construct meaning, the student must reach into long-term memory and pull relevant, previously stored background knowledge into working memory. In this example, that might include vocabulary terms such as *melt*, *freeze*, *rust*, *burn*, and *ferment*. It might include facts such as "matter comes in three states: gas, liquid, solid" and "heat is a form of energy" and perhaps a principle such as "some state changes, like freezing, can be undone, but other state changes, like burning, cannot be undone."

Once that information is in working memory, the student adds in the new vocabulary terms *physical changes* and *chemical changes*. To organize that new knowledge, the student puts *melt* and *freeze* under *physical changes* and *rust, burn, and ferment* under *chemical changes*, as shown in figure 3.2. That hierarchy of vocabulary terms is then stored in long-term memory.

To add the new generalization "all changes in matter are either physical changes or chemical changes," the student pulls the hierarchy of vocabulary terms back into working memory and adds a descriptive structure to contain facts such as the following.

Physical changes

- Do not produce new substances
- Usually reversible
- Do not involve breaking or forming chemical bonds

Chemical changes

- Transform one or more substances into new substances
- Often irreversible
- Involve breaking and forming chemical bonds
- Involve the release or absorption of energy in the form of heat, light, or sound

The vocabulary terms and facts get organized into a new structure that incorporates the generalization and might look like figure 3.3 (page 44).

This new structure (generalization with descriptive details and examples) then heads into long-term memory for storage. Later, the student might realize that they don't really understand the term *chemical bonds*. So that piece gets pulled back into working memory for new information to be added and new meaning constructed, which gets organized and stored. This cycle goes on somewhat indefinitely, as long as new learning is occurring.

To summarize the three declarative knowledge–development phases, consider the metaphor of constructing a model plane.

1. **Constructing meaning:** Finding the connection points between pieces and putting glue on them

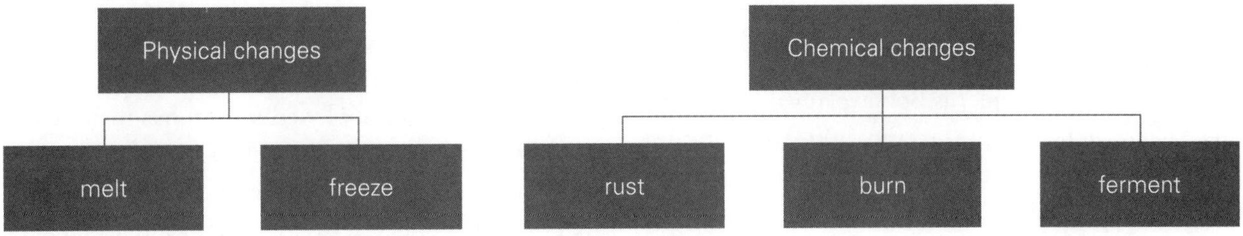

Figure 3.2: Organizing details.

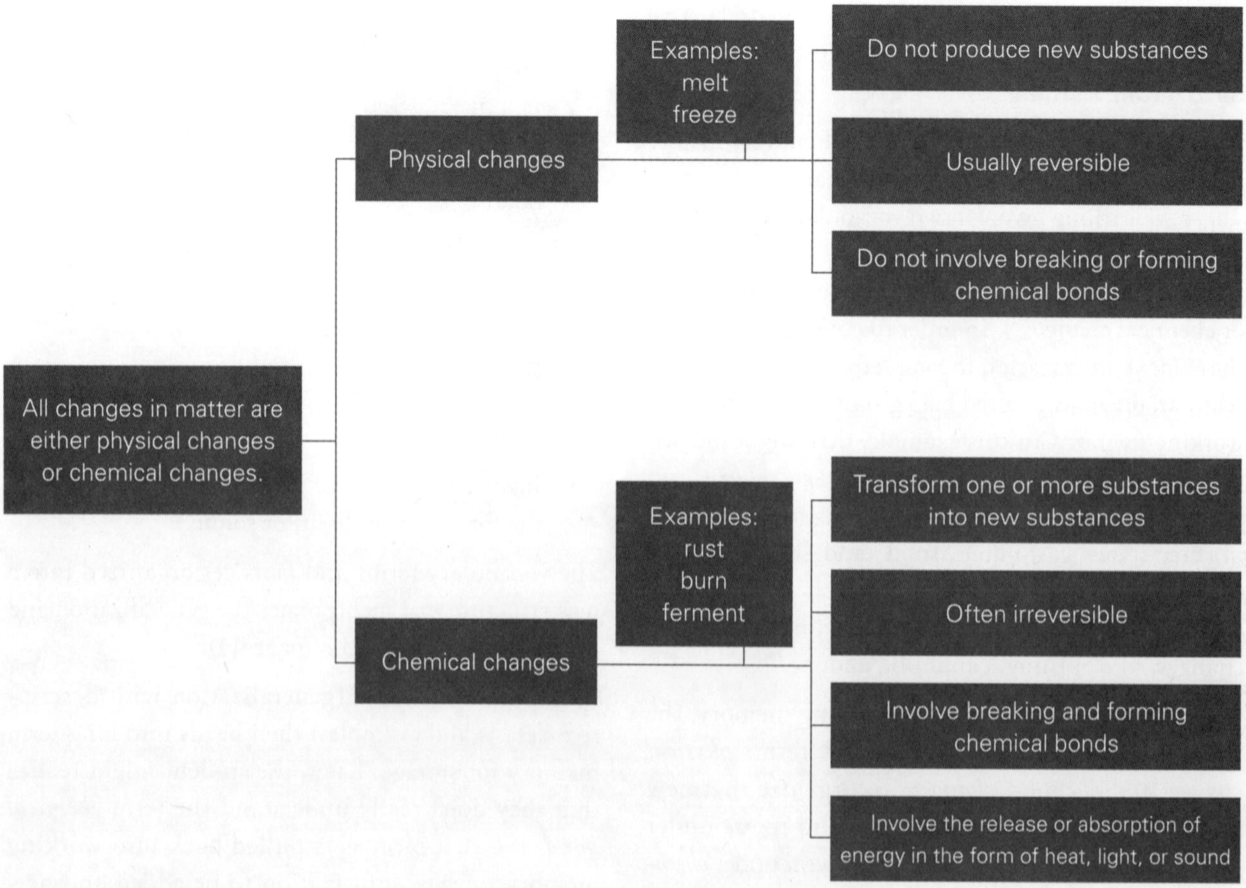

Figure 3.3: Organizing details and generalizations.

2. **Organizing:** Figuring out how the pieces fit together
3. **Storing:** Pressing the pieces together, waiting for the glue to dry

As the model grows (as the student cycles through the phases), the individual pieces change; they get bigger and more complex, and there are more potential connection points.

Understanding the nature of declarative knowledge makes research findings related to it a lot more comprehensible. For example, as Bob explained in *The Art and Science of Teaching* (Marzano, 2007), declarative knowledge develops through review and revision, and students need to encounter new knowledge about three to four times, with a one-to-two-day gap between exposures. That makes perfect sense once you understand the cyclical nature of declarative knowledge. Every time a student draws a piece or structure of declarative knowledge into working memory and adds something to it (corrections and revisions also happen during this time), the structure stored in long-term memory becomes bigger, more elaborate, and more complete. Waiting a day or two between additions gives the new structure time to solidify (or to use the model plane metaphor, it allows time for the glue to dry).

Finally, note that declarative knowledge is the most common form of content articulated in academic standards (McREL International, n.d.a; n.d.b). Bob computed that 77.41 percent of the content articulated in standards is declarative (Marzano, 2019b). This may be one of the reasons why education has historically involved learning methods such as reading, writing, and direct instruction; those instructional approaches are best suited to declarative knowledge. It also makes sense, given that students need a solid foundation in declarative knowledge before they can learn procedural knowledge effectively. We'll expand on how declarative knowledge develops in the next chapter, but for now, let's move on to procedural knowledge.

PROCEDURAL KNOWLEDGE

In his earlier writings (DuFour & Marzano, 2011; Marzano & Kendall, 2007, 2008), Bob made a distinction between two types of procedural knowledge: mental procedures (procedures you do with your mind, like addition or subtraction) and psychomotor procedures (procedures you do with your body, like throwing a baseball). I must admit that I find this distinction confusing and unduly complex. In all my experience dealing with standards and standards statements (for example, Simms, 2016), I have not found any notable benefits arising from this distinction. In my defense, Bob also seems to have abandoned this distinction in his later work, opting for a simple declarative-procedural dichotomy (Marzano, 2009a; Marzano et al., 2019). Additionally, in 2007, he and Kendall explicitly stated:

> The stages of development for acquiring psychomotor procedures are similar to, if not identical with, those involved in acquiring mental procedures: They are first learned as information, during initial practice they are shaped, and then finally they are learned to a level of automaticity or near automaticity. (p. 31)

They also stated that psychomotor procedures "are stored in memory in a fashion identical with mental procedures" (Marzano & Kendall, 2007, p. 31). Therefore, I will henceforth not make a distinction between mental procedures and psychomotor procedures, and I think Bob will forgive me (and I hope you will, too) for keeping this simple.

As with declarative knowledge, we can distinguish procedural knowledge in terms of process size or complexity. Short, simple processes are called *skills*, and there are two types.

- **Algorithms:** Steps performed in a set order that guarantee a certain result (like long division)
- **Strategies:** General-purpose sets of moves that can be performed in a varying order (like reading a map)

Skills can usually be learned to *automaticity*, a level of fluency that no longer requires active thought to execute them.

Long, complex processes are called *macroprocesses*; examples include problem solving, writing, scientific inquiry, and historical analysis. The distinction between skills and macroprocesses is that macroprocesses cannot be learned to automaticity. They can only be learned to a level called *controlled processing*, which means you must think about the steps of the macroprocess as you execute them, but you are good at them and they flow smoothly.

The first phase of learning procedural knowledge (modeling) is where students learn the declarative knowledge associated with a process. That's right, the first step of learning procedural knowledge is understanding declarative knowledge about the process; you must learn the steps of a process before you can execute them. As an example, if students are learning to simplify algebraic expressions by combining like terms, the teacher might present the following steps during the modeling phase.

1. Identify like terms.
2. Combine coefficients for the like terms.
3. Write the resulting terms.
4. Include any remaining terms.
5. Write the simplified expression.

The students must acquire this declarative knowledge (organized in a sequence structure) before they can attempt to carry out the procedure; you must know the steps before you can do them. Also, the students need to know that *like terms* are elements of an expression with the same variables raised to the same exponents (vocabulary); this is also declarative knowledge. And they'd need to know facts like "keep the variable parts of the like terms unchanged; just add or subtract the coefficients" and "arrange the simplified terms in logical order, usually starting with the highest exponent and moving to the lowest." Facts are declarative knowledge. So far, they haven't done anything—this is just the information they need to know to try out the process. This fact—that the modeling phase of developing procedural knowledge deals with declarative knowledge—will be critically important when we discuss the cognitive system in chapter 4 (page 47).

The shaping phase is where students try out and practice the process. There are four important things to remember about the shaping phase.

1. If students make errors, it's important to catch them and correct them quickly.
2. Students can tinker with the process to make it their own.
3. The emphasis should be on accuracy, not speed.
4. Teachers should provide examples (especially worked examples).

The goal of this phase is for students to be able to perform the process smoothly and without errors. To illustrate the shaping phase using the algebraic expression simplification example, the teacher might give students a list of algebraic expressions (challenging but not too difficult) and ask them to identify the like terms in each expression, combine the coefficients for each like term, write the resulting terms, include any remaining terms, and write the simplified expression. As students work, the teacher should quickly point out any errors, explaining why they made the error and how to avoid it in the future. The teacher might also encourage students to experiment with different ways to simplify algebraic expressions; students could discuss their approaches with each other. In addition to providing students with worked examples, the teacher might also ask students to create their own worked examples of the process.

The final phase is the internalizing phase. This is where the emphasis includes speed (in addition to accuracy). For skills, the goal is automaticity; for macroprocesses, the goal is controlled processing. The best way to achieve those goals is through lots of accurate repetition. With the algebraic expressions example, the teacher might ask students to simplify expressions without referring to a checklist or worked example during this phase of practice. The teacher might have them time themselves to see how many expressions they can simplify correctly in a minute. This is also where the teacher might introduce more challenging problems or problems that require students to simplify algebraic expressions in other contexts than they encountered during the shaping phase.

As with declarative knowledge, we'll talk more about the development of procedural knowledge (and how teachers can support it) in the next chapter.

SUMMARY

In this chapter, we discussed the difference between declarative and procedural knowledge. Declarative knowledge is stuff you know, while procedural knowledge is stuff you do. Declarative knowledge is learned in three phases: constructing meaning, organizing, and storing. Procedural knowledge is learned in three different phases: modeling, shaping, and internalizing. Understanding the distinction between the two types of knowledge is essential as we explore how the cognitive system interacts with each in different ways.

CHAPTER 4

THE COGNITIVE SYSTEM

In terms of educational action, the cognitive system is where the rubber meets the road because it articulates the types of tasks that students engage in during learning. In his work, Bob (2007; 2009a), made a strong distinction between *what students are learning* (learning targets) and *the activities they complete* (learning tasks): "Activities are things students do. . . . They constitute the means by which the ends or learning goals are accomplished" (Marzano, 2007, p. 17). Understanding this critical distinction opens up many possibilities in terms of offering students choice. To explain this statement, I'll first give an overview of learning tasks and the cognitive system (with examples) and then investigate each of the five types of learning tasks individually.

OVERVIEW OF LEARNING TASKS AND THE COGNITIVE SYSTEM

As Bob explained in 2003, "learning is enhanced when students are presented with tasks that are similar enough for them to ascertain their sameness" (Marzano, 2003b, p. 112). That means that students need a consistent menu of content-agnostic *learning tasks* that they have learned to perform. As they encounter various *learning targets*, they (or the teacher, but ideally the students) select an appropriate task based on the nature of the content and where they are in the process of learning it. In other words, teachers and students analyze the nature of the content to be learned—and the students' existing background knowledge of that content—and then select appropriate learning tasks that will move the students closer to the learning target.

Of course, this requires that students and teachers (1) can classify learning targets according to their nature (declarative or procedural) and (2) can classify learning targets according to which phases of learning they involve (constructing meaning, organizing, or storing; modeling, shaping, or internalizing). I'll start with a list of the task options in the cognitive system, then organize those options into a flowchart to show how the tasks relate to each other and to both declarative and procedural knowledge. There are five types of tasks in the cognitive system.

1. **Acquisition tasks:** Acquiring new declarative knowledge
   - For declarative knowledge (including the declarative components of procedural knowledge)
   - Involves the constructing meaning (declarative) and modeling (procedural) phases
   - Used when students don't have knowledge and need to acquire it
2. **Execution tasks:** Shaping and internalizing procedural knowledge
   - For procedural knowledge only
   - Involves the shaping and internalizing phases
   - Used when students know the process or steps for a procedure and need to get better and faster at doing it
3. **Organization tasks:** Organizing declarative knowledge
   - For declarative knowledge (including the declarative components of procedural knowledge)
   - Not always necessary for the declarative components of procedural knowledge
   - Involves the organizing and storage phases
   - Used after students have encountered new declarative knowledge, need to organize it into a structure, and store that structure in long-term memory
4. **Analysis tasks:** Analyzing declarative knowledge
   - For declarative knowledge (including the declarative components of procedural knowledge)
   - Not always necessary for the declarative components of procedural knowledge
   - Adds complexity to previously stored declarative knowledge structures
   - Used when students need a deeper understanding of declarative knowledge (which isn't always the case)
5. **Utilization tasks:** Using declarative and procedural knowledge
   - Leverages already-learned declarative and procedural knowledge
   - Involves self-directed projects in which students use a combination of already-learned declarative and procedural knowledge
   - Usually involves going above and beyond the expectations of any single learning target

This list is an adaptation of Bob's New Taxonomy (Marzano & Kendall, 2007, 2008). The cognitive system in the New Taxonomy is composed of four levels of processing: retrieval, comprehension, analysis, and knowledge utilization. Analysis is the only one that made it into my list unscathed. Here's why I changed the names of the other three.

- *Acquisition* better describes the type of learning and learning tasks at the first level of cognition. *Retrieval* describes what happens when students function at that first level during assessment. This is a normal result of the fact that most taxonomies (including Bloom's, Webb's Depth of Knowledge, and others) are designed for assessment situations, not learning.
- The word *comprehension* is so overused in education that it is almost meaningless. Usually, it just means *understand,* and the learning tasks at the second level are more specific than that. They concern getting new information into a structure that can be stored in long-term memory—that is, *organizing* it.
- The *knowledge* part of *knowledge utilization* is redundant, and there is enough knowledge-related terminology already (declarative knowledge, procedural knowledge, and so on). So, just *utilization* is sufficient.

I also added *execution tasks* between acquisition tasks and organization tasks. In the New Taxonomy, execution was a subset of retrieval. But from a learning perspective, execution is so crucial that it needs its own category of tasks. In 2019, Bob and colleagues advocated for this perspective, highlighting the need to view execution as an important category in its own right.

To bring declarative and procedural knowledge together with the five types of learning tasks in the cognitive system, consider the flow chart in figure 4.1.

The primary thing to remember when looking at figure 4.1 is that the start of every arrow is a decision point. Before moving to the next step, the teacher or student (whoever is regulating the learning) must first answer the following question.

- Does this knowledge need more learning or can we stop here with this knowledge?

As we will discuss in the next chapter, the answer to that question is usually determined by the expectations in the learning target (drawn from the standards). If more learning is needed and the arrow has multiple branches, another decision is required.

- What kind of learning is needed for this knowledge?

I'll give four examples of how declarative and procedural knowledge flow through learning tasks within the cognitive system:

1. A straightforward declarative knowledge example
2. A straightforward procedural knowledge example
3. A nonstraightforward declarative knowledge example
4. A nonstraightforward procedural knowledge example

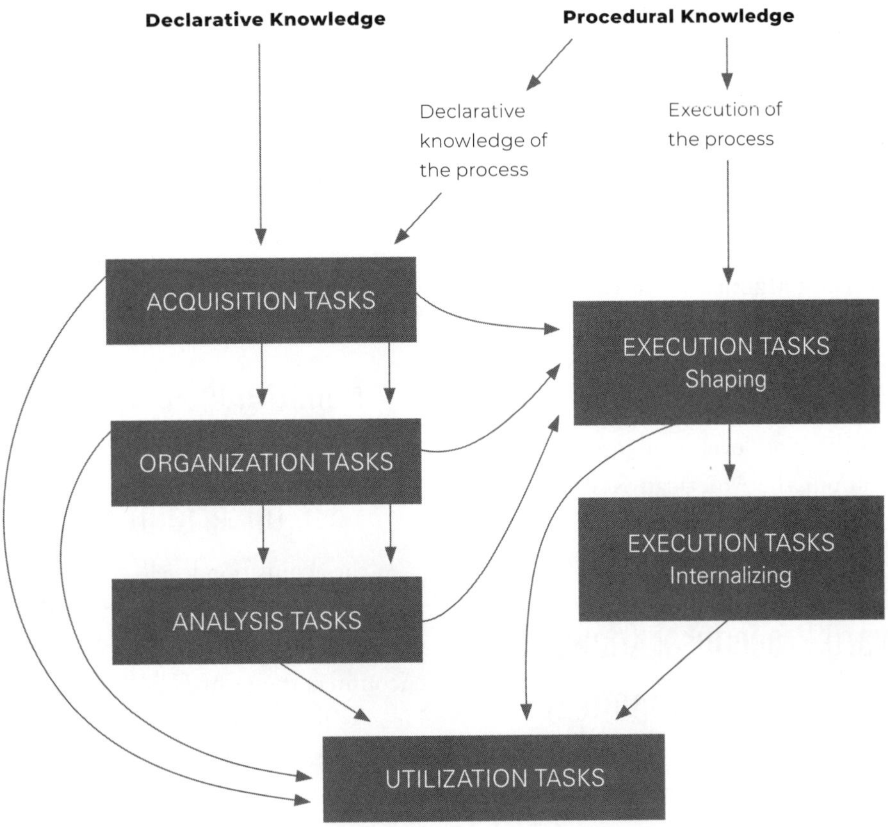

Figure 4.1: Declarative and procedural knowledge in cognitive learning tasks.

Straightforward Declarative Knowledge: Impact of the American Revolutionary War

At the acquisition level, students learn vocabulary terms (*colonies, independence, Great Britain, America*) and details associated with the American Revolutionary War. Details might include events (battles of Lexington, Concord, Bunker Hill, Saratoga; crossing of the Delaware River), documents (Declaration of Independence, Treaty of Paris), and people (George Washington, Thomas Jefferson, Benjamin Franklin).

At the organization level, students figure out how all this information fits together. They might put them all in order—starting in 1775 and progressing until 1783—or they might use a descriptive web to show how the details relate to each other.

At the analysis level, students engage in tasks that add complexity to the descriptive web structure in their long-term memory. They could compare the events, documents, and people of the Revolution to each other and to other topics they've studied. Or they could draw conclusions about the Revolution and defend their conclusions using arguments. In this case, the student might defend their claim that "The American Revolution sparked a wave of revolutions across Europe and South America over the following century."

Finally, at the utilization level, students might use what they know about the American Revolution to decide that it was (or wasn't) the most influential revolution of the past 250 years.

Straightforward Procedural Knowledge: Writing a Multi-Paragraph Text

At the acquisition level, students learn vocabulary terms (*topic, purpose, audience, structure, outline, introduction, body, conclusion*) and a set of steps such as the following.

1. Identify the topic you will write about.
2. Determine your purpose for writing.
3. Identify your target audience.
4. Gather information about your topic.
5. Organize the information into a logical structure.
6. Create an outline to show how big ideas and supporting details fit together and will be sequenced.
7. Write the introduction, body, and conclusion.
8. Revise and edit your text, including proofreading.
9. Publish or present your text to your target audience.

At the execution-shaping level, students try out the process by attempting to follow the steps to create a text. They receive feedback from the teacher and peers about where they are making errors and how to fix them.

At the execution-internalizing level, students write multiple texts. They track how long each one took to write (with the goal of becoming faster with the process) and collect self, peer, and teacher feedback about each one to determine whether quality is increasing.

At the utilization level, students use the process to write a text explaining their decision that the American Revolutionary War was the most influential revolution of the past 250 years.

Nonstraightforward Declarative Knowledge: Heisenberg's Uncertainty Principle

At the acquisition level—while studying the relative properties of elements based on the patterns of electrons in the outermost energy level of atoms—a student encounters the term *Heisenberg's uncertainty principle.* He asks his teacher about it, and she says, "This principle states that we can't know certain properties of particles, like electrons, at the same time. If we want to know an electron's position very accurately, we can't also know how fast it is moving. And if we want to know how fast it is moving, we can't also know exactly where it is. We can only measure one of those things at a time."

Moving to the organization level, she says, "Heisenberg's uncertainty principle is important to quantum mechanics" and quickly draws a diagram to show how quantum mechanics is a branch of physics dealing with matter and energy at the atomic and subatomic scales.

Then she helps the student refocus on the periodic table and the properties of elements, saying, "For this discussion, we are primarily interested in the position of electrons, rather than their velocity." The student considers whether he wants to learn more about Heisenberg's uncertainty principle and decides he does not. In this case, the expectations of the learning target do not require him to deepen this declarative knowledge any further. However, several months later, while working on a utilization task concerning electromagnetic radiation, the student encounters Heisenberg's uncertainty principle again. He reminds himself of its main ideas and incorporates it into his discussion of wave models used to describe electromagnetic radiation, thus refining and extending the structure of this information in his memory through an analysis task.

Nonstraightforward Procedural Knowledge: Multidigit Multiplication

At the acquisition level, students learn that multidigit multiplication (like single-digit multiplication) is repeated addition. They learn the standard algorithm for multiplying multidigit numbers. They also learn at least one other strategy for multiplying multidigit numbers.

At the execution-shaping level, students practice with the algorithm and other strategies using worked examples and practice problems. The goal is error-free execution of each algorithm or strategy.

At the organization level, students organize the strategies that they have learned in terms of which they find the easiest and most useful.

At the analysis level, students compare the strategies they have learned (including the standard algorithm) to identify similarities and differences between them.

At the execution-internalizing level, students practice with the strategy or strategies they have identified as most productive until execution becomes automatic.

At the utilization level, students use their knowledge of effective multiplication strategies to solve the problem of multiplying 123,456,789 × 987,654,321 in a limited amount of time. They conclude that the standard algorithm is functionally useless in such a situation since it would require an unreasonable amount of time and paper to complete.

Here are a few takeaways I hope you will understand after reading those examples.

- **The nature of knowledge (declarative or procedural) determines the tasks students use to learn it.** Not all learning tasks are appropriate for all kinds of knowledge. For example, you will never execute declarative knowledge.
- **Not all knowledge needs to be learned deeply (that is, at every level of the cognitive system).** Sometimes a surface-level understanding (what is it and where it fits) is enough. The expectations in standards help determine the desired depth of understanding.
- **You can skip from lower levels to higher levels.** Not all declarative knowledge needs to be analyzed before it can be utilized. Not all procedural knowledge needs to be internalized before it can be utilized.
- **While sometimes profitable, it is often unnecessary to take the declarative components of procedural knowledge past the acquisition level.** With a lot of procedural knowledge, students just need to be able to execute it.

From here, we'll spend the rest of this chapter diving deep into each of the five levels of cognitive tasks. Note that these levels are deeply intertwined with Bob's instructional model, *The New Art and Science of Teaching* (Marzano, 2017), which I discuss in chapter 8 (page 117). If you're already familiar with *The New Art and Science of Teaching*, you might make connections to your background knowledge as we progress through these sections, but I don't explicitly address those links here.

ACQUISITION TASKS

Acquisition tasks are like first dates. New knowledge meets current knowledge; if they have enough in common, speak the same language, and understand details about each other, a new relationship might be born. In the same way, during an acquisition task, if students draw background knowledge related to new knowledge out of long-term memory and into working memory, if they understand vocabulary related to new knowledge, and if they understand the details of the new knowledge, further learning can occur. Here, we explore these three elements of acquisition tasks: background knowledge, vocabulary, and details.

Background Knowledge

Job one for acquisition tasks is drawing relevant background knowledge from long-term memory into working memory. Background knowledge is a very big deal in learning, but it also may be slightly misunderstood. In their very large 2022 meta-analysis, which included 293 studies and 8,776 effect sizes involving 126,050 participants with an average age of eleven years across forty-seven countries, Bianca Simonsmeier, Maja Flaig, Anne Deiglmayr, Lennart Schalk, and Michael Schneider (2022) investigated the impact of domain-specific background knowledge on students' subsequent status and growth.

Relative to *status*, which is simply a student's current level of achievement, Simonsmeier and colleagues (2022) found that background knowledge in a specific domain strongly predicted a student's overall status in that domain:

> A main finding of our study is that individual differences in knowledge are highly stable over the course of learning. The effect size of r_p^+ = .525 found in our meta-analysis is equivalent to Cohen's *d* of 1.23. Hattie (2009) reported a meta-analytic rank order of 138 variables associated with academic achievement, which did not include domain-specific prior knowledge. If included, it would be among the strongest three effect sizes of all 138 effects in the rank order. This demonstrates that domain-specific prior knowledge predicts individual differences in knowledge and achievement after learning better than almost all other variables. (p. 48)

This is great news and validates the entire educational endeavor. Knowledge is power, and the more we can help students acquire it, the better they'll be able to continue to acquire it.

Relative to student growth, which this study interchangeably calls *knowledge gain* and *learning*, Simonsmeier and colleagues' (2022) findings are surprising. They hypothesized that there would be a small, or weak, positive correlation between domain-specific prior knowledge and knowledge gain during a learning episode. But they found that:

> The average correlation between prior knowledge and knowledge gains was *not* weakly positive. It was virtually zero, and the prediction interval around this mean was very large. Thus, broad and general conclusions about prior knowledge being a strong or weak predictor of learning cannot be drawn. Our findings indicate that *studies differed strongly in how prior knowledge affected learning*. (p. 45; emphasis added)

They continue (being both cautionary and technical):

> The fact that averaged over previous studies, prior knowledge did not predict learning should not be misinterpreted as indicating that prior knowledge generally does not predict learning. This inference cannot be drawn, because the effect sizes varied strongly around their common mean. . . . The very broad prediction interval found in our study indicates that *all is possible*. In some studies, prior knowledge was a strong negative predictor of learning; in some studies, prior knowledge was a strong positive predictor of learning; and in many other studies, prior knowledge barely predicted learning or did not predict it at all. (pp. 46–47; emphasis added)

Essentially, the results were across the board: sometimes background knowledge led to lots of growth, sometimes it led to growth, and sometimes it led to no growth, and sometimes it led to negative growth (that is, loss). Such findings usually indicate that a lot is riding on exactly how an educator uses background knowledge during a learning episode.

Others have noticed this as well. Courtney Hattan and Patricia Alexander (2021) pointed out that background knowledge (and the traditional strategies for activating it, like K-W-L charts or concept mapping) can backfire in the following ways.

- **Traditional strategies often require a sufficient base of relevant knowledge to be helpful.** If the strategies being used don't elicit enough relevant knowledge from students, they might just be a waste of time.
- **Traditional strategies might elicit inaccurate knowledge from students.** Those inaccuracies (if not voiced and corrected) could negatively impact students' subsequent learning.
- **Students who do not have the necessary background knowledge may become frustrated or give up.** In other words, asking students to produce relevant knowledge that they don't have might serve as a demotivator for their learning.
- **Students might have a lot of background knowledge that they don't realize is relevant to the topic at hand.** If students' lives and experiences are vastly different from or in conflict with the topic they're learning, they might not access their background knowledge, even though it could be helpful.

Hattan and Alexander (2021) designed a new strategy, which they called *relational reasoning* (RR), for activating background knowledge that aimed to address these issues. I offer a general description of it here as an example of a more positive technique than those traditionally employed.

1. **Students receive a text on the topic they're studying.** If students are too young to read, the teacher can read the text to them. The text could also be in video form. The content of the text is the focus of this activity, not the act of reading.
2. **At the end of each section of the text, students pause to answer four questions.**
    a. *How is this content similar* to something you have seen, read, or heard in school or out of school?
    b. *How is this content unusual or unexpected* in comparison to something you have seen, read, or heard in school or out of school?
    c. *What about this content is completely opposite* to something you have seen, read, or heard of in school or out of school?
    d. *What about this content could never be* seen, read, or heard today?
3. **Students respond to the questions orally or in writing.** They could write their answers, record verbal responses, or use a speech-to-text app. Similar to step 1, answering the questions is the focus of the activity, not the act of writing.

While Hattan and Alexander (2021) were careful to qualify their findings due to the small sample size (n = 143 fifth- and sixth-grade students at a rural school in the southeastern United States), they did find that students who used this approach demonstrated better understanding of the topic at hand than students who used a K-W-L strategy or a note-taking strategy to activate their background knowledge. They commented:

> The RR prompts encouraged students not only to make connections to prior topic knowledge, but to other sources of relevant knowledge as well, such as their personal knowledge. For example, some students noted that the columns described in the training text were similar to the columns they saw as part of the architecture of prominent local buildings in their town. Further, the RR prompts encouraged students to confront discrepancies between textual content and their own lives and experiences. For example, many students in this rural town attend church on Sundays and Bible study in the evenings. Therefore, a number of students commented on discrepancies between their religious beliefs and the Greeks' belief in multiple gods, which was mentioned in the training text. Additionally, students noted that the Roman Colosseum is similar to stadiums today. However, they also commented that gladiators fought to the death in the Colosseum, whereas today we watch sports like football in stadiums. Moreover, rather than treat these discrepancies as some kind of learner deficit, the RR prompts allow the students to use these discrepancies to critique the content of the readings. (Hattan & Alexander, 2021, p. 893)

In conclusion, background knowledge is a very important factor in acquisition tasks, but it is important to use it carefully. Traditional strategies for activating background knowledge can backfire, but newer strategies like relational reasoning can be more effective. Educators should carefully consider how they will use background knowledge during a learning episode to maximize student growth.

Vocabulary

Job two for acquisition tasks is vocabulary. Bob has explored every facet of vocabulary learning in his work (consult *Teaching Basic, Advanced, and Academic Vocabulary* [Marzano, 2020] for an overview). Rather than attempt to rehash it all, I'll use this opportunity to talk about incidental learning and the power of knowing "just a little bit" about a vocabulary term.

Remember the nonstraightforward declarative knowledge example in the previous section where the student learned a bit about Heisenberg's uncertainty principle and then used that knowledge later? The research consistently shows that kind of implicit learning and surface-level understanding of vocabulary terms is incredibly useful. In 1957, Anthony Downs defined incidental learning as "instances when individuals (1) are exposed to information and (2) acquire a lasting trace of it, both without the intention of doing so" (as cited in Greene, Copeland, & Deekens, 2021, p. 886). Work from the 1970s on *fast mapping* builds on this concept:

> Susan Carey (1978) noted students initially start learning a word by rather quickly associating a new term with some general meaning, even though that meaning is very general or vague. This is referred to as *fast mapping*. As students experience the word in the future, they add new characteristics to their understanding, as well as correct their previous misconceptions. This is referred to as *extended mapping*, which can go on indefinitely as a student has more and more encounters with a term. (Marzano, 2020, p. 19)

In 2004, Bob extrapolated:

> The fact that even surface-level background knowledge is useful greatly increases the viability of a program that seeks to enhance students' academic background knowledge. The goal of such programs *need not be deep conceptual understanding* of the target information. Such a goal would require massive resources and time. Rather, the goal should be to develop a surface-level understanding of the target information. (Marzano, 2004, p. 30; emphasis added)

In 2021, Ueli Studhalter and colleagues found that "simply being exposed to . . . specific vocabulary helps children infer common underlying properties. . . . Teachers can contribute to a rich language environment by referring to objects in a careful and correct way" (p. 12).

So, while there is ironclad evidence for the importance of direct vocabulary instruction (again, see Marzano, 2020), I also strongly encourage educators not to underestimate the power of briefly introducing or simply using words that students might not know. Every time students hear a word in context, there is an opportunity to infer just a little bit more about the target concept and all the concepts connected to it.

Details

Finally, job three for acquisition tasks involves learning details (for declarative knowledge) or the steps of a procedure (for procedural knowledge). Though it is now older, the best research I've found on this is still Bob's 2001 synthesis of work by Graham Nuthall (1999) and Graham Nuthall and Adrienne Alton-Lee (1995) around the effects of types of instruction on learning.

When presenting details during acquisition tasks, a teacher can use at least three methods: verbal instruction, visual instruction, or dramatic instruction. Verbal instruction encompasses both speaking and reading, such as telling students details and having them read about details. Visual instruction provides a picture or diagram that shows the details and how they relate to each other, such as using a descriptive web or an animation that shows the relationships of details to one another. Dramatic instruction embeds details into a story or narrative; you could tell the story to students or ask them to act it out.

Bob's (2001) synthesis found that dramatic instruction is drastically more effective than verbal or visual instruction, both immediately after instruction and when measured twelve months after instruction. The effect sizes immediately after instruction were as follows.

- Dramatic instruction: 1.12
- Visual instruction: 0.90
- Verbal instruction: 0.74

And the effect sizes twelve months after instruction:

- Dramatic instruction: 0.80
- Visual instruction: 0.74
- Verbal instruction: 0.64

In sum, students remembered details much better when they were embedded into a story or narrative. As teachers are already aware, there are many book-length narrative texts with embedded details on a wide variety of topics (especially for science and social studies topics). However, for teachers seeking shorter narrative texts that present details for a learning topic they can't find a book for, artificial intelligence has much to offer. For example, I used the queries in table 4.1 to generate details and a narrative text that used those details related to ratios, proportions, and percents.

TABLE 4.1: Using Artificial Intelligence to Generate a Narrative Text Presenting Details for a Mathematics Topic

Query	Response from Google Bard
What are five foundational details that students need to know to do this standard: students will be able to apply their understanding of ratios, proportions, and percents to solve real-world problems.	Here are five foundational details that students need to know to apply their understanding of ratios, proportions, and percents to solve real-world problems: **What is a ratio?** A ratio is a comparison of two quantities. It can be written in a few different ways, such as 3:2, 3/2, or "3 to 2." Ratios can be used to compare anything, such as the number of boys to girls in a class, the amount of flour to sugar in a recipe, or the distance traveled to the time it takes to travel it. **What is a proportion?** A proportion is a statement that two ratios are equal. It can be written in the form a/b = c/d, where a, b, c, and d are any quantities. Proportions can be used to solve a variety of problems, such as finding a missing value in a ratio or calculating a unit rate. **What is a percent?** A percent is a way of expressing a fraction as a hundredth. For example, 50 percent is the same as 50/100, which is also equal to 0.5. Percents can be used to compare quantities, calculate discounts, and find sales tax. **How to use ratios and proportions to solve real-world problems.** To use ratios and proportions to solve real-world problems, students need to be able to: · Identify the relevant quantities in the problem · Write ratios for the quantities · Set up and solve proportions · Interpret the solution to the proportion in the context of the problem **How to use percents to solve real-world problems.** To use percents to solve real-world problems, students need to be able to: · Calculate percentages · Apply percentages to quantities · Interpret percentages in the context of the problem
Please write a narrative text that incorporates those five details.	Once upon a time, there was a young girl named Sarah who was fascinated by ratios, proportions, and percents. She loved to use these mathematical concepts to solve real-world problems.

continued →

Query	Response from Google Bard
Please write a narrative text that incorporates those five details.	One day, Sarah was helping her mother bake a cake. The recipe called for two cups of flour and three cups of sugar. Sarah knew that this meant that the ratio of flour to sugar in the recipe was 2:3. Sarah also knew that she could use proportions to calculate the amount of each ingredient she needed for a different batch size. For example, if she wanted to make a half-batch of the cake, she would need to use one cup of flour and one-and-a-half cups of sugar. After Sarah and her mother had baked the cake, Sarah decided to use percents to calculate the amount of frosting they needed. The recipe called for enough frosting to cover the top and sides of the cake. Sarah knew that the cake was ten inches in diameter and three inches tall. She also knew that the surface area of a cylinder is calculated by using the formula $2\pi rh + 2\pi r^2$, where r is the radius and h is the height. Sarah plugged the values for the cake's diameter and height into the formula and calculated that the surface area of the cake was 146.5 square inches. She then decided that she wanted to use enough frosting to cover the cake with a 1/4 inch thick layer of frosting. This meant that she needed 36.625 cubic inches of frosting. Sarah used percents to calculate how much frosting she needed to make. She knew that one cubic inch of frosting is equivalent to 16.387 percent of a cup of frosting. This meant that she needed to make 2.24 cups of frosting. Sarah and her mother made the frosting and frosted the cake. The cake looked and tasted delicious. Sarah was proud of herself for using ratios, proportions, and percents to solve a real-world problem.

Source: Google, 2023.

Teachers should review (and edit, if necessary) any AI-generated content before using it with students. In table 4.1, you might reverse the flour and sugar in the ratio (to avoid an unreasonably sugary cake) and correct and clarify errors and inconsistencies in the frosting calculations. AI is not perfect. Nevertheless, it provides an excellent starting point and can save teachers the time and trouble of composing their own narratives involving details. However teachers access or generate them, narratives provide a powerful tool for presenting details during acquisition tasks.

EXECUTION TASKS

As explained previously, all procedural knowledge involves a declarative knowledge component: an understanding of the steps or moves involved in the process. Students can deepen that declarative knowledge using the other cognitive tasks, but to be able to perform procedures, *they need to practice them*. Execution tasks take center stage for procedural knowledge. There are three important things to keep in mind with execution tasks:

1. When to use worked examples
2. How to leverage the spacing effect
3. How to optimize interleaving

Worked Examples

A worked example is a list of the steps of a process with an example to illustrate each step. In Bob's words, "Worked examples provide students with clear exemplars of what a procedure looks like when it is executed properly" (Marzano, 2019b, p. 59). Figure 4.2 shows a worked example for the process of solving a linear equation.

Solve the equation 2x + 5 = 13

Step 1: Simplify both sides of the equation as much as possible.

$2x + 5 - 5 = 13 - 5$

$2x = 8$

Step 2: Isolate the variable term on one side of the equation.

$(2x)/2 = 8/2$

$x = 4$

Step 3: Check the solution by substituting the value you found for the variable back into the original equation.

$2(4) + 5 = 13$

$8 + 5 = 13$

$13 = 13$

The checked solution satisfies the equation, so x = 4 is the correct solution.

Figure 4.2: Linear equation worked example.

The research on worked examples clearly illustrates the distinction between the shaping and internalizing phases of procedural learning. As Shana Carpenter, Tino Endres, and Luotong Hui (2020) explained:

> Studies have shown that the effectiveness of worked examples depends on a learner's level of knowledge. Novice learners who have low prior knowledge on a given topic learn as well or better by starting with worked examples compared to problem-solving practice, whereas more advance learners who have developed high prior knowledge on the topic benefit more from problem-solving practice (Kalyuga et al. 2003; Kalyuga et al. 2001; Kalyuga 2007; Reisslein et al. 2006). (pp. 1035–1036)

When students have just learned the steps of a procedure and are trying it out for themselves, give them lots of worked examples; it is counterproductive to ask them to figure out answers to practice problems all by themselves at this point. But as they become more comfortable with the process, provide fewer worked examples. Fries and colleagues (2021) connected this back to cognitive load theory: there comes a point in procedural learning where worked examples switch from intrinsic load (productive use of working memory) to extraneous load (a distraction). Once students have moved into the internalizing phase, they simply need to practice the process with large numbers of problems—which is an excellent segue to the spacing effect.

The Spacing Effect

Spaced practice and massed practice are opposites: *massed practice* is one long practice session; *spaced practice* is multiple practice sessions with downtime in between. As highlighted by Ouhao Chen, Fred Paas, and John Sweller (2021) in a systematic review of forty-eight studies on the spacing effect (first observed by Ebbinghaus in 1885), spaced practice consistently results in superior learning. The histogram in figure 4.3 (page 58) shows the range of effect sizes they found. All are positive, and quite a few are very large.

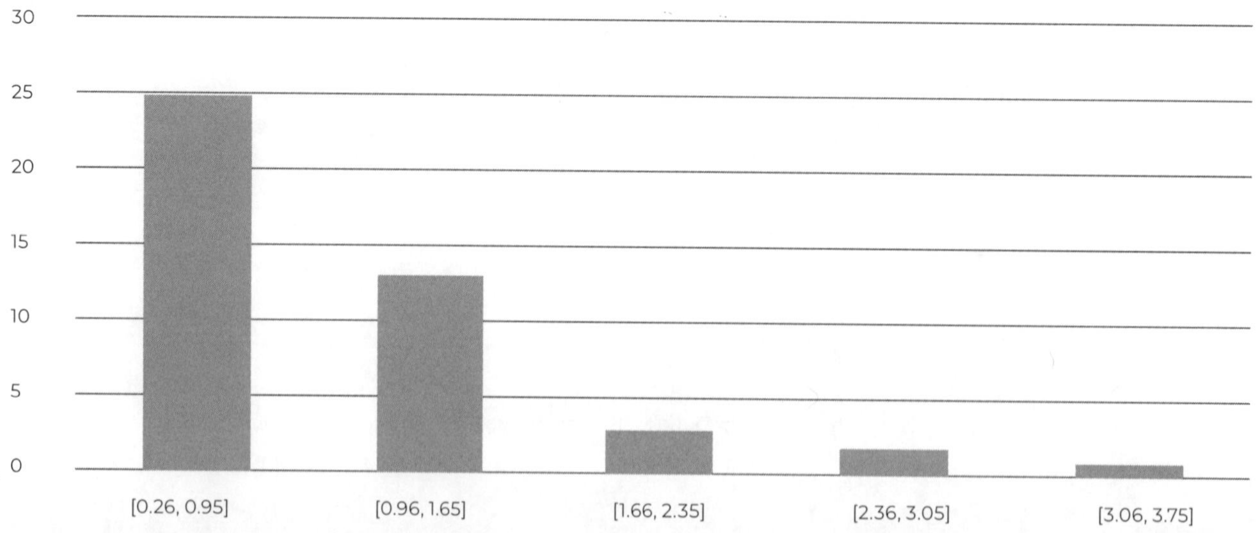

Figure 4.3: Distribution of effect sizes (Cohen's *d*) for spaced practice.

Bob and Abbott (2022) pointed out that the ideal length of time between sessions varies: "If practice sessions are spaced too far apart in the beginning, students will forget the steps involved and have to be reminded of what to do each time they use the procedure" (p. 51). Start with practice sessions closer together (so students don't forget how to do the process between sessions), and once they've got a handle on the process, gradually add more time between the practice sessions.

Interestingly, the efficacy of spaced practice also seems to be related to working memory capacity. Brandon Schmeichel (2007) demonstrated *working memory resource depletion*: after completing a task that uses a lot of working memory, the capacity of working memory shrinks. James Tyler and Kathleen Burns (2008) found that if you take a mental break you can restore your working memory resources. If students are stuck on either the shaping or internalizing phase of procedural learning, encouraging them to take a break to restore their working memory resources can be a very effective strategy.

Interleaving

Finally, we come to the interesting case of interleaving. When students are in the internalizing phase of procedural learning, it might be tempting to give them a large set of the same type of problem to practice (*blocked practice*). But research shows that it is better to alternate one type of problem with a different type of problem (*interleaved practice*). As Doug Rohrer, Robert Dedrick, and Marissa Hartwig (2020) explained, "interleaving prevents students from safely assuming that each practice problem relates to the same skill or concept as the previous problem, thus forcing them to choose an appropriate strategy on the basis of the problem itself" (p. 873). They elaborated:

> The scaffolding provided by blocked practice has a downside, as illustrated by the following example:
>
> A bug crawls 24 cm west and then 7 cm north. How far is the bug from where it started?
>
> To solve this problem, students must first infer that they need to use the Pythagorean theorem ($24^2 + 7^2 = c^2$, so c = 25 cm). Yet this inference is unnecessary when the problem appears as part of a blocked assignment, especially if the block immediately follows a lesson on the Pythagorean theorem. Put another way, the solution of a mathematics problem requires students to both choose and execute a strategy, yet blocking often allows students to infer an appropriate strategy for a problem before they read the problem. In effect, blocked practice denies students the opportunity to learn how to choose a strategy on the basis of the problem itself. (pp. 875–876)

Chen and colleagues (2021) reviewed sixty-seven studies on the interleaving effect and reported the range of effect sizes shown in the histogram in figure 4.4. All are positive, and a few are extremely large.

While some may find it counterintuitive (Won't students develop fluency more quickly if they do the same type of problem repeatedly?), the research is unequivocal: interleaved practice works better than blocked practice. Robert Bjork, John Dunlosky, and Nate Kornell (2013) explained that teachers and students must remember that *developing fluency* is very different from *experiencing fluency*. The type of study activities that lead to fluency often do not feel very fluent or easy:

> Activities such as spacing and interleaving . . . are known as desirable difficulties (Bjork 1994, Bjork & Bjork 2011). They impair performance—and hence, apparent learning—during acquisition, but enhance long-term learning. The fundamental problem with using fluency as a basis for study decisions is that learners often interpret high fluency as signaling a high rate of improvement when it can actually, under some circumstances, signal just the opposite. (p. 16.18)

We will return to this notion of desirable difficulties in chapter 8 (page 117) when we discuss retrieval practice. For now, help students remember that a certain amount of difficulty while developing fluency is desirable.

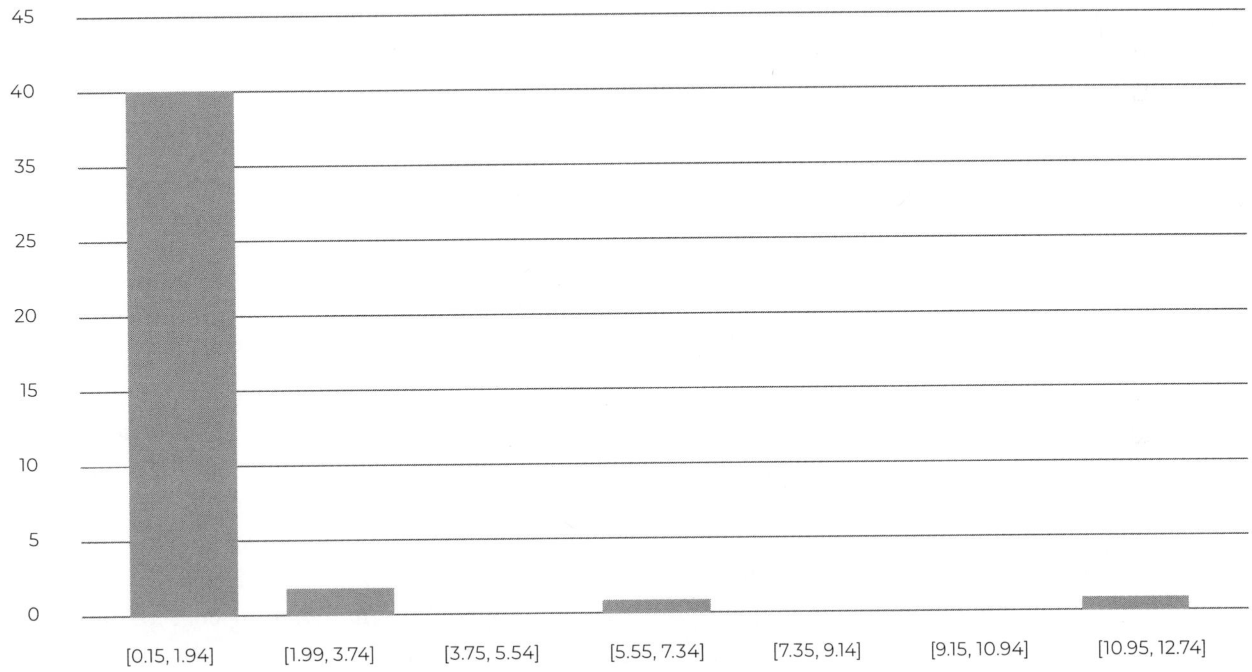

Figure 4.4: Distribution of effect sizes (Cohen's *d*) for interleaved practice.

ORGANIZATION TASKS

Students need to identify the structure of information and create representations of those structures to store information in long-term memory. Closely related to structures and representations is Richard E. Mayer's (2014b) cognitive theory of multimedia learning. It is based on three assumptions (as articulated by Sascha Schneider, Maik Beege, Steve Nebel, Lenka Schnaubert, and Günter Daniel Rey [2022]).

1. Information is processed via two cognitive channels (linguistic and nonlinguistic; Paivio, 1986).

2. The working memory system is limited in capacity (Baddeley, 1992).
3. Actively processing information requires learners to build mental representations and models.

We have already discussed the second point as cognitive load theory (chapter 2, page 33). We'll get to the first point shortly, but for now, let's focus on point three: representations and models.

You have already seen a number of knowledge representations and models in this book.

- **List structures:** Most of the tables involve some sort of list structure.
- **Cause-effect structures:** Figure 1.1 (interaction between types of memory; page 18) is a cause-effect structure.
- **Descriptive structures:** Figure 1.5 (quadrants of valence and activation for emotions; page 22) is a descriptive structure, and so is figure 3.3 (organizing details and generalizations; page 44) in the example of how declarative knowledge develops.
- **Comparison structures:** The two histograms in the previous sections of this chapter, figure 4.3 (page 58) and figure 4.4 (page 59), are comparison structures.
- **Process structures:** Figure 3.1 (phases of learning declarative and procedural knowledge; page 42) has two process structures in it, and the flowchart in figure 4.1 (declarative and procedural knowledge in cognitive learning tasks; page 49) at the beginning of this chapter is also a process structure.

The purpose of telling you what kind of structures you've seen so far is twofold: (1) highlighting some of the major structures that organize information (others include sequence, problem-solution, argumentation, episode, and generalization); and (2) showing that representations and models are not as neat and tidy as the designers of graphic organizer templates would have you believe.

First, not everybody calls the structures by the same names. What I call a comparison structure, Xue Wang, Richard E. Mayer, Pu Zhou, and Lin Lin (2021) call "compare-and-contrast," and what I call a descriptive structure, Wang and colleagues call "hierarchy." Second, multiple visualizations can represent a given structure. For example, bar charts, Venn diagrams, and histograms are all comparison structures expressed in different ways. Finally, assigning a structure to a set of information isn't an objective exercise. Two people might (equally productively) assign different structures to the same set of information. As Bob has repeatedly pointed out, this is fine:

> Different patterns can be used to organize the same information. . . . Most passages contain information that is loosely organized. . . . When students synthesize information, they should be required to justify the pattern they select. (Marzano & Arredondo, 1987, p. 61)

> Organizing information is a somewhat subjective process in which the learner structures information in ways unique to her perspective. She highlights some ideas, makes others subordinate, and even disregards a few. (Marzano, 1992, p. 47)

Noah Schroeder, John Nesbit, Carlos Anguiano, and Olusola Adesope (2018)—note that Nesbit and Adesope are pioneers in the field of knowledge structures and mental representations—performed a meta-analysis of the influence of concept maps (another term for knowledge structures) on learning. They synthesized 142 effect sizes (involving 11,814 participants) and found an overall effect size of $g = 0.58$. But they also found that *creating* concept maps ($g = 0.72$) had a much larger effect than *studying* concept maps ($g = 0.43$). Based on this (and other) research, Hyoung Seok Shin and Allan Jeong (2021) stated that "improving students' knowledge structures is best achieved by having students construct their own maps as opposed to presenting them with maps constructed by experts" (p. 2). The purpose of using representations and models is to help students process information and structure it for storage in long-term memory. There is no reason to impose particular structures, premade representations, or graphic organizers on the information students learn. If they can explain why they chose a particular structure or created a particular representation, they are on the right track.

A study by Keith Thiede and colleagues (2022) further illustrated the power of student-created representations and models. They taught one group of fifth-grade science students how to create an organizational representation for a text: "instruction emphasized the importance of connecting ideas in the text to one another and including the actions described in the text and connecting these actions to other key elements" (p. 3). The control group was simply asked to draw a representative picture of the text. They found that those students who drew organizational sketches (showing how elements of the text and actions in the text related to one another) scored higher on a comprehension test (effect size $d = 0.64$).

One final word on representations and models: organization tasks ask students to find basic relationships between ideas and draw or describe them. It is a labeling and diagramming activity, not an analysis activity. Analysis tasks go a step further and ask students to examine similarities and differences and the relationships between ideas in detail. We'll talk about that in the next section.

Now, let's consider the first item from Mayer's (2014b) cognitive theory of multimedia learning. Information is processed via two cognitive channels, linguistic and nonlinguistic (Paivio, 1986). This theory of *dual-channel processing* asserts that there are two channels from working memory to long-term memory: a linguistic channel (words) and a nonlinguistic channel (pictures). Liru Hu, Gaowei Chen, Pengfei Li, and Jing Huang (2021) explained that each channel "is limited in terms of working memory capacity, but their combined capacity is additive. . . . Individuals can access greater processing capacity when materials are presented through the two symbolic systems" (pp. 1718–1719). This means that you can expand working memory capacity by presenting and processing information using both words and pictures; working memory uses separate resource pools for each. Bob has leveraged this idea for years to advocate for having students record their learning using both words and pictures; in 2007, he explained:

> Information can be encoded in nonlinguistic or imagery form. [Allan] Paivio (Paivio, 1969, 1971, 1990; Sadoski & Paivio, 2001) provides a detailed explanation of the dynamics of this type of processing. The linguistic aspect of processing is most observable as the ability to talk about what one has read, heard, or experienced. The nonlinguistic aspect of information processing is most observable as the mental images associated with one's experiences. (Marzano, 2007, p. 35)

Returning to our cognitive load theory equations, using both words and pictures to process information seems to increase *germane load*—the cognitive resources available for a task—as shown in figure 4.5.

Intrinsic load		Germane load		Extraneous load
6		4	+	2
6		5	+	2
6		6	+	2

Figure 4.5: Increasing germane load.

More up-to-date research has extended this idea to include physical actions as an additional way to access untapped working memory resources, an idea called *embodied cognition*. Carolien Duijzer, Marja Van den Heuvel-Panhuizen, Michiel Veldhuis, Michiel Doorman, and Paul Leseman (2019) found that having students move their own bodies in ways that were related to the target content—or even just having students watch others move their bodies in ways related to the target content—resulted in learning gains. For example, students might use their arms to show acute and obtuse angles. Or they might move small props (like toy cars or cubes) to show the relationship between two objects moving at different speeds. An oft-used example is when students collaborate to act out the movement and rotation of planets, moons, and other solar bodies by standing and moving in various positions around a room. Alexander Skulmowski and Günter Rey (2018) compared studies where movement was strongly or weakly linked to the target content; stronger links to the target content resulted in greater learning gains. Because of the importance of linking movement to target content, researchers investigating the educational uses of virtual reality tools (for example, Araiza-Alba, Keane, Chen, & Kaufman, 2021) have become very interested in these theories. Regardless of the application, the principle is the same as dual-channel processing:

> Physical interactions and bodily cues can lighten the cognitive load required in the learning process, resulting in better task completion and learning outcomes. In other words, this theory implies that there is a connection between our motor and visual senses; therefore, the more explicit the connection, the easier learning becomes (Johnson-Glenberg, 2018; Mayer, 2014). (Araiza-Alba et al., 2021, p. 3)

Although this field of research is nascent and it is too early to draw strong conclusions, it does support the idea that students can productively organize content using words, pictures, and gestures.

ANALYSIS TASKS

Bob has probably written more about analysis tasks (which he typically calls *cognitive analysis tasks*) than any other topic. He defined *analysis* as "the reasoned extension of knowledge. Analysis . . . involves the generation of new information not already possessed by the individual" (Marzano & Kendall, 2008, p. 17). As already mentioned and highlighted in the flowchart in figure 4.1 (page 49), not all declarative information needs to be analyzed. Learning statements (such as standards) usually provide fairly overt guidance about whether information needs to be analyzed. Terms like *compare, contrast, relationships, claim, evidence*, and *reasoning* all signal the need for declarative information to be the subject of analysis tasks.

The big idea here is that *you must teach students how to do analysis tasks*. That is, you ought not to ask them to examine relationships, evaluate information, or construct arguments until after you teach them how to examine relationships, evaluate information, or construct arguments. Analysis tasks are procedural knowledge in and of themselves. And as with all procedural knowledge, teachers should give students a process (modeling), guide them to practice slowly with that process (shaping), and then—if they are to reach controlled processing or automaticity—let them practice it repeatedly (internalizing).

Bob has been advocating for teaching students cognitive processes (also known as *thinking skills*) since (at least) 1987. In *Tactics for Thinking*, he and Daisy Arredondo said, "Overt instruction in thinking skills means that students are explicitly taught processes for specific cognitive operations" (Marzano & Arredondo, 1987, p. 1). The rest of that book is essentially twenty-two thinking skills and the processes for teaching them. In almost all of his books since then, Bob has included explicit processes for thinking skills; it is a hallmark of his work. However, for several reasons, I don't present specific processes for teaching thinking skills in this book. First, I am sacrificing depth for breadth in this book. Second, from the very beginning, Bob has acknowledged that his processes aren't gospel:

> Even though a specific process is identified for each skill taught in the program, a given process should not be considered the only way to perform the skill. Instead they should be considered a starting point for students and teachers—a frame within which to consider specific cognitive activities. (Marzano & Arredondo, 1987, p. 1)

Educators can find such processes in other resources or generate them using their own expertise or technology tools (including AI). Here, I present three categories that house most (if not all) of the analysis processes: examining relationships, evaluating information, and constructing arguments.

Examining Relationships

If you've read Bob's work, you've probably run into the phrase "similarities and differences." Over the years, Bob has articulated four specific activities that fall into this category (Marzano, 2007).

1. **Comparing:** Identifying similarities and differences
2. **Classifying:** Grouping things that are alike into categories
3. **Creating metaphors:** Identifying a pattern that connects seemingly unrelated information
4. **Creating analogies:** Identifying the relationship between two sets of items

At the heart of any task that involves similarities and differences is the idea that looking closely at how two or more things relate to each other draws attention to the specific attributes of each thing. As Bob and Pickering explained:

> Consciously putting things into different categories influences how we perceive the items. When a round, purple object is grouped with other round objects, you notice it is round; when it is grouped with other purple objects, you notice it is purple. (Marzano & Pickering, 1997, p. 123)

Comparison and classification are quite straightforward (please consult Marzano 2019b for in-depth treatments). Here, I'll offer some brief thoughts on metaphor and analogy.

Bob's favorite metaphor is "love is a rose"; he uses it almost every time he talks about metaphors. The relationship in the metaphor draws attention to the beauty and prickliness of love. Relative to helping students construct metaphors, I have found Jonan Donaldson and Ayana Allen-Handy's (2020) definition helpful:

> Metaphors are a class of analogical thinking with complex mapping of characteristics from a source domain onto a target domain in which the source and target domains are dissimilar (Hofstadter and Sander 2013; Lakoff and Johnson 1980, 1999). For example, in the metaphor *time is money*, the source domain is economic transactions and the target domain is time. (pp. 547–548)

In other words, you identify important characteristics of one object (the one in the target domain) and then think of another object (from a source domain) that has those same characteristics. For example, rational numbers (target domain) encompass a wide range of values and include different types of numbers, like whole numbers and fractions. What else encompasses a wide range with different types? Flowers. Music. There are lots of possibilities. From an educational perspective, the source domain doesn't matter, but the target domain needs to match the learning goal this analysis task focuses on. As this example illustrates, students must list and explain the characteristics they identified in the target domain; using metaphor can often help with those explanations, but students need to be able to clearly identify the characteristics they are focusing on in the target domain.

The point of analogies is to strip away distracting details and make knowledge more portable and generalizable (Fries et al., 2021). I have personally found analogies to be extremely helpful in answering the question, "Why is this important to learn?" For example, why do we need to be able to describe and analyze the physical features and landforms of different regions? In response, the student first connects physical features and landforms to something else that they have previously learned about in the same domain (social studies)—for example, the development and characteristics of ancient civilizations. That's relationship 1: landforms have a relationship with the civilizations located on them. To articulate what kind of relationship this is, students look for another relationship that is similar. Relationship 2 could be the relationship between a foundation and its building, arteries and the body, or between a canvas and the painting on it. Each analogy highlights a different aspect of the landforms-civilization relationship. Again, as with metaphor, students need to explain the relationship they're describing. There is no need to belabor either metaphors or analogies; remember that the goal is to help students notice specific attributes of the content at hand. Once that has happened, feel free to move on.

Evaluating Information

Whereas examining relationships involves examining the characteristics of specific content, evaluating information is about examining the accuracy and credibility of new information related to a topic. As Bob and his colleagues (1988) defined them, "Evaluating skills involve assessing the reasonableness and quality of ideas" (Marzano et al., 1988, p. 109). Once again, not all information needs to be the subject of an analysis task:

> The rigor with which we must analyze information for errors depends on the extent to which the information can affect us. When the stakes are high, more attention to an argument is required. Recognizing high-stakes situations and increasing our level of attention and depth of analysis will

> decrease the possibility of doing things we later regret (Marzano, Paynter, & Doty, 2003, p. 40)

Analysis tasks that involve evaluating information deepen students' understanding of a topic by asking them to determine whether new information should or should not be added to their current knowledge about that topic. One of the main ways that students make that determination is by examining and evaluating sources of new information, a critical skill when using digital texts and online sources.

Over the past few decades, researchers and theorists have engaged in much hand-wringing about the challenges associated with digital texts and online sources, so I'll just mention them in passing rather than dwelling on them. As summarized by Joel Breakstone and colleagues (2021, p. 505):

- "Outside of school and homework, [teens] spend more than 7 hours a day online."
- "Three quarters [of teens] say they get news from social media 'often' or 'sometimes,' and nearly 70% do so through internet videos."
- "Young people, like many Americans, struggle to evaluate online sources."
- "Students who said they would base evaluations on source information rarely did so when observed in real time."
- "Students frequently ignored source information . . . focusing instead on the relevance of the information provided . . . and basing their conclusions on a website's surface-level features."

The good news is that students' sourcing skills are highly susceptible to intervention. In their review of sourcing interventions, Eva Brante and Helge Strømsø (2018) identified many interventions that had significant positive effects on students' sourcing behavior, as shown in table 4.2.

In table 4.2, I want to draw particular attention to Mônica Macedo-Rouet, Jason Braasch, M. Britt, and Jean-François Rouet's (2013) study with fourth and fifth graders. While this is just a single study, I always take notice when an intervention works better with less-skilled students than it does with more skilled students, because that data pattern indicates that the intervention may have the potential to close achievement gaps rather than widen them (per the Matthew Effect I mentioned in chapter 1, page 15).

A strategy called lateral reading shows particular promise toward improving students' sourcing behaviors. Sam Wineburg and Sarah McGrew (2017) compared how university students, university professors, and professional fact-checkers interact with websites. They found that students and professors read websites "vertically," starting at the top and reading to the bottom. The fact-checkers took a radically different approach, as indicated by Breakstone and colleagues (2021):

> Landing on an unfamiliar website, they clicked away from it and engaged in lateral reading. . . . They opened up new tabs across the horizontal axis of their browser and searched for information about the organization or individual behind it. Only after surveying what other sites had to say did they return to their original starting place. Using this approach, fact checkers quickly sized up sites that masked their intent and backers. (p. 506)

Lateral reading focuses less on the content of a website and more on the evidence behind the website. That's an important consideration for evaluating information and a perfect segue into constructing arguments.

TABLE 4.2: Interventions for Evaluating Digital Sources

Study	Level	Number of Students	Intervention	Affected Outcome	Effect Size
Argelagós & Pifarré, 2012	Seventh and eighth graders	40	Students were prompted to define the problem, search for information, identify a site's author and purpose, and present information.	Selected results evaluation (usability and reliability)	1.84
De La Paz & Felton, 2010	Eleventh graders	160	Students were instructed to analyze sources; for example, consider the author (position, knowledge) and the date the document was published, identify the form of document and understand the underlying assumptions in the document.	Document use	0.75
				Rebuttals in essay	0.71
Kammerer, Meier, & Stahl, 2016	Ninth graders	45	Students were prompted to attend to and tag content to source by classifying websites according to category.	Memory for sources	2.26
				Source-to-content links	1.20
Kingsley, Cassady, & Tancock, 2015	Fifth graders	418	Students were taught to locate source information, question author, check accuracy of information, and detect bias by triangulating data.	Locating information	0.34
				Synthesizing information	0.23
Macedo-Rouet, Braasch, Britt, & Rouet, 2013	Fourth and fifth graders	96	Students were guided to identify the sources present in the texts, to identify who said what and to assess the knowledge level of the source with respect to the topic of the text.	Source-content questions (less-skilled readers)	0.76
				Source-content questions (skilled readers)	-0.01 ns
				Source evaluation—less skilled	0.60
				Source evaluation—skilled	0.03 ns
Mason et al., 2014	Ninth graders	134	Students read about what to consider when assessing how reliable websites are; answered questions about the author's knowledge and motivation.	Time on least reliable sites	0.51
				Rank order according to reliability	0.62
				Justification criteria most reliable sites	0.39
				Justification criteria least reliable sites	0.37
				Argumentation in essay	0.54
Walraven, Brand-Gruwel, & Boshuizen, 2013	Ninth graders	100	Students attended to source features via process worksheet with questions such as: When was the site last updated? What does the author of the information want to achieve?	Evaluation of hit list	1.12
				Evaluation of websites	0.64
Zhang & Duke, 2011	Fourth and fifth graders	242	Students were encouraged via worksheets to pay attention to who wrote this, why did they write it and when was it written?	Website judgments (trust reasons)	1.01
				Website rank order	0.97

Constructing Arguments

The focus for this category is on students making claims and defending them. Bob has provided a great deal of useful detail relative to making and defending claims, including the components of an effective argument—claim, grounds, backing, qualifiers—in many of his books (for example, Marzano, 2003b, 2019a, 2019b; Marzano & Brown, 2009; Marzano & Pickering, 1997). I will not replicate that information here. Instead, I want to focus on two aspects of constructing arguments: making a claim and supporting that claim.

You'll notice that this section on constructing arguments comes after the section on evaluating information. In my experience listening to educators share about their use of argumentation in their classrooms, it seems as if the hardest part is getting students to make substantive claims. Making a substantive claim—one worth defending—is not an easy task. Therefore, I strongly recommend that educators begin not by asking students to make a claim but by asking them to consume information on a topic until they have enough ideas to formulate a claim. In 1981, Bob advised writers that they should be "full of ideas" (p. 112) before they attempt to start writing. I believe the same is true for students making claims; they need to be full of ideas first.

Bob has also said much in his work about the various reasoning processes used to formulate claims: induction, deduction, and retroduction. If those labels are useful to you and your students, please use them. However, in my review of Bob's work, I find the verb *generalizing* to be the most useful when it comes to formulating claims. Here is Bob's brief explanation: "The skill of generalizing involves inferring new generalizations and principles from information that is known" (Marzano & Kendall, 2007, p. 87). And here's the extended one:

> The process of generalizing, as defined in the New Taxonomy, is neither purely inductive nor purely deductive. . . . Many philosophers have advanced the concept of *retroduction* as a more fruitful approach to understanding the nature of inferential thinking. Retroduction is the act of generating and shaping an idea based on one or more cases. Sometimes inferences made during the process are more inductive in nature; sometimes they are more deductive. In the New Taxonomy, generalizing is best described as a retroductive process that is oriented more toward induction than deduction but involves both during different aspects of the process. (Marzano & Kendall, 2007, pp. 49–50)

The bottom line is that making a claim involves using what you know to make an assertion, and it may be just as productive for students to make an indefensible claim—and realize the claim is indefensible while trying to defend it—as it is for them to initially make a defensible one. In support of such an assertion, Maria Tulis, Gabriele Steuer, and Markus Dresel (2016) cited research supporting their learning-from-errors model, as shown in table 4.3. As explained in chapter 2 (page 33), these findings come with the caveat that positive outcomes from a learning-from-errors model are contingent on the presence of an error-friendly climate in the classroom.

Relative to defending claims, I agree with Bob and Kendall (2007) that "a student does not have to understand the technical aspects of grounds, warrants, backing, and qualifiers, such as their names and defining characteristics" (p. 46). I also agree with Stelios Christodoulou and Irene-Anna Diakidoy (2020) that argumentation can and does look different depending on the issue at hand, the available information about the issue, and the goals of constructing the argument. They stated, "In its simplest form, an argument consists of a claim and a reason supporting it (Toulmin, 1958; Voss & Means, 1991)" (p. 2). In some cases, an argument might only have one reason supporting it. Students need to understand that, especially in academic contexts, it is appropriate to provide evidence to support their reasons. I argue that many students (and educators) get stuck trying to generate multiple reasons for a claim and multiple pieces of evidence for each reason (not to mention qualifiers). It might be more productive (and timely) to switch that focus to a simpler claim-reason-evidence structure that both students and educators can use more frequently and more flexibly in everyday classroom life.

TABLE 4.3: Research on Learning From Errors

Reflecting on and correcting errors increases the accuracy of mental models.	Kapur, 2008; Mathan & Koedinger, 2005; Siegler, 2002; Van Lehn, Siler, Murray, Yamauchi, & Baggett, 2003
Including errors in worked examples (and asking students to find and explain them them) leads to enhanced learning outcomes.	Grosse and Renkl, 2007
Feedback which allows students to detect, correct, and reflect on their own errors fosters learning at a faster rate, conceptual understanding, and (transfer) performance.	Mathan & Koedinger, 2005
Delaying instruction enables reflection on incorrect solution attempts by students.	Kapur, 2008; Westermann & Rummel, 2012
Reaching impasses and clarifying errors turned out to have stronger impact on effective learning than when a tutor modeled the correct action.	Van Lehn et al., 2003

UTILIZATION TASKS

At their core, utilization tasks (which Bob has many names for, including *knowledge application lessons* and *cognitively complex tasks*) are projects. I love the way Bob and Diane Paynter defined *projects* in 1994: "A project is a task that mirrors the complexity and holistic nature of real-world tasks. Specifically, projects are tasks that are (a) partially specified, (b) multidimensional, (c) student-directed, and (d) long-term" (Marzano & Paynter, 1994, p. 113). Over the years, Bob has stuck with this definition, although he has refined it. In 2017, he clarified "student-directed":

> The discovery learning teachers execute during knowledge application lessons is not pure discovery, where students are pretty much left to their own devices in their exploration of specific declarative or procedural knowledge. Such *unassisted discovery* is highly ineffective. . . . In contrast, *enhanced discovery* is a very powerful instructional tool. (Marzano, 2017, p. 47)

In 2019, Bob clarified "partially specified": "Projects tend to devolve into students selecting topics of interest and reporting out on them. I present a way of designing projects . . . that require the application of knowledge and have discernible structures" (2019b, p. 105). Bob and Abbott described six of these structures:

> - **Decision making** is the process of generating and applying criteria to select between alternatives that appear equal.
> - **Problem solving** is the process of overcoming obstacles or constraints to achieve a goal.
> - **Invention** is the process of creating a new process or product that meets a specific identified need. . . .
> - **Experimental inquiry** is the process of generating a hypothesis about a physical or psychological phenomenon and then testing your hypothesis.
> - **Investigation** is the process of identifying and then resolving differences of opinion or contradictory information about concepts, historical events, or future possible events.
> - **Systems analysis** is the process of describing and analyzing the parts of a system with particular emphasis on the relationships among the parts. (Marzano & Abbott, 2022, p. 56)

As with analysis tasks, I do not give you the details on these; if you need them, please see chapter 5 of *The Handbook for the New Art and Science of Teaching* (Marzano, 2019a). Here, we focus on other research regarding the teacher's role during utilization tasks.

Greg Ashman, Slava Kalyuga, and John Sweller (2020) conducted a series of randomized, controlled experiments to investigate whether students benefited more from (1) explicit instruction before student-directed exploration or (2) student-directed exploration before explicit instruction. The second scenario, referred to as "productive failure" (Kapur & Bielaczyc, 2012), involves having "learners first struggle to solve a problem on their own before being given full guidance" (Ashman et al., 2020, p. 230). Ashman and colleagues found that novice learners benefit more from explicit instruction first, which makes perfect sense given the tenets of cognitive load theory. Explicit instruction brings the level of challenge involved with learning new material down to a level appropriate for the capacity of working memory.

But the problem is that there are also studies (Kapur, 2012, 2014; Jacobson et al., 2017; Lai, Portolese, & Jacobson, 2017; Loibl & Rummel, 2014a, 2014b) that support the opposite conclusion: student exploration first leads to better learning. Why this contradiction? Ashman and colleagues (2020) present a compelling explanation (which will resonate with educators familiar with gradual release models): as students become more skilled with content, and their mental representations become more sophisticated, it frees up working memory capacity to handle the cognitive load of learning by exploration. I review this corner of research controversy for two reasons.

1. Before asking students to use knowledge in utilization tasks, it is critical that they have (at least) acquired the knowledge and organized it (for declarative knowledge) or shaped it (for procedural knowledge). Otherwise, it is likely that the intrinsic load of a utilization task will overload their working memory capacity.
2. Educators can adjust their level of support for students during utilization tasks depending on (a) students' familiarity with the knowledge involved and (b) students' familiarity with the structure and expectations of utilization tasks.

Relative to this second point, Margaret Blanchard and colleagues (2010) provided a set of levels of support that teachers can provide to students during what they called *inquiry instruction* and which I have adapted here for use during utilization tasks.

1. The teacher provides a student with the topic for their utilization task, selects the type of task the student will engage in, and provides relevant resources. The teacher and student meet several times per week during the task.
2. The student selects the topic for their utilization task, and the teacher selects the type of task the student will engage in. The teacher and student share responsibility for collecting resources. The teacher and student meet once a week during the task.
3. The student selects the topic for their utilization task and the type of task they will engage in. The student collects relevant resources. The teacher and student meet once at the outset of the task, once in the middle of the task, and once at the end of the task.

These levels of support provide a structure in which teachers can help students move toward engaging in utilization tasks with what Cai-Ting Wen and colleagues (2020) call "minimal but nonzero" (p. 3) guidance.

SUMMARY

In this chapter, we discussed the intersection of declarative and procedural knowledge with the cognitive tasks that students use to learn that knowledge. Acquisition tasks are used to initially learn details related to both declarative and procedural knowledge; for procedural knowledge, those details are usually a process or set of steps. Procedural knowledge then moves into execution tasks where students focus first on using the process accurately and then increasing their speed with the process. Declarative knowledge moves into organization and analysis tasks. Utilization tasks allow students to bring together both declarative and procedural knowledge to complete tasks that mimic and mirror real-world situations. For all tasks within the cognitive system, students need to clearly understand the parameters of the task; especially for analysis and utilization tasks, students will likely need to learn the processes for those tasks and practice them (as procedural knowledge) before applying them to content. This chapter's discussion of the cognitive system completes our survey of the self-, metacognitive, cognitive, and knowledge systems. As we have seen, each of these systems is an important element of K–12 education. In the next chapter, we will discuss how to bring all these systems together in a guaranteed and viable curriculum.

CHAPTER 5

CURRICULUM

In this final chapter of part 1, we bring together the self-, metacognitive, cognitive, and knowledge systems to create a comprehensive answer to the question, "What do students need to know and be able to do as a result of schooling?" Specifically, we will focus on how to create and implement a *guaranteed and viable curriculum*. Bob coined this phrase in 2003 to describe the need for a curriculum that is clearly articulated and teachable in the time available. To begin our exploration of the guaranteed and viable curriculum, we will start where Bob always starts this discussion: the standards movement.

STANDARDS

In the 20th century, textbooks articulated what students should know and be able to do as a result of schooling. Hypothetically, this made sense: as long as teachers used the same textbook to teach the same course, there was a reasonable expectation that students would be exposed to similar content. But in one really important way, this system wasn't satisfactory. If textbooks determined what students learned, the textbook authors were in a position of exceptional power regarding what students needed to know. Over time, sentiment and research have both found these authors' judgments to be somewhat unsatisfactory. Therefore, the standards movement emerged, and it has seen two distinct phrases.

The Standards Movement—Phase 1

As early as the 1940s, educators such as Ralph Tyler advocated for a different approach to education than the textbook-driven system. Tyler (1949a, 1949b as cited in DuFour & Marzano, 2011) advocated for something radical: statements that clearly specify the knowledge students are expected to acquire as a result of schooling. Tyler called these statements *objectives*. In 1983, a report called *A Nation at Risk* (National Commission on Excellence in Education, 1983) stimulated significant concerns among the American public and government about the U.S. education system. The report stated:

> the educational foundations of our society are presently being eroded by a rising tide of mediocrity that threatens our very future as a nation and as a people . . . We have, in effect, been committing an act of unthinking, unilateral educational disarmament. (p. 5, as cited in Marzano, 2004, p. 107–111)

In response, President George H. W. Bush convened a panel, resulting in *The National Education Goals Report* (National Education Goals Panel, 1991). This report articulated a host of goals:

> By the year 2000, American students will leave grades four, eight, and twelve having demonstrated competency in challenging subject matter including English, mathematics, science, history, and geography; and every school in America will ensure that all students learn to use their minds well, so they may be prepared for responsible citizenship, further learning, and productive employment in our modern economy. (p. 4, as cited in Marzano, 2004, p. 107–111)

This was the beginning of the standards movement.

At this point in the story (as Bob always mentions), the National Council of Teachers of Mathematics was already working on standards. They published their first set in 1989. Over the next decade, all the subject-area groups jumped on board. By 2000, there were more than a hundred national and state standards documents written for science, history, social studies, language arts, the arts, civics, economics, foreign language, geography, health, physical education, and technology.

Between the beginning of the standards movement around 1990 and the advent of the Common Core State Standards (CCSS) around 2010, schools and districts who wanted to implement standards-based education had to construct their own standards. They could either use national documents or state documents. Using national documents posed the following problems.

- Multiple documents related to each content area, each with varying definitions of what constituted a "standard"
- Varying levels of generality in each standard
- Varying levels of subordination (for example, expectations nested within benchmarks nested within standards)

The greatest problem when trying to use state documents was, according to Bob and Kendall (1996), that "Most state documents simply have weak standards. . . . The vast majority of states have standards that are so vague that they will probably have to be reworked—or even totally rewritten—by schools and districts in those states" (p. 27).

To address these issues, Bob and Kendall dedicated years to designing and constructing a standards database that would make it easier for schools and districts to create local sets of standards. They analyzed all the relevant national standards documents across various content areas and translated the information into a common format, thus creating the McREL standards database (McREL International, n.d.a, n.d.b).

But the major problem with the standards movement was that there were simply *too many standards*. This makes sense when you think about it. If you convene a group of content experts in a field (such as mathematics, science, ELA, or social studies) and ask them to identify the content they think students need to learn from their field, they will identify *a lot of content*. It's natural; they have dedicated their lives to their field, and the content is very important to them. Bob's colleague Ron Brandt (1995) articulated this dilemma:

> I would describe [the standards] as an ambitious conception of what professional educators, most of whom are advocates or specialists in the various school subjects, want students to learn in those subjects. It's the classic curriculum dilemma faced by every principal, central administrator, and generalist teacher: specialists naturally expect a lot; they love their subject and they know its possibilities. Taken as a whole, however, such statements of aspirations are overwhelming. (p. 5)

In many ways, the processes used to generate the standards guaranteed that there would be too much content. So in 2010, the Council of Chief State School Officers and the National Governors Association tried to fix that.

The Standards Movement—Phase 2

The Common Core State Standards (CCSS; www.thecorestandards.org) were intended to define standards for mathematics and ELA that all states could adopt, thus creating an unprecedented level of consistency in American education. In 2013, a similar effort to create consistent science standards across the U.S. resulted in the Next Generation Science Standards (NGSS; www.nextgenscience.org). While these efforts represented a step forward for the standards movement in the United States—and did solve some of the issues with previous standards documents—they met with strong resistance in some regions and stirred controversy around the federal role in education.

One of the explicit goals of the CCSS and NGSS projects was to create a set of fewer, clearer, and higher standards (Rothman, 2013). It is doubtful whether they accomplished this; Andrew Porter, Jennifer McMaken, Jun Hwang, and Rui Yang (2011) compared the CCSS to different sets of state standards and found that "the Common Core has more focus than some states' standards and less focus than other states' standards" (p. 108). In 2017, Bob commented more strongly:

> After decades of evolution, one might think that standards in every subject area have been fine-tuned to a high degree of precision and focus. However, this is not the case. . . . I believe [this] is one of the most serious issues plaguing K–12 education: namely a curriculum that is so bloated and cumbersome that it is impossible for teachers to teach well and, therefore, difficult for students to learn efficiently. (pp. 18, 20)

In some ways, the standards movement has achieved its goals. More up-to-date research indicates that, for the most part, teachers have moved away from textbooks and toward standards as the basis for curriculum decisions. Research by David Blazar and colleagues (2019) found that textbook use has declined dramatically over the last decade. In a state-representative sample of schools from six states, only 7 percent of teachers used the textbook exclusively, and 26 percent of teachers used online curriculum materials in more than half of their lessons.

But in other ways, the standards movement has failed. In 1999, Bob and Kendall estimated that there are about 9,042 hours of instructional time available across the K–12 interval. They also estimated that the current standards would require 15,465 hours to teach. In a now famous statement (at least among educators), Bob (2003b) asserted that "schooling would have to be extended from kindergarten to grade 21 or 22 to accommodate all the standards and benchmarks in the national documents" (p. 26). Even with the adoption of later standards, such as the CCSS, NGSS, and sets of standards derived from those documents, the problem of too much content remained rampant. And the amount of available instructional time seems to have actually decreased. In 2018, the Organisation for Economic Co-operation and Development (OECD) estimated that students worldwide only spend an average of 7,533 hours in the classroom (as cited in Forsblom, Pekrun, Loderer, & Peixoto, 2022). In sum, the sheer volume of standards is a millstone around educators' necks. Fortunately, there is a way forward.

GUARANTEED AND VIABLE CURRICULUM

Bob first introduced the concept of a guaranteed and viable curriculum in 2003 in the book *What Works in Schools* (Marzano, 2003b). *Guaranteed* means that all teachers who teach the same levels or courses teach the same content. The content students learn does not vary depending on the teachers they are assigned. *Viable* means that the content is teachable in the time available. Viable is where we're going to start. A curriculum is *viable* when "teachers have sufficient time in the school year to adequately teach and reinforce the content" (Marzano & Kosena, 2022, p. 87). Notice the inclusion of the term *reinforce* in this definition. Students often (maybe always) need more than one chance to learn something to master it. High-quality learning involves opportunities for students to revisit and refine their understanding as they move through the curriculum. We will consider this in more depth when we discuss review strategies in chapter 8 (page 117).

Narrowing Down

Since we can't increase instructional time (and actually seem to be losing it year by year), educators must—absolutely must—select which standards to directly teach and assess. Bob has been saying this since the early 2000s: "Schools should drastically reduce the amount of content teachers are required to address in class" (Marzano, 2003b, p. 27). He proposed a simple rating process for this, involving three choices.

> - This is an important benchmark/standard, and it should be required of every student.
> - This is an important benchmark/standard, but should be optional.
> - This should not be a benchmark/standard. (Marzano & Kendall, 1996, p. 43)

In 2002, Bob unpacked the National Council of Teachers of Mathematics's 241 benchmark statements on mathematics standards into 741 individual dimensions. Then, he asked ten mathematics educators to identify from that list those that were essential for all students to learn. After the educators rated each dimension, Bob combined the ratings and produced a list of 404 essential dimensions. This represented a reduction in the list of 46 percent, or close to half. (Details of this study are in Marzano, 2003b.) In fact, Bob (2003b) noted that "143 or 19.3 percent of the instructional concepts were not identified by any of the mathematics educators as essential" (p. 28).

Over the years, Bob and his colleagues have proposed various target numbers indicating exactly how far the standards need to be narrowed down, as shown in table 5.1.

But before you commit to a target number (which could be anywhere from eight to thirty-five), here's another problem: despite their extent, the standards don't articulate everything that students need to know and be able to do as a result of schooling.

TABLE 5.1: Recommendations for Narrowing Down the Standards

Citation	Number of topics per subject per grade or course
Marzano, 2006	No more than twenty
Marzano & Haystead, 2008	No more than twenty
Marzano & Waters, 2009	About fifteen
Marzano et al., 2016	Eight to fifteen
Marzano, 2017	Fifteen to twenty-five
Marzano, 2018	No more than twenty-five
Marzano et al., 2018	Twelve to thirty-five

Adding In

Traditionally, K–12 education has emphasized academic content and skills. But Bob has made the case—thousands of times since the early 1990s—that students need more.

- "Acquiring content knowledge is very important, but perhaps it should not be the most important goal of the education process. Ultimately, it might be better to help students develop mental habits that will help them learn" (Marzano, 1992, p. 131).
- "Without positive attitudes and perceptions, students have little chance of learning proficiently, if at all" (Marzano et al., 1993, p. 1).
- "Developing mental habits that will enable individuals to learn on their own whatever they want or need to know at any point in their lives is probably the most important goal of education" (Marzano et al., 1993, p. 3).
- "Enhancing metacognitive and self-system thinking is central to developing self-regulation" (Marzano & Kendall, 2007, p. 123).

- "The acquisition of metacognitive and life skills is considered at least as important as academic knowledge skills" (Marzano & Abbott, 2022, p. 146).

If some of those terms sound familiar, that's because this is where the topics of the first four chapters come in. In 1998, Bob and Kendall meta-analyzed over 2,500 effect sizes to determine the effects of instructional strategies focused on nonacademic knowledge and skills (that is, self-system, metacognitive, and cognitive skills). They found that teaching students self-system skills resulted in an effect size of 0.74, metacognitive skills resulted in an effect size of 0.72, and cognitive skills resulted in an effect size of 0.55.

Recall that self-system skills are those used to interact with oneself and others, metacognitive skills are those used to regulate oneself when interacting with specific tasks, and cognitive skills are those used to learn academic content. Bob explained, "The self-system exerts more influence over learning than does the metacognitive system, which, in turn, exerts more influence over learning than does the cognitive system" (Marzano & Kendall, 2007, p. 122).

These systems are not only important for understanding how students learn or helping students learn more while they are in school. Joseph Rios, Guangming Ling, Robert Pugh, Dovid Becker, and Adam Bacall (2020) analyzed 142,000 job advertisements and found that "oral and written communication, collaboration, and problem-solving skills are in high demand by employers, with particular emphasis on the pairing of oral and written communication" (p. 84). These researchers acknowledged that their study was limited in several ways:

> This study assumed that all 21st-century skills mentioned in job advertisements were of great importance to employers. . . . Given the limited space available in job advertisements, it is unclear whether employers may have been interested in 21st-century skills that they did not explicitly state. (p. 85)

All the same, their findings reinforced the idea that the standards do not articulate everything that students need to know to succeed in the 21st century and beyond.

The knowledge and skills associated with the cognitive, metacognitive, and self-systems go by many names in the research literature and discussions of what students should learn and are often mixed together. For example, since the 1980s, educational researchers and theorists (Bers, 2018; Papert, 1980; Wing, 2006, 2011) have discussed a concept they call *computational thinking*. Emily Relkin, Laura de Ruiter, and Marina Bers (2021) listed concepts associated with Bers's (2018) seven powerful ideas of computational thinking. These align directly to self-system, metacognitive, and cognitive skills, as shown in table 5.2.

TABLE 5.2: Computational Thinking Skills and the Self-, Metacognitive, and Cognitive Systems

Bers's (2018) Eight Powerful Ideas	Associated Concepts (Relkin, de Ruiter, Bers, 2021)	Self-System, Metacognitive, and Cognitive Skills
Algorithms	Sequencing and order, logical organization	Cognitive—organizing
Modularity	Breaking up larger task into smaller parts, instructions	Metacognitive—preparatory phase
Control Structures	Recognizing patterns and repetition, cause and effect	Cognitive—organizing, analysis
Representation	Symbolic representation, models	Cognitive—organizing
Hardware/Software	Smart objects are not magical, objects are human engineered	Metacognitive—preparatory and performance phases

continued →

Bers's (2018) Eight Powerful Ideas	Associated Concepts (Relkin, de Ruiter, Bers, 2021)	Self-System, Metacognitive, and Cognitive Skills
Design Process	Problem solving, perseverance, editing and revision	Self-system—interacting with self Metacognitive—appraisal phase Cognitive—utilization
Debugging	Identifying problems, problem solving, perseverance	Self-system—interacting with self Metacognitive—performance and appraisal phases Cognitive—utilization

Another example of self-system, metacognitive, and cognitive skills being mixed together and labeled occurred with the advent of the phrase *social-emotional learning* (SEL). Three meta-analyses, shown in table 5.3 have demonstrated that SEL results in increased academic achievement.

Over the years, Bob has provided many lists of nonacademic skills that students should learn in school and has used various names and labels as he refined his conceptions of how best to articulate the discrete skills and which systems to assign them to. Table 5.4 (page 76) summarizes his past work on translating the self-system, metacognitive system, and cognitive system into skills that educators can include in curricula.

As illustrated by table 5.4, Bob has long believed that academic standards don't articulate everything that students need to know and be able to do as a result of K–12 education. The knowledge and skills related to the self-system, metacognitive system, and cognitive system are as important to students' education as the knowledge and skills that comprise traditional curricula built around the knowledge system. In sum, the dual problems of too much content in the academic standards and the need to expand the curriculum to include nonacademic skills create quite a challenge for educators. In the subsequent sections, I'll explore how to reconcile these issues and develop a guaranteed and viable curriculum, defined through proficiency scales.

TABLE 5.3: Effects of Social-Emotional Learning

Meta-analysis	Number of Studies	Effect Size (*g*)	Percentile Gain
Durlak, Weissberg, Dymnicki, Taylor, & Schellinger, 2011	Thirty-four	0.27	11
Sklad, Diekstra, De Ritter, Ben, & Gravesteijn, 2012	Eight	0.33	13
Corcoran, Cheung, Kim, & Xie, 2018	Forty	0.25 reading 0.26 mathematics	10 10

Articulating a Viable Curriculum

Before discussing how to select essential knowledge and skills and articulate them as a guaranteed and viable curriculum, it is important to note that this work should be done at least at the school level and ideally at the district—or even the state—level. It makes very little sense (and threatens the concept of a guaranteed curriculum) to have individual schools, or worse, individual teachers, engage in the work of articulating the K–12 curriculum. As Bob and colleagues (2018) observed:

> The district needs to take the lead in these efforts. A district would find it very difficult to replicate the time, effort, energy, and expertise required to develop quality proficiency scales in every single school. A district-level approach eases the burden. (p. 181)

The work of developing proficiency scales could be undertaken by regional education service agencies (composed of two or more districts) or even state-level education groups. For example, the Alabama Math,

Science, and Technology Initiative (AMSTI) and the Alabama Reading Initiative (ARI) developed proficiency scales that educators across the state could use. Such large-scale efforts are possibly one of the highest-impact activities a regional or state-level education group could undertake, as they foster a guaranteed (and viable, if the content is appropriately narrowed during the process) curriculum regionwide or statewide. Therefore, in the subsequent discussion, I'll examine the work in terms of what the school or district does rather than what the teacher does. However, teachers—as the educators who are actually teaching and assessing the content in the classrooms each day—must comprise the groups that a school, district, region, or state convenes to accomplish this work.

As you'll recall from earlier in the chapter, Bob proposed that schools or districts identify between eight and thirty-five topics per subject per grade or course. That is, he recommends that ELA identify eight to thirty-five topics for each grade or course, mathematics identify eight to thirty-five topics for each grade or course, science identify eight to thirty-five topics for each grade or course, and social studies identify eight to thirty-five topics for each grade or course, and so on. However, in *Classroom Assessment and Grading That Work*, Bob (2006) offered a list of measurement topics for ELA, mathematics, science, and social studies, which was not restricted by grade level or course. It was simply a list of topics to cover *across the K–12 interval*. He explained that "it is important to note that the list . . . is a sample only. Districts must articulate their own topics, reflecting the content in their state standards and the priorities of their teachers and the community" (Marzano, 2006, p. 23). He explicitly points out that the list does not include grade spans, explaining that, "in practice, all measurement topics do not span all grade levels. . . . Even though mathematics has 18 measurement topics, any particular grade level has fewer than 18" (Marzano, 2006, p. 23). He also noted that the list groups individual topics under larger categories, which he called *strands*.

I would argue that this approach of articulating the strands and topics *for the entire K–12 interval* first and then filling in content from state standards documents is a better way to form a curriculum than the current prevailing method of starting with the standards and trying to wrestle them into a viable curriculum (which is very difficult, given the overwhelming volume of the standards). Once a district has identified the strands and topics that K–12 curricula will cover and is ready to fill in specific content from their state standards, I suggest that they use grade bands (such as K–2, 3–5, 6–8, and 9–12) rather than thirteen individual grade levels. Let me explain why.

From 2014 to 2019, I served on the team of analysts who created the Critical Concepts proficiency scales (Dodson, 2019; Simms, 2016). As we analyzed standards documents and synthesized them into proficiency scales, we were struck by the amount of redundancy in standards documents. Especially in ELA, the standards writers sometimes did backflips to articulate how each skill gets a tiny bit more complex from one grade level to the next. For example, compare the fourth- and fifth-grade writing standards in figure 5.1—the differences are minute.

Grade 4 students	Grade 5 students
Write opinion pieces on topics or texts, supporting a point of view with reasons and information. a. Introduce a topic or text clearly, state an opinion, and create an organizational structure in which related ideas are grouped to support the writer's purpose. b. Provide reasons that are supported by facts and details. c. Link opinion and reasons using words and phrases (such as *for instance, in order to, in addition*). d. Provide a concluding statement or section related to the opinion presented.	Write opinion pieces on topics or texts, supporting a point of view with reasons and information. a. Introduce a topic or text clearly, state an opinion, and create an organizational structure in which ideas are logically grouped to support the writer's purpose. b. Provide logically ordered reasons that are supported by facts and details. c. Link opinion and reasons using words, phrases, and clauses (such as, *consequently, specifically*). d. Provide a concluding statement or section related to the opinion presented.

Source: NGA & CCSSO, 2010, p. 20.

Figure 5.1: Comparison of fourth- and fifth-grade writing standards.

TABLE 5.4: Self-System, Metacognitive, and Cognitive Skills in Marzano's Books

	Marzano & Arredondo, 1987	Marzano et al., 1988	Marzano, 1992	Marzano & Kendall, 1996	Marzano & Pickering, 1997	Marzano & Kendall, 1998
Self-System	Attention control	Attention	Being aware of your own thinking		Monitor your own thinking	
	Power thinking	Attitudes	Positive attitudes and perceptions		Positive attitudes and perceptions	
	Responsibility frame	Commitment Executive control		Leadership skills Considers risks		
	Examination of value					
		Observing	Being sensitive to others		Respond appropriately to others' feelings and level of knowledge	
				Communication skills		Effectively communicates in a variety of ways
						Effectively communicates for a variety of purposes
		Oral discourse				
Metacognitive System	Goal setting	Setting goals		Sets and manages goals		Setting and managing progress toward goals
				Contributes to the effort of a group		Works toward the achievement of group goals
				Uses conflict-resolution techniques		

arzano, 2000	Marzano, Pickering, & Pollock, 2001	Marzano, 2007	Marzano & Kendall, 2007	Marzano & Heflebower, 2012	Marzano, Norford, et al., 2017	Marzano, 2019b	Marzano & Kosena, 2022
				Focus			
			Examining efficacy Examining overall motivation	Cultivating useful ways of thinking Avoiding negative ways of thinking			Growth mindset thinking
			Examining importance Examining emotional response				
				Responsible interaction			
Communicates effectively in written form Communicates effectively in a medium other than writing or speaking							
Effectively communicates for a variety of purposes							
Communicates effectively in oral form							
	Goal setting				Planning for goals and making adjustments		Setting goals and making plans
				Controversy and conflict resolution			

continued →

	Marzano & Arredondo, 1987	Marzano et al., 1988	Marzano, 1992	Marzano & Kendall, 1996	Marzano & Pickering, 1997	Marzano & Kendall, 1998
Metacognitive System				Works well with diverse individuals in diverse situations		Effectively communicates with diverse audiences Effective interpersonal skills
			Planning Being aware of necessary resources		Plan appropriately Identify and use necessary resources	
			Evaluating the effectiveness of your actions	Performs self-appraisal	Evaluate the effectiveness of your actions	
			Analyzing perspectives		Analyzing perspectives	Analyzing perspectives
			Being sensitive to feedback		Respond appropriately to feedback	
			Being accurate and seeking accuracy		Be accurate and seek accuracy	
			Being clear and seeking clarity		Be clear and seek clarity	Expresses ideas clearly
			Being open-minded		Maintain an open mind	Seeking multiple perspectives
			Resisting impulsivity	Restrains impulsivity	Restrain impulsivity	Restraining impulsivity
			Engaging intensely in tasks even when answers or solutions are not immediately apparent	Perseverance	Persevere	Persevering
			Pushing the limits of your knowledge and ability		Push the limits of your knowledge and abilities	Pushing the limits of one's abilities
			Generating, trusting, and maintaining your own standards of evaluation	Healthy self-concept	Generate, trust, and maintain your own standards of evaluation	
			Generating new ways of viewing situations outside the boundaries of standard convention		Generate new ways of viewing a situation that are outside the boundaries of standard conventions	

arzano, 2000	Marzano, Pickering, & Pollock, 2001	Marzano, 2007	Marzano & Kendall, 2007	Marzano & Heflebower, 2012	Marzano, Norford, et al., 2017	Marzano, 2019b	Marzano & Kosena, 2022
Effectively communicates with diverse audiences							
					Seeking incremental steps	Taking incremental steps	Seeking incremental steps
			Process monitoring				
				Perspective taking			Analyzing perspectives
			Monitoring clarity and accuracy		Seeking accuracy	Seeking accuracy	Seeking accuracy
Expresses ideas clearly					Seeking clarity	Seeking clarity	Seeking clarity
				Becoming aware of the power of interpretations			
					Resisting impulsivity	Resisting impulsivity	Resisting impulsivity
					Staying focused when answers and solutions are not immediately apparent	Staying focused when answers and solutions are not apparent	Staying focused when answers and solutions are not immediately apparent
					Pushing the limits of one's knowledge and skills		Pushing the limits of one's knowledge and skills
					Generating and pursuing one's own standards of excellence		Generating and pursuing one's own standards for performance
				Divergent and convergent thinking			

continued →

	Marzano & Arredondo, 1987	Marzano et al., 1988	Marzano, 1992	Marzano & Kendall, 1996	Marzano & Pickering, 1997	Marzano & Kendall, 1998
Cognitive System	Deep processing Memory frameworks	Encoding Recalling	Storing		Storing	
	Concept attainment Concept development	Concept formation Identifying attributes and components	Organizing		Organizing	
	Proceduralizing	Ordering	Construct models Shaping Internalizing		Constructing models Shaping Internalizing	
	Synthesizing	Comprehension Identifying main ideas Summarizing Restructuring				
	Nonlinguistic patterns	Representing	Using physical and symbolic representations Using graphic organizers			
	Elaboration	Elaborating				
		Formulating questions	Questioning			
	Extrapolation	Inferring	Inducing Deducing	Logic and reasoning	Inductive reasoning Deductive reasoning	Induction Deduction
		Comparing	Comparing	Comparing Contrasting	Comparing	Comparison
		Classifying	Classifying	Classifying	Classifying	Classification
	Pattern recognition	Principle formation Predicting Identifying relationships and patterns	Using organizational patterns Abstracting		Abstracting	Abstracting
	Macro-pattern recognition					
	Analogical reasoning					

rzano, 2000	Marzano, Pickering, & Pollock, 2001	Marzano, 2007	Marzano & Kendall, 2007	Marzano & Heflebower, 2012	Marzano, Norford, et al., 2017	Marzano, 2019b	Marzano & Kosena, 2022
		Mnemonic devices employing imagery	Retrieval	Generating mental images Performing mental rehearsal	Generating and manipulating mental images		Generating mental images
	Organizing ideas						
	Skills					Developing fluency Proceduralizing Analyzing errors	
	Summarizing	Summarizing	Integrating		Seeking cohesion and coherence	Seeking cohesion and coherence	Seeking cohesion and coherence
	Nonlinguistic representations	Nonlinguistic representations Graphic organizers	Symbolizing	Creating graphic representations Drawing and sketching			
		Elaborative interrogations				Elaborating	
	Questions	Questioning					
Induction Deduction			Generalizing Specifying	Generating conclusions	Generating conclusions		Analyzing inferences
Comparing and contrasting	Comparing	Identifying similarities and differences	Matching	Identifying basic relationships between ideas	Identifying basic relationships between ideas	Comparing	Comparing
Classifying	Classifying		Classifying			Classifying	Classifying
Analyzing relationships	Metaphors						
	Analogies						Analogical reasoning

continued →

	Marzano & Arredondo, 1987	Marzano et al., 1988	Marzano, 1992	Marzano & Kendall, 1996	Marzano & Pickering, 1997	Marzano & Kendall, 1998
Cognitive System	Evaluation of evidence	Identifying errors Verifying Establishing criteria	Analyzing errors Constructing support Taking and defending a position	Presenting an argument	Constructing support Analyzing errors Taking a position when the situation warrants it	Error analysis Constructing support
	Decision making	Decision making	Decision making	Decision making	Decision making	Decision making
	Solving everyday problems Solving academic problems	Problem solving Defining problems	Problem solving	Trouble-shooting and problem solving	Problem solving	Problem solving
	Invention	Composition	Invention		Invention	Invention
		Research (scientific inquiry)	Experimental inquiry	Hypothesis testing and scientific inquiry	Experimental inquiry	Experimental inquiry
			Investigation		Investigation	Investigation
					Systems analysis	

At the high school levels, the authors of the CCSS abandoned a strict grade-by-grade approach, banding grades 9–10 and grades 11–12 together. I believe this was a step (albeit a small one) in the positive direction of creating a more viable curriculum. Articulating content by grade band lifts the restriction that every important topic must be addressed every year. In some cases, a topic might only need to be taught once during a grade band; in other cases, it might need to be taught every year. A grade-banding approach gives teacher teams more freedom to determine how to teach and review the content across a three- to four-year period.

In figure 5.2 (page 84), I present my version of the figure Bob offered in 2006. I present it with the same caveat: it is a sample only. Districts and schools must identify those strands and topics that reflect the content in their state standards and the priorities of their teachers and community.

There are three important differences between Bob's figure and mine. First, I have added in grade bands. I believe doing so provides a useful amount of specificity (approximately when content should be taught) without being over-restrictive in terms of requiring every topic to be taught every single year. Second, I have added in the self-system, metacognitive, analysis, and utilization skills discussed in chapters 1–4. Third, and perhaps most importantly, I did not articulate topics; each item in figure 5.2 should be considered a *strand* and might have one or more topics associated with it.

The main reason I recommend articulating curriculum in this manner is that it allows school and district leaders to consider the viability of the curriculum across subject areas and grade levels *first*. Starting from a narrow set of strands and topics and then determining which content is important enough to include is—I believe—a more effective approach than starting from the bloated standards and deciding what to leave out.

The K–12 curriculum needs to be drastically narrowed. If educators were able to achieve such a vision, it would create instructional space for more utilization tasks and projects, more review and revision of knowledge, and more instruction in self-system, metacognitive, and cognitive skills.

rzano, 2000	Marzano, Pickering, & Pollock, 2001	Marzano, 2007	Marzano & Kendall, 2007	Marzano & Heflebower, 2012	Marzano, Norford, et al., 2017	Marzano, 2019b	Marzano & Kosena, 2022
Argumentation		Error analysis Effective support	Analyzing errors	Identifying common logical errors Presenting and supporting claims	Identifying common logical errors Presenting and supporting claims	Constructing support Analyzing errors	Constructing support Analyzing errors in reasoning
Decision making	Decision making	Decision-making tasks	Decision making		Using decision making	Decision making	Decision making
Problem solving	Problem solving	Problem-solving tasks	Problem solving	A problem-solving protocol	Using problem solving	Problem solving	Problem solving
	Invention					Invention	Invention
Experimental inquiry	Experimental inquiry	Experimental inquiry tasks	Experimenting	Conducting thought experiments	Experimenting	Experimental inquiry	Experimental inquiry
Investigation	Historical investigation	Investigation tasks	Investigating	Navigating digital sources	Navigating digital sources Investigating	Investigation	Investigation
	Systems analysis					Systems analysis	Systems analysis

Guaranteeing the Curriculum

Once a school or district has identified a viable number of topics across each grade band, the next step is to add clarity. Clearly articulating the curriculum is the first step toward making it guaranteed. A guaranteed curriculum is so clearly articulated that there is no doubt in anyone's mind (educators, students, parents) about what content is taught in each grade level or course. It also comes with a guarantee: the articulated curriculum is what will actually be taught in each grade level or course. And this brings up a very interesting point that Bob and Kendall made in 1996:

> A district or school can adopt the position that standards and benchmarks should identify *only a portion of the content* that teachers will address in a particular course or at a particular grade level. In other words, a district or school can consciously keep the number of benchmarks down to allow individual teachers to add content they believe will be meaningful to a particular group of students at a particular point in time. Matthew Gandal (1995), author of the American Federation of Teachers study of state standards . . . notes that standards and benchmarks should cover 60–80 percent of the curriculum. Similarly, the Core Knowledge Sequence designed by E. D. Hirsch, Jr., author of *Cultural Literacy* (1987), recommends that standards and benchmarks constitute 50 percent of the curriculum only. (p. 87; emphasis added)

In my experience, schools and districts typically take the view that the guaranteed curriculum will take up all the available instructional time. But teachers are professionals. In the same way that one doctor might not prescribe exactly the same treatment as another doctor (but both can be relied on to provide quality care), one teacher might not conduct class in exactly the same way as another teacher. To honor the professionalism, beliefs, and personalities of individual teachers, Bob recommends that schools and districts (1) only guarantee content for a percentage of the available instructional time and (2) create a supplemental topic within the curriculum. Bob describes the supplemental topic as one that:

Grade Band	Self-System Skills	Metacognitive Skills	Analysis Tasks	Utilization Tasks	Mathematics	Science	ELA	Social Studies
K–2	Attention Emotions Awareness	Preparatory Phase	Examining Relationships	Decision Making Problem Solving	Place Value Addition Subtraction Multiplication Measurement Geometry Categorical Data	Energy Force Motion Weather Organisms Material Properties Geology	Decoding Analyzing Expository Texts Analyzing Narrative Texts Generating Expository Texts Generating Narrative Texts	Timelines Communities American History Rights and Justice Economics Geography
3–5	Emotions Beliefs Communication	Performance Phase	Evaluating Information	Experimental Inquiry	Multiplication Division Fractions Decimals Measurement Geometry Exponents Coordinate Plane	Energy Force Motion Magnets Climate Organisms Geology Matter Ecosystems Engineering	Analyzing Expository Texts Analyzing Narrative Texts Generating Expository Texts Generating Narrative Texts Editing	Timelines Exploration American History Communities Government Civic Responsibility Economics Geography
6–8	Beliefs Communication Collaboration	Appraisal Phase	Constructing Arguments	Investigation Invention	Factors and Multiples Proportional Relationships Algebra Geometry Measurement Distributions Statistics Probability Roots Irrational Numbers Functions	Energy Force Motion Chemical Reactions Geology Climate Organisms Genetics Ecosystems Engineering	Analyzing Expository Texts Analyzing Narrative Texts Generating Expository Texts Generating Narrative Texts Revising and Editing	Geography Economics Civics American History World History
9–12	Beliefs Collaboration	All Three Phases	All Three Types	Systems Analysis	Algebra Geometry Statistics Trigonometry	Energy Force Gravity Atomic Structure Chemical Reactions Nuclear Processes Astronomy Geology Organisms Genetics Ecosystems Engineering	Analyzing Expository Texts Analyzing Narrative Texts Generating Expository Texts Generating Narrative Texts Revising and Editing	Geography Economics Civics American History World History

Figure 5.2: Sample measurement topics with grade bands.

> Involves content considered important by a teacher but not reflected in the measurement topics articulated by the district or school. In effect, this option allows teachers to supplement the district or school curriculum in a way that recognizes the unique set of experiences and background they bring to the subject matter. (Marzano, 2006, p. 28)

We will return to the supplemental topic in chapter 7 (page 103) during our discussion of grading and reporting. For now, we turn to the tool that Bob recommends schools and districts use to clearly articulate their guaranteed curriculum: proficiency scales.

PROFICIENCY SCALES

A *proficiency scale* is "a continuum that articulates distinct levels of knowledge and skill relative to a specific topic" (Marzano, 2010a, p. 44). Figure 5.3 shows an example of a proficiency scale. The topic for this proficiency scale is the writing process, as defined by the target level. I have simplified this scale down to the essentials; there are three things you must have in a proficiency scale:

1. The learning target
2. Simpler and complex content
3. Scale values (including static 1.0 and 0.0 levels)

4.0 Complex	Use the writing process to compose a text about the solution to a problem.
3.0 Target	Use the writing process (*prewriting, drafting, revising, editing*, and *publishing*) to create texts.
2.0 Simpler	Understand vocabulary such as *prewriting, drafting, revising, editing*, and *publishing*. List activities associated with each phase of the writing process. Produce artifacts that show their use of each phase of the writing process.
1.0	With help, some of the content.
0.0	Even with help, none of the content.

Figure 5.3: Sample proficiency scale.

Learning Target

The *learning target* defines what all students are expected to learn or be able to do relative to the topic of the proficiency scale. The learning target should be either declarative or procedural knowledge. While Bob has provided a structure to articulate learning goals that include both declarative and procedural knowledge, having worked with proficiency scales for over a decade (including discussing scales with educators, creating scales from standards, and reviewing scales created by educators), I have found that simple, straightforward scales are the most useful to teachers.

The learning target should also be unidimensional. This means that it refers to *just one thing*. Most standards are multidimensional; they refer to a lot of things. For example, look back at the standards in figure 5.1 (page 75)—see how they refer to a long list of things? Write opinion pieces, support a point of view, introduce a topic, create an organizational structure, and on and on. In 2013, Bob highlighted multidimensionality as a problem with standards, and Erika Landl (2020) listed just a few of the problems this causes:

> The multidimensional nature of the standards not only makes it difficult for states to clearly define and articulate the target of assessment, but it makes it difficult for peer reviewers to evaluate the degree to which a state's test design provides for adequate alignment to [standards]. (p. 25)

One of the primary uses of a proficiency scale is assessment, so given the assessment issues caused by multidimensionality, it makes sense to make a proficiency scale learning target unidimensional. Unidimensional learning targets are easier for educators, students, and parents to understand and act on.

Last but not least, the primary goal of the language in a proficiency scale is *clarity*. Remember that proficiency scales are a tool used to articulate a guaranteed curriculum so clearly that there is no doubt about what content is taught in each grade level or course. In figure 5.3 (page 85), the learning target is procedural knowledge that needs to be learned to the level of internalization, and the wording makes that clear. Educators have often overfocused on verbs when it comes to the language used to express learning targets, but the same verb can apply to all sorts of levels of complexity depending on context (see Heflebower, Hoegh, & Warrick, 2014). I strongly recommend that educators use the simplest and most concise language possible to convey the learning target, regardless of the "level of complexity" supposedly associated with specific verbs or other phrases. Brevity is the soul of a proficiency scale.

Simpler and Complex Content

Simpler content is foundational knowledge underlying the scale's learning target that the teacher intends to directly teach and assess. *Complex content* is usually a utilization task that requires students to use the scale's learning target in a way that goes above and beyond the expectations of the target. Articulating simpler content depends on whether the learning target is procedural or declarative. If it is procedural knowledge, then the simpler content is likely vocabulary associated with the process and an understanding of the steps of the process (as in figure 5.3, page 85). If it is declarative, then the simpler content is likely vocabulary and facts or details associated with the knowledge in the learning target. If you can, limit the simpler content to three items (with all vocabulary grouped as one item). This is another lesson learned from the hundreds of educators and thousands of proficiency scales I've had the privilege of interacting with. In a proficiency scale, less is more.

If the learning target is declarative knowledge, the nature of simpler content depends on whether the learning target is an acquisition task (just being exposed to knowledge), an organization task (encoding knowledge), or an analysis task (applying an analysis process to content). Consider the following examples.

- In kindergarten, students typically need to be able to rote count. That is an organization task; they need to store the counting sequence structure in long-term memory. So simpler content would include acquisition tasks: knowing the names of the numbers (at least up to twenty and then the tens after that) and the order of the numbers.
- In intermediate and secondary grades, students typically need to compare two texts. That's an analysis task; they need to describe the relationship between two things. So simpler content would include organizing tasks: describing the structure of one text, identifying the main idea of one text, and identifying the important details of one text.

Learning goals (if they are truly unidimensional) will not be utilization tasks. By definition, utilization tasks (problem solving, decision making, and so on) bring multiple learning goals together. Utilization tasks are usually an excellent fit for the more complex level of a proficiency scale, regardless of the learning target's level of complexity. Just because a student hasn't analyzed declarative knowledge or internalized procedural knowledge doesn't mean they can't use it (see figure 4.1, page 49). In fact, utilizing it is likely to help boost that knowledge toward the next level of complexity. Importantly, whatever utilization task you write for the complex level of a proficiency scale should be completely negotiable if a student wants to use the target knowledge in a different utilization task to demonstrate more complex mastery. For example, if you wrote a problem-solving task and a student would prefer to engage in a decision-making task related to the same learning target, the student can and should do so. We'll discuss student-designed tasks and assessments in chapter 7 (page 103), but when students take ownership of their learning to the extent of articulating how they will show their learning, they should be encouraged at every turn.

Scale Values

The values of the scale levels will be most pertinent when we reach chapter 7 (page 103) and discuss measurement. For now, it is enough to note, as Bob did in 2010, that:

> Scores 4.0, 3.0, and 2.0 involve different content . . . while scores 1.0 and 0.0 do not.

> A score of 1.0 indicates that, independently, a student cannot demonstrate competence in the score 2.0 or 3.0 content, but with help, he or she demonstrates partial competence. Score 0.0 indicates that even with help, a student does not demonstrate competence or skill in any of the content. (Marzano, 2010a, p. 45)

If teachers want to make finer distinctions for scoring, they could use half-point scores (Marzano, 2007), one-third point scores (Marzano, 2010a), or even quarter-point intervals (Marzano et al., 2019). We discuss half-point scores in more detail in chapter 7 (page 103).

In figure 5.3 (page 85), I've used the simplest language possible for scores 1.0 and 0.0. Some schools and districts leave off the 0.0 level because they believe that every student, with help, can access some background knowledge relative to a learning target. As long as everyone in the school or district understands why the 0.0 level is not being used, that's fine.

I'll close this section with a quote from Bob about what *help* means in a proficiency scale. Bob and colleagues (2016) explained *help* as:

> Extensive probing questions and prompting by the teacher to discern any proficiency on the student's part at score 2.0 or 3.0. It is not considered help if a teacher simply restates or clarifies a question for a student. On the other hand, if a student requires assistance with many assessment components and demonstrates little to no independence with the content, that student would likely receive a "with help" designation. (p. 45)

In sum, a proficiency scale—when well-composed—is a simple tool that makes curriculum (and also assessment, instruction, and grading) transparent to all stakeholders.

SUMMARY

In this chapter, we discussed the standards, their history, and the fact that there are simply too many of them. We also highlighted the knowledge and skills from the self-, metacognitive, and cognitive systems that are missing from the standards. We discussed how schools and districts can identify and articulate the components of a guaranteed and viable curriculum and how to organize learning targets, simpler content, and more complex content into a proficiency scale, as well as how that scale ensures transparency of the curriculum for all stakeholders. We now turn our attention away from what students need to learn (curriculum that covers all four systems) and toward the critical roles of teachers in classrooms.

PART II

TEACHERS

In part II, it's time to talk about teachers. By 2010, it was "common knowledge that a classroom teacher is probably the single most powerful influence on student achievement that is within the control of the educational system" (Marzano, 2010b, p. 213). My favorite Bob quote (because he almost *never* uses exclamation points) about this is from *The Art and Science of Teaching*: "One can conclude that the question as to whether effective teachers make a significant difference in student achievement has been answered. They do!" (Marzano, 2007, p. 2).

Branching out to the field of economics for a moment, in 2014, Raj Chetty, John Friedman, and Jonah Rockoff linked data for the years 1989–2009 from a large urban school district in the United States with tax records for the years 1996–2011. They compared teacher quality to student outcomes such as earnings, college attendance, and teenage birth rates. After analyzing data from approximately one million students, they found that teacher quality:

> Has substantial impacts on a broad range of outcomes. A one standard deviation improvement in teacher [quality] in a single grade raises the probability of college attendance at age 20 by 0.82 percentage points. . . . A one standard deviation increase in teacher quality in a single grade raises annual earnings by 1.3 percent. . . . Improvements in teacher quality significantly reduce the probability of having a child while being a teenager, increase the quality of the neighborhood in which the student lives (as measured by the percentage of college graduates in that zip code) in adulthood, and raise participation rates in 401(k) retirement savings plans. (p. 2634)

They continued: "We estimate that replacing a teacher whose current [performance] is in the bottom 5 percent with an average teacher would increase the mean present value of students' lifetime income by $250,000 per classroom over a teacher's career" (Chetty et al., 2013, p. 2635). David Blazar and Casey Archer (2020) called teachers "the most important in-school resource we can provide to students" (p. 298). Thomas Kane, Daniel McCaffrey, Trey Miller, and Douglas Staiger in 2013 and Nye and colleagues in 2004 both found large, positive, and significant relationships between teacher quality and student success.

As such, this part of the book investigates the profile of a high-quality, effective teacher. Specifically, we are looking at what I see as the three most important roles of teachers: self-regulation, measurement, and instruction. Before we consider the practical details of instructing and assessing students, we're going explore what Bob—and other researchers—have said about teacher wellness. Specifically, our next chapter explores teachers' self- and metacognitive systems and how both relate to their critically important work in the classroom.

CHAPTER 6

SELF-REGULATION

On one hand, findings about the major impact of teaching quality on students highlight the importance and value of classroom teachers, and the urgency of cultivating cultures focused on teacher development. On the other hand, findings like these put a lot of pressure on teachers to be high-quality teachers. This pressure comes in addition to all the other pressures facing teachers. It is not surprising that K–12 education is facing a worldwide epidemic of teacher burnout and teacher turnover (Rankin, 2016).

We discussed student burnout in chapter 1 (page 15); obviously, it happens to teachers, too. Educator burnout has three components: exhaustion, depersonalization, and low efficacy. Table 6.1 (page 92) provides three definitions from the research.

Teacher burnout impacts teachers' mental health (see Durlak, Domitrovich, Weissberg, & Gullotta, 2015), but it also impacts teachers' work performance, the climate of classrooms, and students' well-being, as detailed by Kimberly Schonert-Reichl in 2017. And it leads to teacher turnover: in a 2020 study, the American Psychological Association (n.d.) found that half of teachers leave the profession in their first five years. Mariana Haynes (2014) estimated that K–12 educator turnover costs up to $2.2 billion annually (that breaks down to $12.2 million per school day of a 180-day year). Furthermore, the COVID-19 pandemic that began in 2020 made a difficult educational situation more difficult. Dora Gicheva (2022) explained:

> Evidence from specialized surveys conducted in 2020 [showed] that teachers worked longer hours during the pandemic and that this may have caused burnout and lowered morale (Diliberti & Kaufman, 2020; Kaufman & Diliberti, 2021; Kraft et al., 2021; Pressley, 2021), which could affect student achievement negatively (Greenberg et al., 2016). (p. 85)

So, what do we do?

First, it is important to acknowledge that when we talk about educators in general, and teachers in particular, we are talking about a host of positions with different working conditions, stressors, and pressures. Educators working at the regional or state level are differently situated than educators working at the district

TABLE 6.1: Definitions and Components of Burnout

Citation	Definition
Califf & Brooks, 2020	"Traditionally, burnout has been associated with three components: **emotional exhaustion, depersonalization, and lack of personal accomplishment** (Montgomery & Rupp, 2005). These three components are measured using Maslach's Burnout Inventory, which is commonly employed today (Malach-Pines, 2005)." (p. 4)
Junker, Donker, & Mainhard, 2021	"Repeated exposure to **stressors that cannot be adequately managed** may give rise to psychological symptoms of burnout (Maslach & Leiter, 2016) and a physiological effect called 'allostatic overload' (McEwen, 2005). According to previous research, the **main psychological symptoms of burnout are 'overwhelming exhaustion, feelings of cynicism and detachment from the job, and a sense of ineffectiveness and lack of accomplishment'** (Maslach & Leiter, 2016, p. 103)." (p. 2)
Oliveira, Roberto, Veiga-Simão, & Marques-Pinto, 2021	"According to Maslach's model, teachers' burnout is defined as a three-dimensional **syndrome** characterized by **emotional exhaustion** (also referred to as exhaustion; i.e., feelings of emotional distress and depletion of emotional resources, loss of energy, and fatigue), **depersonalization** (also referred to as cynicism; i.e., negative, detached feelings and behaviors toward students, irritability, loss of idealism, and psychological withdrawal), and a **reduced personal accomplishment (also referred to as low sense of professional efficacy**; i.e., loss of feelings of competence and efficacy at work, reduced productivity, demoralization, and inability to cope with one's work demands), which is driven by chronic teaching stressors (Maslach, 1976; Maslach et al., 2001; Maslach & Leiter, 2016)." (p. 1780)

Emphases added.

level, who in turn are differently situated than educators working as administrators or other building-level leaders, instructional coaches, and specialized teachers. And those building-level positions are vastly different from the roles of teachers in classrooms. As Robert Roeser and colleagues (2022) pointed out, even the differences between elementary and secondary classroom teachers differ significantly:

> The work environments of middle and high school teachers can differ considerably from those of elementary school teachers: secondary teachers often work in larger schools with primarily adolescents rather than children; they teach several classes of students each day rather than just one; and they are responsible for specific school subjects rather than a comprehensive curriculum (see Eccles & Roeser, 2016). (p. 411)

Therefore, it is potentially of limited practical help to make generalizations about educators or even teachers. However, the research does provide helpful guidance regarding the adult self-system and metacognitive system, which educators of all kinds can apply to their individual situations.

Before we dive into the self- and metacognitive systems of educators, I want to acknowledge that the body of research supporting these areas is younger than the body of research supporting the student self- and metacognitive systems. As Fani Lauermann and Ruth Butler (2021) explained, "Until about a decade ago, teachers' psychological characteristics—in particular, their teaching-related emotions, motivations, and self-regulation—and corresponding implications for teachers and students were largely overlooked in educational research" (p. 244). Please read this chapter with the understanding that, while there *is* a research base here, it is simply not as robust as those underlying other areas, so I invite you to scrutinize it more carefully.

COMPONENTS OF THE EDUCATOR SELF-SYSTEM

In 2022, Lisa Bardach, Robert Klassen, and Nancy Perry conducted an integrative review of teachers' psychological characteristics. In simple terms, they collected numerous meta-analyses (which produce overall effect sizes from a group of studies on the same topic) and *systematic reviews* (which summarize a group of studies on the same topic without producing an overall effect size) and synthesized them. They categorized the studies they collected into eight characteristics that define the educator self-system:

1. Expectations
2. Self-efficacy
3. Personality
4. Attributions
5. Emotional labor
6. Emotional intelligence
7. Mindfulness
8. Enthusiasm

In this section, we focus on three of those categories: expectations, emotions, and enthusiasm. Self-efficacy and attributions will be a part of our discussion of expectations, we won't delve into personality very much, and mindfulness will be discussed in the context of emotions.

Expectations

There are two types of expectations that educators (especially teachers) must be aware of: student expectations and self-expectations. Bob has written extensively about teachers' student expectations:

> If the teacher believes students can succeed, she tends to behave in ways that help them succeed. If the teacher believes that students cannot succeed, she unwittingly tends to behave in ways that subvert student success or at least do not facilitate student success. (Marzano, 2007, p. 162)
>
> Teachers must pay special attention to students for whom educators wittingly or unwittingly have developed low expectations. It is not so much that these students need dramatically different strategies to feel valued and respected, but sometimes teachers don't use typical instructional strategies as rigorously or completely with these students as they do with other students. (Marzano, 2017, p. 97)

Research on the impact of teachers' student expectations goes back over five decades, largely beginning with Robert Rosenthal and Lenore Jacobson's seminal book in 1968, *Pygmalion in the Classroom*. Table 6.2 (page 94) summarizes the research history in this area.

The good news about student expectations is that when teachers change their behaviors toward students for whom they have low expectations, those students respond in productive ways. In a study conducted in New Zealand, Christine Rubie-Davies, Elizabeth Peterson, Chris Sibley, and Robert Rosenthal (2015) found that when teachers were trained in behaviors designed to communicate high expectations to students, the students in their classrooms exhibited greater learning gains (effect size was $d = 0.24$) compared to a control group. The behaviors taught in the study were based on the work of Elisha Babad (2009), Rubie-Davies (2007), and Rhona Weinstein (2002), and included the following.

- Both high- and low-expectation teachers taught core subjects such as reading and mathematics with students in ability-based instructional groups, but whereas the low-expectation teachers kept their students in ability groups for learning activities, the high-expectation teachers did not. Instead, they gave all students a choice in the activities they could complete and allowed them to work with a variety of peers.
- High-expectation teachers created a much warmer socioemotional environment for their students than did low-expectation teachers. High-expectation teachers were very positive toward students, focused on mastery goals both at the class and individual level, encouraged cooperation and collaboration among students, promoted student autonomy, and used positive, preventive behavior management strategies.
- High-expectation teachers monitored student progress closely, set clear individual learning goals with students, provided feedback on progress, and taught students how to set their own goals.

TABLE 6.2: Research on Teachers' Expectations of Students

Teacher expectations vary according to student characteristics.	
Aronson & Steele, 2005; Halberstadt, Castro, Chu, Lozada, & Sims, 2018; Rowley et al., 2014; Weir, 2016	Teachers view Black students as more aggressive, overemotional, and more likely to repeat a problematic behavior as compared to White students.
Auwarter & Aruguete, 2008; Ferguson, 2003; McKown & Weinstein, 2008; Meissel, Meyer, Yao, & Rubie-Davies, 2017; Ready & Wright, 2011; Rubie-Davies, 2010; Tenenbaum & Ruck, 2007	Teacher expectations are lower for minoritized groups (African American, Latinx, low-income).
Brophy & Good, 1974	Teachers tend to have lower expectations for low-achieving students.
Hachfeld, Anders, Schroeder, Stanat, & Kunter, 2010	Teachers tend to have lower expectations for students with immigration status.
Hagan, Halberstadt, Cooke, & Garner, 2020	Teachers' misperceptions of seeing anger when anger was not actually present were racialized.
Hughes, Gleason, & Zhang, 2005; Muntoni & Retelsdorf, 2018; Ready & Chu, 2015; Ready & Wright, 2011	Teacher expectations are higher for girls, high-socioeconomic status (SES) students, and students from cultural-ethnic majorities, and lower for boys, low-SES students, and students from cultural-ethnic minorities.
Kunter et al., 2013	Teachers' perceptions of a student's disengaged and insubordinate behavior described in a vignette differ based on the race of the child described.
Lazarides & Watt, 2015	Teachers tend to have lower expectations for boys in some situations.
Morris & Perry, 2016; Nicholson-Crotty, Grissom, Nicholson-Crotty, & Redding, 2016	Teachers perceive Black students as academically inferior and more behaviorally problematic compared to White students.
Myhill & Jones, 2006	Teachers tend to have lower expectations for girls in some situations.
Quinn, 2017	In a nationally representative data set, 4 percent of preK–12 teachers reported believing that inequities were due to innate differences between Blacks and Whites, 31 percent believed inequities were due to Black Americans' lack of motivation, and 56 percent reported Black Americans did not have access to the same educational opportunities as White Americans.
Rubie-Davies, Hattie, & Hamilton, 2006	Teachers tend to have lower expectations for Indigenous students.
Tenenbaum & Ruck, 2007	Teachers tend to have lower expectations for ethnic minority groups.
VanWeelden & Whipple, 2007	Teachers tend to have lower expectations for special needs students.
Wedin, 2010	Teachers tend to have lower expectations for students whose second language is English.
Westphal et al., 2016	Teachers tend to have lower expectations for students with low socioeconomic status.
Teacher expectations correlate with teacher characteristics.	
Chin, Quinn, Dhaliwal, & Lovison, 2020	Teachers' implicit White-Black biases vary depending on teacher gender and race or ethnicity: female teachers appear slightly less biased than male teachers, and teachers of color appear less biased than White teachers.
Copur-Gencturk, Cimpian, Lubienski, & Thacker, 2020	A bias favoring White students was detected among teachers of color.
Legette, Halberstadt, & Majors, 2021	The more a teacher adhered to cultural deficit beliefs, the more that teacher saw Black boys' behaviors as threatening, stable, and serious compared to White boys' behaviors.

Students are aware of and impacted by teacher expectations.	
McKown, Gregory, & Weinstein, 2010	Students are generally good at perceiving teachers' expectations.
McKown & Weinstein, 2003	Students as young as six years old can recognize when people hold stereotypes.
Perry, Steele, & Hilliard, 2003; Steele & Aronson, 1995	Low expectations can impede student performance by causing challenge avoidance, disidentification with school, and rejection of teacher feedback.
Taylor & Walton, 2011	Low expectations can impede student performance by causing student stress.
Teachers' expectations for students influence the decisions teachers make concerning those students.	
Burkam, LoGerfo, Ready, & Lee, 2007	Teachers' expectations for students influence grade retention decisions.
Oakes, 2005	Teachers' expectations for students influence track placement decisions.
Page, 1987	Teachers' expectations for students influence instructional quality and characteristics.
Tach & Farkas, 2006	Teachers' expectations for students influence within-class ability grouping.

Source: Chin et al., 2020; Denessen, Hornstra, van den Bergh, & Bijlstra, 2022; İnan-Kaya & Rubie-Davies, 2022; Legette, Halberstadt, & Majors, 2021; Umansky & Dumont, 2021.

The research indicates that (1) teacher expectations do exist, (2) they have an impact on students, and (3) teachers can prevent the negative impacts of expectations and promote positive impacts by supporting the growth and development of students' self- and metacognitive systems (as already discussed in chapters 1, page 15, and 2, page 33). The remainder of this section focuses on teachers' self-expectations because I believe that teaching students about their self- and metacognitive systems means that teachers and educators must understand and be able to regulate their own self- and metacognitive systems. As Tina Boogren (2018) said, "Educational strategies and pedagogy are only as good as the person providing them" (p. 4).

Teacher self-expectations, or—as this idea is known in the research literature—teacher self-efficacy, concerns how teachers answer the question, "Can I do this?" As you may recall from chapter 1 (page 15), self-efficacy is simply the belief that you can do something. Rebecca Lazarides and Ulrich Schiefele (2021) defined *teacher self-efficacy* as "teachers' conviction that they will be able to successfully execute teaching behaviors that bring about desired outcomes of student engagement and learning, even among students who are difficult or unmotivated" (p. 2). The most important question here is, How can teachers increase their self-efficacy? In a critical review of the emerging literature on the sources of teacher self-efficacy, David Morris, Ellen Usher, and Jason Chen (2017) identified mastery experiences (Bandura, 1997) as a potential source of teaching self-efficacy: "Mastery experiences involve the achievement of goals . . . through direct, personal action. . . . People who view their past efforts as successes are more likely to approach similar tasks with confidence" (p. 5). Essentially, teachers who experience success in teaching are likely to believe that success will continue.

So how can teachers increase their likelihood of success in the classroom? Obviously, there are many options. The one I want to address here is reducing stress in the classroom through student-centered instruction. Studies by Monika Donker, Lian van Vemde, David Hessen, Tamara van Gog, and Tim Mainhard (2021) and Robin Junker and Manfred Holodynski (2022) have found that teacher-centered activities (like explaining concepts or giving instructions) were more stressful for teachers (measured through their electrodermal activity and heart rate) than student-centered activities. Robin Junker, Monika Donker, and Tim Mainhard (2021) also measured teacher heart rate and found that "teachers showed an increased heart rate in situations where they had more interactional dominance" (p. 2). Interestingly, they found that:

> Students' disrespectful-disruptive behavior . . . and negative interpersonal teacher behavior. . . were not predictive of heart rate. However, low student engagement and motivation . . . as well as teacher-centered activities . . . were significantly

> associated with an increase in teachers' physiological stress. (p. 5)

In other words, it seems as if teacher stress is less associated with students' choices in the classroom and more associated with how the teacher perceives their performance in the classroom—that is, with the teacher's sense of mastery.

It stands to reason that teachers may be able to reduce their stress and increase their self-efficacy by utilizing more student-centered approaches in the classroom. Junlin Yu, Pia Kreijkes, and Katariina Salmela-Aro (2022) provided a typology of teaching practices that contrast a more teacher-centered classroom with a more student-centered classroom, as shown in table 6.3.

Using student-focused teaching approaches isn't only beneficial for reducing teacher stress and increasing teacher self-expectations. Research by Keith Trigwell (2012) found a link between student-focused teaching approaches and positive teacher emotions, which is what we'll discuss next.

TABLE 6.3: Comparing Teacher-Centered and Student-Centered Classrooms

Type of Teaching Practice	Teacher-Centered Classroom	Student-Centered Classroom
Autonomy	Learning directed by teachers, few opportunities for students to exercise control	Learning constructed through guided inquiry, opportunities for self-direction
Tasks	Differentiate the amount and difficulty level of assigned tasks based on students' ability	Offer multiple difficulty levels and the choice to attempt challenging tasks with teacher support
Grouping	Homogeneous and hierarchical ability groups that remain stable over time	Students work in varying groups not defined by ability
Evaluation	Focus on social comparison and how smart a student is	Focus on individual improvement and how able a student is becoming

Source: Adapted from Yu et al., 2022.

Emotions

Teachers' emotions matter, both the emotions they actually experience and the emotions they show to students. Bob recommended that teachers "project a sense of emotional objectivity. This approach does not mean that teachers will be unemotional at all times. It does mean that teachers provide students with a consistent tone in the classroom" (Marzano, 2007, p. 158). According to Bob, "emotional objectivity involves an avoidance of emotional extremes when dealing with students" (Marzano, 2003a, p. 72). Research supports this; positive teacher emotional affect and tone are associated with the following positive outcomes.

- Cognitive and motivational stimulation and social support (Frenzel, Goetz, Stephens, & Jacob, 2009)
- Positive student affect and student engagement (Mazer, McKenna-Buchanan, Quinlan, & Titsworth, 2014)
- Better learning opportunities and experiences for students and teachers (Hagenauer, Hascher, & Volet, 2015; Meyer, 2014)
- Teacher perceptions of student performance, motivation, and discipline (Zembylas, 2002)
- Student engagement and teacher-student relationships (Demetriou & Wilson, 2009)

This is also where I want to discuss implicit bias because of the similarities between emotions and implicit bias. Emotions and implicit bias are alike in the following ways.

- **They can both occur subconsciously:** We are not always aware of our emotions or our implicit biases. They can operate below the level of our conscious awareness.
- **They can be influenced by our past experiences:** Our emotions and implicit biases are shaped by the things we have seen and

heard, the people we have interacted with, and the culture in which we live.

- **They can lead to biased behavior:** Our emotions and implicit biases can cause us to make decisions or take actions that are unfair or discriminatory.
- **They can be difficult to change:** It can be challenging to overcome our emotions and implicit biases, even when we are aware of them.

For example, we may experience negative emotions, such as fear or anxiety, when we encounter people from a different social group. This can be due to implicit biases that we have developed about that group. It is important to note that emotions and implicit bias are not always negative. For example, we may experience positive emotions, such as empathy or compassion, when we encounter people from different social groups. However, it is important to be aware of how our emotions and implicit biases can influence our behavior, both positive and negative.

This section examines how teachers can regulate their responses to both emotions and implicit bias. While these important factors cannot be controlled, teachers are able to influence them, though this requires emotional labor. *Emotional labor* is the work teachers do to make their expressions match certain *display rules* (Taxer & Frenzel, 2015): "Teachers are expected to show positive emotions (e.g., enjoyment and pride) when students strive and make progress, and to suppress or hide negative emotions (e.g., anger and hopelessness) when students misbehave in class" (Burić, Kim, & Hodis, 2021, p. 1227). There are two types of emotional labor: deep acting and surface acting (Grandey, 2000; Hochschild, 1983). According to Irena Burić, Lisa Kim, and Flaviu Hodis:

> *Deep acting* involves the conscious management of internal feelings to experience the supposed emotion and to modulate the observable emotional expression; *surface acting* involves the modification of outward displays of emotions by hiding and faking to comply with the emotional display rules. (pp. 1227–1228, emphasis added)

The research is very clear about surface acting: it is associated with decreased teacher well-being (Grandey & Gabriel, 2015), increased teacher stress (Hülsheger, Lang, & Maier, 2010), more frequent teacher burnout (Akin, Aydın, Erdoğan, & Demirkasimoğlu, 2014; Cheung & Lun, 2015; Näring, Briët, & Brouwers, 2006; Taxer & Frenzel, 2015), and decreased teacher job satisfaction (Yin, Lee, Zhang, & Jin, 2013).

The research is less clear about deep acting. In their 2019 meta-analysis, Hui Wang, Nathan Hall, and Jamie Taxer found that there was no relationship between deep acting and psychological well-being. But other studies have found positive and negative impacts of deep acting (Brotheridge & Lee, 2002; Grandey, 2003; Hülsheger & Schewe, 2011). To tease apart the complexity associated with deep acting, Burić and colleagues (2021) measured three emotional labor strategies in a sample of over two thousand Croatian teachers: deep acting, hiding emotions, and faking emotions.

Within the parameters of this study, profiles with high levels of faking emotions and hiding feelings (that is, surface acting) exhibited lower levels of positive emotions and self-efficacy. Profiles with high levels of deep acting exhibited higher levels of all the positive indicators. But interestingly, the two unhealthiest profiles (regulators and suppressors) also exhibited high levels of deep acting. Burić and colleagues (2021) concluded, "relying predominately on deep acting while keeping the use of hiding feelings and faking emotions at low to moderate levels of frequency appears to be the most adaptive pattern" (p. 1238).

So how does a teacher consciously manage their internal feelings to experience desired emotions and avoid implicit bias? The following are simple strategies that a teacher might use toward this end.

- **Become more aware of their own emotions and biases:** Teachers can do this by reflecting on their own thoughts and feelings and by taking implicit bias tests.
- **Challenge their own assumptions:** When people experience strong emotions or encounter someone from a different social group, they should ask themselves if they are making any assumptions based on emotions or biases.
- **Seek out diversity in their lives:** The more people put themselves in new situations, the more likely it is that they will experience a

variety of emotions and interact with people from different social groups.

- **Be mindful of their emotions:** When interacting with themselves and others, people should be aware of their own emotions and how they influence behavior.

Relative to the last bullet, research suggests that mindfulness training is a good option. Bob has advocated for mindfulness since 2003:

> The construct of a mental set in classroom management is quite similar to the construct of "mindfulness" in psychology. . . . Mindfulness involves a heightened sense of situational awareness and a conscious control over one's thoughts and behavior relative to that situation. (Marzano, 2003a, p. 65)

In 2017, Bob and the coauthors of *Motivating and Inspiring Students* expanded:

> Mindfulness is a deliberate focus on thinking that results in intentionality. The premise behind mindfulness is that people are typically filled with so many thoughts and related emotions that they are often incapable of making the best decisions or noticing what is happening around them. (Marzano, Scott, et al., 2017, p. 23)

Subsequent research agrees. David Klingbeil and Tyler Renshaw (2018) performed a meta-analysis of twenty-nine studies (including 347 effect sizes and 1,493 teachers) on mindfulness training for teachers in grades preK through 12. They found an overall effect size of $g = 0.60$ of mindfulness training on increasing teacher psychological well-being and decreasing teacher psychological distress. Roeser and colleagues (2022) investigated the effects of mindfulness training in a large urban school district in the Pacific Northwest region of the United States and found a particularly strong benefit for new teachers:

> Beneficial program impacts on teacher and classroom outcomes were strongest for newer teachers (5 years or less of teaching experience) and for teachers working in middle (Grades 6–8) versus K–8 schools who undertook the training, especially at follow-up during a new school year. In fact, newer teachers who undertook mindfulness training not only showed the strongest improvements in the ways they managed students' behavior in their most stressful classroom at 4-month follow-up, they also were observed to reduce behaviors like expressed negative emotion, sarcasm and use of punitive language with students. (pp. 420–421)

Given the worldwide teacher shortage, mindfulness training and the practice of mindfulness presents a potentially high-impact strategy to promote teacher well-being.

Enthusiasm

Finally, we turn our attention to educator enthusiasm. As Bob described it in 2019, "enthusiasm involves viewing a topic as interesting, meaningful, and important and communicating those views to students while studying the topic" (2019a, p. 193). At its core, teacher enthusiasm has to do with beliefs about value: when teachers value the content they are teaching and feel that it is valuable for their students to learn, it can contribute to positive outcomes for both teachers and students (Dicke, Rubach, Safavian, Karabenick, & Eccles, 2021; Lazarides, Fauth, Gaspard, & Göllner, 2021; Parrisius, Gaspard, Trautwein, & Nagengast, 2020).

However, there may be a downside to teacher enthusiasm. Because education is such a powerful mission and so many educators are deeply committed to their students and their work, it can be hard to detach from that work. Many teachers find themselves engaged in *work-related rumination*, intensive involvement in work-related thoughts, usually related to negative or worrisome issues. In their systematic review of studies of work-related rumination, Yasemin Türktorun, Gerald Weiher, and Holger Horz (2020) highlighted the fact that teachers have "blurred work-home boundaries when parts of the work are completed at home, extending working hours into the evening and making rumination until bedtime more likely" (p. 14). Work-related rumination is unsurprisingly associated with a host of negative impacts on teacher well-being, including fatigue, stress, sleep issues, burnout, and depression.

There are two strategies that teachers can use to combat work-related rumination: problem-solving pondering and psychological detachment. In contrast to work-related rumination, problem-solving pondering involves an intentional, goal-directed approach to work problems (Cropley & Zijlstra, 2011). Teachers could adapt Bob's problem-solving process for such an application:

1. What is the goal?
2. What obstacle or constraint makes it difficult to accomplish the goal?
3. What are some ways I might overcome the obstacle or constraint?
4. Which solution do I predict will work best, and why?
5. What actually happened?
6. Do the results fit with my original prediction?
7. If not, how should I change my thinking regarding the problem? (Marzano, 2019a, p. 95)

Alternatively, teachers could engage in psychological detachment. According to Sabine Sonnentag and Charlotte Fritz (2015), psychological detachment involves mentally disengaging from one's job while away from work. Research has found that psychological detachment was associated with positive outcomes such as an increase in positive emotions, a decrease in sleep onset problems (and therefore a decrease in fatigue and exhaustion), and greater life satisfaction (Bennett, Bakker, & Field, 2018; Gluschkoff et al., 2016; Wendsche & Lohmann-Haislah, 2017).

Sabine Sonnentag and Undine Kruel (2006) found that higher job involvement—that is, the extent to which a teacher identifies with and finds their job relevant to their life goals—is associated with lower psychological detachment. Since preserving teacher enthusiasm is desirable, teachers must find ways to psychologically detach from work. A diary study by Sonnentag in 2001 indicated that low-effort (sitting still, reading) and social activities can promote psychological detachment. Additionally, refraining from work-related activities for a specified period before bedtime also seems to help, especially with sleep issues that stem from work-related rumination. Finally, it seems that mindfulness practice and training is also beneficial for cultivating psychological detachment.

COMPONENTS OF THE EDUCATOR METACOGNITIVE SYSTEM

As noted in chapter 2 (page 33), the metacognitive system consists of the skills people use to regulate their performance on specific tasks. Charlotte Dignath and Marcel Veenman (2021) emphasized the importance of teachers using metacognitive skills—or self-regulated learning (SRL)—to regulate their practice:

> Research on teachers' own SRL has shown that teachers are more motivated to promote SRL when they are convinced of the effectiveness of self-regulation strategies (Dembo 2001). Moreover, in order to model strategy use, teachers need to be experienced strategy users themselves (Paris and Winograd 2003; Kohen and Kramarski 2018). To become aware of self-regulation strategies, teacher training curricula have to address SRL and strategy use explicitly (Randi 2004) in order to develop self-regulating teachers who can then develop self-regulating students later on. (pp. 524–525)

For educators, the tasks on which they need to regulate their performance are quite varied. Classroom teachers are primarily focused on providing high-quality instructional experiences for students, building-level administrators are focused on cultivating systems and processes that ensure a safe and orderly environment and lead to high-quality teaching and learning, and so on. Therefore, as with self-system skills, this discussion of the educator metacognitive system will be general for the most part. We will begin by focusing on the overarching metacognitive skill of goal setting.

As in our discussion of goals in chapter 2 (page 33), we will view educator goals through the lens of achievement goal theory. However, the categories of goals for educators are slightly different from those for students (Butler, 2007, 2012).

- **Mastery approach:** I'm seeking to develop my own competence and promote student learning.

- **Performance approach:** I'm seeking to demonstrate that my performance is superior to that of others.
- **Performance avoidance:** I'm seeking to avoid demonstrating that my performance is worse than that of others.
- **Work avoidance:** I'm aiming to minimize the amount of effort I have to exert.

Which goal orientation do you think is most productive for educators? If you picked the mastery-approach goal orientation, you're right! According to Helen Watt, Ruth Butler, and Paul Richardson (2021), mastery-approach goals are associated with:

> Constructive, problem-focused strategies, interest in teaching and professional development, positive emotions, self-efficacy and job satisfaction. Mastery goals also associate with mastery-orienting, autonomy-supportive, and cognitively stimulating instruction that emphasizes and promotes student effort, progress, and learning for understanding. (p. 2)

But guess what? If you picked the performance-approach goal orientation, you're right, too. Again, according to Watt and colleagues, performance-approach goal orientations were beneficial for "interest, engagement, wellbeing and achievement" (p. 3). In contrast, both performance-avoidance and work-avoidance goal orientations were associated with negative outcomes for both teachers and students.

Whether teachers are seeking to demonstrate mastery or superior performance, their goals should focus on specific aspects of teaching that they want to improve. To identify those specific aspects, an instructional model, such as the one articulated in Bob's 2017 book, *The New Art and Science of Teaching*, can be used. We will discuss instructional models in depth in chapter 8 (page 117), but for our purposes here, a summary will suffice. *The New Art and Science of Teaching* instructional model articulates forty-three elements of effective teaching. This granularity is the model's strength. These elements constitute moves that teachers can execute at different times in the classroom. Teachers can select one or more of the elements as goal areas to improve their practice. Critically, the success of a teacher move (or strategy) is dependent on the outcomes it produces in students. If students don't respond to a move in productive ways, then it didn't work, and the teacher needs to either improve their execution of the strategy or try something else to get the desired student outcomes.

After choosing a goal, the teacher can practice executing that element (and observing students' responses) in the classroom. To use the metacognitive phases introduced in chapter 2 (page 33), this moves them from the preparatory phase of metacognition to the performance phase of metacognition. During this phase, teachers must make decisions about when to use specific strategies (including the strategies they've selected as their growth areas). But how do teachers know which moves to use at which moments? One way is to cultivate metacognitive awareness of the scripts they are using in the classroom.

In the 2015 book *Managing the Inner World of Teaching*, Bob and his wife, Jana, defined a *script* as "a mental structure that defines an appropriate sequence of actions in a particular situation" (Marzano & Marzano, 2015, p. 6). Scripts differentiate the performance of novice teachers from that of expert teachers. Rebekka Stahnke and Sigrid Blömeke (2021) explained:

> The superior performance of experts is not only based on teachers' knowledge, but also on their situation-specific skills (Blömeke et al., 2015; Lachner et al., 2016). During the development from novice to expert, the initially isolated and explicit knowledge base of novices is restructured and evolves towards more integrated and organized scripts. (p. 2)

Charlotte Wolff, Halszka Jarodzka, and Henny Boshuizen (2021) pointed out that the gateway to leveraging scripts in the classroom lies in *noticing*.

> In the professional domain of teaching, scripts provide the background knowledge that helps teachers understand the complex world of the classroom and they expand as teachers learn through experience in the classroom. Scripts provide connectivity between events and are more tightly connected to specific types of events than to the overarching situations. Teachers' ability to recognize the relevance of different events is crucial to

> their knowledge acquisition. Whenever an existing script is violated or expectations (about actors and events) are challenged, teachers' scripts are rewritten and their knowledge is restructured accordingly. (pp. 136–137)

Educators must notice specific events, identify them as requiring a specific script, activate that script in their background knowledge, and then execute it. Additionally, effective teachers are constantly reworking their scripts to make them more effective.

One way that novice teachers could improve the quality of their scripts is to focus on their noticing behavior. Tina Seidel, Katharina Schnitzler, Christian Kosel, Kathleen Stürmer, and Doris Holzberger (2021) found that "expert teachers tended to pay more attention than novices did to those students who might be in particular need of further support" (p. 85). Stahnke and Blömeke (2021) noted that "teachers' noticing, reasoning and acting skills help to apply . . . scripts to situations that are not pre-structured" (p. 2). Additionally, they used eye-tracking methodology to collect data on what novice teachers and expert teachers notice in both whole-class and partner-work formats.

Novice teachers noticed more preventive teacher events, student discipline, and learning events in the partner-work format than they did in the whole-group format. While it might simply take time and experience for novice teachers to develop their noticing and scripts into expert-level constructs, they can immediately take advantage of the benefits that student-centered learning formats (such as partner work) afford them in terms of noticing.

SUMMARY

In this chapter, we explored the teacher self- and metacognitive systems, and how the components of each can be influenced and adjusted to preserve and promote teacher health and well-being. Relative to the teacher self-system, we considered expectations, emotions, and enthusiasm. Relative to the teacher metacognitive system, we discussed goal setting and the importance of scripts and student-centered learning environments. Teachers have a primary responsibility to regulate themselves and their practice as educators. Successfully caring for themselves allows teachers to perform at a high level in the two roles that, I would assert, are among their most important: measurement and instruction. In the next two chapters, we consider these roles.

CHAPTER 7

MEASUREMENT

In this part of the book, we discuss three primary roles of the classroom teacher: self-regulation, measurement, and instruction. That second role—and this chapter—is called "Measurement" and not "Assessment" because *measurement* is the term for the overarching process of determining and communicating student status and growth; *assessment* is one part of that process. Bob (2006) further detailed the distinction:

> *Assessment* is any planned or serendipitous activity that provides information about students' understanding and skill regarding a specific measurement topic; a *test* is one of a number of forms of assessment. Regardless of what type of assessment is used, judgments are made about each student's level of understanding and skill via the process of *evaluation*. These judgments are translated into *scores* using the process of *measurement*. (pp. 35–36)

An assessment is an event or activity that generates data, and there are thousands of different types of assessments. Measurement is the process of translating assessment data into scores that accurately reflect what students know and are able to do.

As teachers engage in the measurement process, there is one fact that ought to inform every decision they make: *all assessments contain error*. Bob has been reiterating this since at least 1987:

> The standard error of measurement (SEM) is a statistic that estimates the magnitude of measurement error in a score. *Because there is error in every test score*, it is important to interpret a student's scores as a range of possibilities rather than as an exact measurement. (Marzano et al., 1987, p. 118; emphasis added)

The classical test theory equation for this is as follows.

True score = observed score + error score

No one can ever really know a student's true score. You can only estimate it using an observed score. As Bob (2018) explained in his most important assessment book, *Making Classroom Assessments Reliable and Valid*:

> Scores for individual students contain some amount of error. Error may be due to careless mistakes on the part of students, on the part of those administering and scoring the test, or both. Such an error is referred to as a *random measurement error*, and is an anticipated part of any assessment. . . . Random error can either increase the score a student receives . . . or decrease the score a student receives. (p. 10)

The last sentence of this quote means that the + in the true score equation can also be a –, depending on whether the error is in the student's favor or not. For example, if a student doesn't know the answer to an item but guesses right, that error is in the student's favor. The observed score will indicate the student knows more than she truly does. On the other hand, if a student knows the answer to an item but accidentally fills in the wrong bubble, that is an error against her. The observed score is going to indicate that she doesn't know something she truly does know.

There are literally thousands of ways that error can occur in an assessment event, so suffice it to say (again) that all assessments contain error. Here's what Stephen Sireci, past president of the National Council on Measurement in Education, said in his 2020 presidential address:

> We as a field have long acknowledged educational tests are imperfect approximations of the constructs we attempt to measure. Publicly acknowledging all educational tests are fallible to some degree by instilling it as a core value grounds our work in an appropriate cloak of humility. Such humility is needed to improve assessment practices and helps inoculate us against hypocrisy. (pp. 12–13)

No test is perfect; all assessments contain error. Even the big ones.

LARGE-SCALE ASSESSMENTS

Large-scale assessments are standardized tests given to large groups of students, typically at the state or national level. They are often used to assess student achievement in specific subjects, such as reading, mathematics, and science. Large-scale assessments are also used to hold schools and districts accountable for student performance.

While large-scale assessments can provide some useful information, they also have a number of problems. These problems include the following.

- **Bias:** Large-scale assessments can be biased against certain groups of students, such as English learners, students with disabilities, and students from low-income families.
- **Validity:** Large-scale assessments are often not valid measures of student learning, meaning that they do not accurately measure what students know and can do.
- **Reliability:** Large-scale assessments are often not reliable measures of student learning, meaning that they produce inconsistent results.
- **Cost:** Large-scale assessments are expensive to develop, administer, and score.
- **Time:** Large-scale assessments take a significant amount of time away from instruction.

Here, we focus on two big problems with large-scale assessments: (1) they're designed to make generalizations across large groups of students (not for individual students), and (2) they're not necessarily aligned with what students are learning in school.

Large-Scale Assessments Are for Large Groups

Large-scale assessments are not designed to provide feedback to individual students. In 1996, Bob and Kendall reminded us that "standardized tests were initially designed for the purpose of identifying which students would most likely succeed in school and which students would most likely fail" (p. 90). In 2017, Bob pointed out that "benchmark assessments and end-of-course assessments are not administered frequently enough to be useful for students and teachers. . . . They don't meet the day-to-day feedback needs of teachers and students" (p. 115). And in 2018, "large-scale assessments represent reliability in terms of scores for *groups of students* as opposed to individual students" (Marzano, 2018, p. 8; emphasis added).

Measurement experts discourage teachers' use of student subscores from large-scale assessments. In their review of international trends in large-scale testing, Louis Volante and colleagues (2020) said:

> Large-scale assessment can occur with sparse sampling of content and rare validity studies relative to the policy uses intended (Baker, 2016). As a result, these exams may neither give full descriptions nor provide comprehensive guidance for specific policy options, but their regular use may convince the authorities that they are upholding managerial principles of guidance, evidence, and accountability. Their true cost is whether teachers can legitimately affect these scores, which has given rise to value-added models and extensive tracking practices as evident in the United States, England, and Singapore, and to a lesser extent in Germany, Canada, and Australia. (p. 26)

In other words, large-scale assessments are simply not designed for many of the purposes they are often used for. Whenever large-scale assessment scores are used to make high-stakes decisions for individual students, remember that *all assessments contain error.*

Large-Scale Assessments Aren't Long Enough to Include All the Content

In 2003, Bob pointed out that large-scale assessments only "sample the content in state standards documents" and that, "sampling the content within a subject area is the basis for all large-scale assessments" (Marzano, 2003b, p. 38). According to Norman Webb's (2007) alignment criteria, an "aligned" assessment needs to contain a certain number of items focused on each standard it purports to measure, with "the recommended minimum being at least six items per standard" (Welch & Dunbar, 2020, p. 9). There are forty-two ELA standards for third grade in the CCSS (not counting the substandards; if you include them, you're up to ninety total). Forty-two standards times six items per standard is 252 items to adequately measure third-grade ELA performance on the standards—and that assumes each standard is unidimensional, which they're not. It would more reasonably take upward of five hundred items to begin to get a clear picture of a student's performance on the third-grade ELA standards alone—and the number of standards just increases after third grade. There is simply no way for large-scale tests to adequately measure everything they purport to measure. Landl (2020) summarized the situation:

> Over the past 5 years, we have seen an unprecedented call for shorter tests and reduced testing times. This is often due to the perceived limited value of large-scale, summative assessments and the desire to prioritize other assessments that provide teachers and students with timely feedback that informs instruction throughout the school year. In response, a large number of states have significantly shortened the time allotted to the state summative assessment by proportionally reducing the test length or strategically reducing or removing selected subdomains. In addition to the technical challenges these modifications pose (e.g., reliability and comparability), these changes make it difficult to defend claims that the full depth and breadth of a state's academic content standards are being addressed. (p. 25)

Even if a test has enough items to adequately measure the standards it purports to measure, the items may not actually align with those standards. Morgan Polikoff is a leader in the field of assessment alignment; he has done extensive research with his colleague Andrew Porter, whose 2002 Surveys of Enacted Curriculum and Webb's (1997) alignment model are the two major alignment approaches in the educational psychometric field. Polikoff (2020) bemoaned the nonobjective nature of current approaches to aligning large-scale assessments to education standards:

> Why has there been so little peer-reviewed research on alignment methods, and why has the science advanced in such a limited fashion? Probably, the simplest answer is that alignment analyses are hard and require actual humans to carry out. While item response theory methods can be improved with a smart statistician and a fast computer, improving alignment

> methods requires sitting down with trained raters and doing careful validation work. And, like classroom observation, alignment analyses feel more "art" than "science," perhaps because there is no obvious right answer or criterion. Furthermore, there has obviously not been demand for improving alignment methods—the federal peer review requirements have not pushed for more rigor in these methods. As a result, the alignment methods have not changed much, and the science of alignment research remains weak relative to other areas of test construction and validation. (p. 18)

To be fair, it's not just large-scale assessments that suffer from error. All assessments contain error, including classroom assessments.

CLASSROOM ASSESSMENTS

Classroom assessments have traditionally been heavily laced with error. As Bob (2000) strikingly said, "Grades are so imprecise that they are almost meaningless" (p. 1). Some of that imprecision is a natural product of the assessment endeavor. As James Pellegrino (2020) reminded us:

> We assess students to learn about what they know and can do, but assessing educational outcomes is not as straightforward as measuring height or weight; the attributes to be judged are mental representations and processes that are not outwardly visible. Thus, educational assessment is a process designed to observe students' behavior and produce data that can be used to draw reasonable inferences about what students know and can do. Deciding what to assess and how to do so is not as simple as it might appear. (p. 82)

Teachers' best hope for an assessment event is to collect information they can use to make productive inferences about what students know and are able to do. The very first step in that endeavor is ensuring that students have had an opportunity to learn the content on which they will be assessed.

Assess Students on Topics They've Had an Opportunity to Learn

The concept of *opportunity to learn* is exactly what it sounds like. Assessment experts in the 1960s (Husén, 1967a, 1967b) articulated the self-evident idea that there is a relationship between a student's opportunity to learn content and their performance on an assessment featuring that content. If we expect students to perform well on assessments, we must ensure they have had adequate opportunities to learn the content.

For students to have the opportunity to learn the content they will be assessed on, the intended curriculum must be aligned to the implemented curriculum, which must be aligned to the attained curriculum. Marzano and colleagues (2018) defined each of these as follows:

- The *intended curriculum* is what is articulated in standards documents.
- The *implemented curriculum* is what teachers actually teach and assess in classrooms (sometimes also referred to as the *taught curriculum* or *assessed curriculum*).
- The *attained curriculum* is what students actually learn in a given course or level.

Aligning these three curricula can be tricky. Misalignment might stem from the resources that teachers use for instruction. Jing Tian, David Braithwaite, and Robert Siegler (2021) analyzed the 2016 versions of mathematics textbooks published by Houghton Mifflin Harcourt, Pearson, and McGraw-Hill in the United States. They found that the textbooks presented more of a specific type of mathematics problem (addition and subtraction problems where both numbers were decimal numbers) and much fewer of a different type (addition and subtraction problems where one number was a decimal and one was a whole number). Despite the fact that adding a whole number and a decimal is easier than adding two decimals, they found that students who used textbooks with these imbalances performed significantly better during testing on two-decimal addition and subtraction problems and worse on addition and subtraction problems with a decimal and a whole number. They replicated these results with three different data sets, as shown in table 7.1.

TABLE 7.1: Impact of Implemented Curriculum on Attained Curriculum

Data Set	Number Of Students	Decimal And Whole Number Problems Correct	Two-Decimal Problems Correct
Historical (1985)	272	Fall—37 percent Spring—38 percent	Fall—70 percent Spring—73 percent
Contemporary Large (2019)	3,359	76 percent	84 percent
Contemporary Small (2016)	66	68 percent	80 percent

Because the implemented curriculum focused disproportionately on a specific kind of problem, the attained curriculum was also skewed toward that kind of problem. This put both of them out of alignment with the intended curriculum, represented by the following standard:

> Add, subtract, multiply, and divide decimals to hundredths, using concrete models or drawings and strategies based on place value, properties of operations, and/or the relationship between addition and subtraction; relate the strategy to a written method and explain the reasoning used. (CCSS.Math.5.NBT.7, NGA & CCSSO, 2010, p. 35)

Proficiency scales have the potential to solve curricular misalignment problems by clearly articulating the intended curriculum in a format that facilitates instruction and assessment. As Bob and Abbott (2022) commented, "to a great extent, proficiency scales can ensure that the intended curriculum, the taught curriculum, and the assessed curriculum are all the same" (p. 21). Proficiency scales empower teachers to maintain a strong link between the intended and implemented curriculum.

Use Proficiency Scales to Score Students Accurately

As Bob and colleagues (2016) explained, "*measurement* . . . is the act of translating the information about students gleaned from assessments onto some scale" (p. 58). Creating high-quality classroom assessments and translating that information can be a challenge, as Henning Fjørtoft (2020) said:

> Classroom assessments must also be practicable for teachers. Conceptualizing this dilemma as a one-handed clock, Stobart (2008) argues that teachers must balance validity, reliability, and manageability, and that meeting all three requirements is generally impossible. Teachers (or test designers) normally are able to satisfy only two in practice. (p. 2)

With a proficiency scale (see chapter 5, page 69), teachers can pretty easily satisfy all three requirements.

- For **validity** (which is "the extent to which an assessment measures what it purports to measure;" Marzano, 2018, p. 7), a proficiency scale clearly defines what is being measured. A teacher can score all different types of assessment events (tests, observations, probing discussions) using the same proficiency scale, thus obtaining a consistent and comparable set of scores that all measure what they aim to.
- For **reliability** (which is consistency in measurement from one assessment opportunity to the next and from one scorer to the next), a proficiency scale clearly defines what performance looks like at each score level, allowing for consistent scoring across teachers, classrooms, and assessment opportunities. As Richard DuFour and Bob (2011) stated, "Scales . . . allow teachers to design their unique individual assessments but still maintain a common interpretation of a standard to score on those assessments" (p. 133).
- For **manageability**, proficiency scales are a simple tool that teachers can use to communicate with students, parents, and colleagues about the expectations for a grade level or course.

If teachers use proficiency scales to assign scores on assessments, they will be able to collect a series of scores that all use the same scale and are comparable to one another. Collecting this series of scores allows teachers to adhere to another important principle of educational measurement: never trust a single assessment.

Never Trust a Single Assessment

To put it bluntly, using the score from a single assessment to determine what a student knows and can do is an egregious violation of the fundamental principles of measurement. To understand this topic, we must begin with the formative-summative distinction in assessment. Paul Black and Dylan Wiliam's (1998) research review popularized formative assessment in education and has been discussed at great length since. But the distinction between formative and summative assessments is flawed for at least two reasons. First, there is no such thing as a formative assessment; *formative* refers to a *use* for assessment, not a type of assessment. Pellegrino (2020) agreed:

> Another issue we must address is whether [we are] using assessment to mean a process or a thing. The literature vacillates between using assessment as a verb or a noun or both. This is not necessarily harmful, but we should be clear when we are adopting one orientation or the other. In many cases we wish to emphasize the process of collecting evidence and then the tools or tasks that we develop to support that process. A somewhat pernicious example of this confusion has arisen with respect to formative assessment. There is often confusion about formative assessment as a process (verb) versus calling something a formative assessment (noun). There is no such thing as a "formative assessment," there can only be assessments that are sufficiently informative that the information they provide can be used as part of the formative assessment process which includes acting on the information to effect subsequent learning. (p. 84)

Educators need to stop talking about "formative assessments"; you use assessment information formatively, you do not administer a formative assessment.

Second, the entire idea of a summative assessment promotes the idea that you can use a single assessment to measure student learning, and that's just not the case:

> In a traditional system, the final score is often determined by a student's performance on a single summative assessment or by averaging a series of summative scores. Both of these methods are problematic. A score on a final exam may not accurately represent a student's true level of knowledge simply because *all assessments contain error*. Averaging test scores is also problematic. Averages assume that a student's level of knowledge has been the same throughout all assessments, which runs contrary to the idea of learning as a progression. (Marzano et al., 2016, p. 59; emphasis added)

Here, Bob reiterated the unreliability of single assessments, as well as the problem with averaging scores. As educators all know, student learning isn't the same across a unit—it should increase! Therefore, when computing final scores, teachers shouldn't penalize students for knowing less at the beginning of a unit (which is what the average does). So, let's talk about formative scores and summative scores.

Determine Summative Scores by Considering Patterns of Formative Scores

The best way to describe formative scores and summative scores is using the visual in figure 7.1. Ignore the linear, curvilinear, and average lines and their numbers for a moment and focus on the gray bars. The bars represent formative scores; a *formative score* is collected from a specific assessment on a specific date for a specific topic using the proficiency scale for that topic. The number below each bar aligns with a specific date. So on January 3 (bar 1), the teacher assessed the student and their score was 1.5. On January 8 (bar 2), the teacher assessed the student again on the same topic and their score was 2.0—same on January 13 (bar 3), then 2.5 on January 18 (bar 4), 3.0 on January 23 (bar 5), and 4.0 on January 28 (bar 6). The teacher assessed the student on the same topic on all these dates and recorded a score from each assessment.

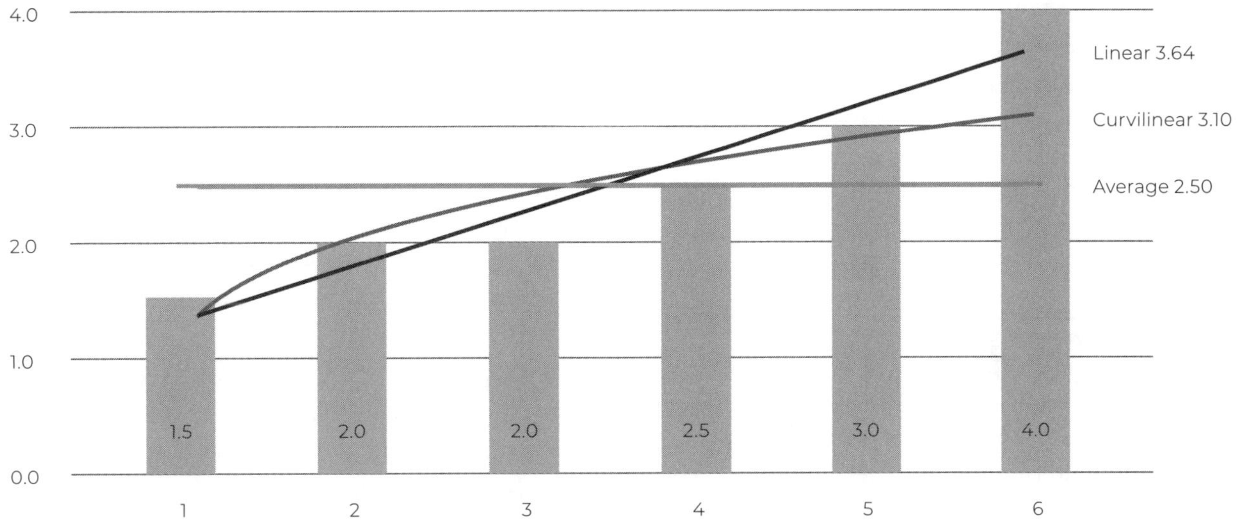

Source: Marzano, 2018, p. 65.

Figure 7.1: Three prediction lines.

Now, it's time for the teacher to assign this student a summative score; a *summative score* summarizes the student's current level of knowledge and skill on a specific topic. It is generated from pattern of formative scores (and is never based on a single assessment). In this example, the teacher looks at the pattern of this student's scores. The teacher could overlay one or more statistically predicted learning trajectories and see which one best fits the pattern.

- The curvilinear trend in figure 7.1 assumes that student learning improves more at the beginning of a unit and levels off toward the end.
- The linear trend assumes that student learning consistently increases (or decreases) during a unit.
- The average trend assumes that student learning neither increases nor decreases during a unit.

Making Classroom Assessments Reliable and Valid (Marzano, 2018) details the calculations for these trends and their use.

To keep things simple, though, when you look at the pattern of observed scores, it should be obvious that this student's current status is at least a 3.0 and possibly as high as 4.0; you might assign a summative score of 3.5. If you have the benefit of being able to see the curvilinear trend, you might be more cautious (since it shows an expected score of 3.10 for that last score) and assign a 3.0 or 3.25. (In general, the curvilinear trend line best represents expected student growth over time; see Bob's 2018 book *Making Classroom Assessments Reliable and Valid* for further explanation of how to analyze residuals to determine the line of best fit.) Or you might give the student one more assessment opportunity if you're just not sure. If they score 4.0 on that last assessment, you're probably justified in assigning them a summative score of 4.0—not because that was their score on the last assessment you gave but because the body of evidence you collected leads you to believe that is their current status on this topic. Never forget that "the primary goal of educational assessment is to infer attributes about a learner from observations of their performance" (DiCerbo, 2020, p. 90). Don't make what Bob and Brian Kosena (2022) call one of education's biggest mistakes:

> In many schools, formative assessments are only considered practice for a summative test. Stated differently, some schools have adopted the position that students' scores on the summative assessment are the only scores that count. In fact, scores on summative tests might be the only ones teachers record in a gradebook. We believe this is one of the biggest and most consequential mistakes currently made in schools, at least in terms of classroom assessment. (Marzano & Kosena, 2022, p. 131)

Summative scores are a product of teacher judgment, based on the evidence from a pattern of scores collected over time. As you've no doubt gathered, those formative scores need to be as accurate as possible. While you can't get rid of all error, you can reduce it as much as possible by ensuring that your assessment opportunities produce valid scores.

ASSESSMENT DESIGN

As articulated in the previous section, classroom assessment should be a process wherein a teacher collects scores from a series of assessment events on a single topic (resulting in a progression of formative scores for that topic over time) and uses that series of formative scores to compute a summative score for that topic. Here, we talk about the nuts and bolts of designing classroom assessment events. To begin, let's hear from Bob and colleagues about the potential precision of classroom assessment:

> Some educators assume they can't use classroom assessments to make decisions about individual students because the assessments do not exhibit the same psychometric properties as the externally designed assessments. While this observation has intuitive appeal, it is actually misleading . . . we assert that classroom assessments can actually be more precise than external assessment when it comes to examining the performance of individual students. (Marzano et al., 2019, p. 2)
>
> Classroom assessments are the front line of the assessment system. Classroom assessment scores represent the evaluation of student knowledge and skill that is closest in time and proximity to the teacher and learning process that occurs each day in classrooms. (Marzano et al., 2019, p. 105)

Moreover, Detlef Urhahne and Lisette Wijnia (2021) performed a literature review on the accuracy of teacher judgments about students and found that "the relative accuracy of teacher judgments is high for students' academic achievement" (p. 15). So yes, teachers can design useful classroom assessments and use their professional judgment to determine students' levels of knowledge and skill.

Assessment Events

Educators have a lot of options when it comes to assessment methods—a point Bob has made countless times. There are three overarching categories: obtrusive, unobtrusive, and student-generated.

- **Obtrusive** means that instruction pauses for assessment to occur. This could be a traditional test with items, a demonstration or performance, or a probing discussion. With this method, students know they're being assessed.
- **Unobtrusive** is assessment "on the sly." Students don't always know they're being assessed, and instruction doesn't necessarily stop. For example, during collaborative work, the teacher might hear a student's explanation of a concept to a peer that illustrates score 3.0 understanding. Or, in reviewing a student's journal entries, the teacher might notice that the student is consistently exhibiting 3.0 competence with English grammar and mechanics.
- **Student-generated** assessment is where a student suggests an assessment event that they will use to demonstrate a specific score on a specific topic. For example, a student might suggest that—to illustrate their 3.0 understanding of civic responsibility—they will create a voter education campaign that highlights the importance of voting, the voter registration process, and a call to action to register and vote in an upcoming election. The teacher agrees (or coaches the student toward an alternative), observes, and scores the student. If the teacher and student disagree about the student's current status, they discuss.

When designing assessments of any type (obtrusive, unobtrusive, or student-generated), teachers should ensure that each assessment clearly focuses on one topic, or if more than one topic is present, that they are scored separately.

Assessment Topics

If you create an assessment opportunity that involves two topics (for example, writing an expository text about nuclear processes), you need to either assign each student two scores for the assessment opportunity (one for the procedural skill of writing an expository text, the other for declarative knowledge of nuclear processes), or you will need to choose which topic the assessment focuses on (and recognize the other may interfere—if you choose nuclear processes, the written format of the assessment may prevent some students from fully displaying their understanding of nuclear processes). Ideally, an assessment focuses on just one topic; in the measurement literature, this concept is known as *unidimensionality*, and we talked about it briefly in chapter 5 (page 69) during our discussion of proficiency scales.

Regarding the potential interference of extraneous topics on an assessment, consider how they contribute to the cognitive load of an assessment. Recall from chapter 1 (page 15) that working memory capacity is absorbed by germane load and extraneous load. If you think about cognitive load in relation to a single assessment item, you can see how important it is to focus assessment items narrowly on the topic you are seeking to assess. Imagine the intrinsic load of an assessment task related to nuclear processes is 4 (again, this arbitrary number is for the purposes of illustration only). But the separate skill of writing exacts a mental load as well (let's quantify it as 1), as does expressing knowledge in English if it is not students' first language (also 1). The writing and the language are extraneous load. See figure 7.2.

Intrinsic load		Germane load		Extraneous load
4		4	+	0
4		3	+	1
4		2	+	2

Figure 7.2: Sample cognitive load of multidimensional assessment task.

As shown here, the increased extraneous load decreases the germane load to a point where the intrinsic load of the assessment task exceeds the available resources in the student's working memory. Thus, the student may not be able to fully demonstrate their understanding of nuclear processes.

Assessment Items

Specific features of assessment items can also increase the cognitive load of an assessment. Teachers can design assessment items to decrease extraneous load and help students better demonstrate what they know and are able to do. Research by Marlit Lindner (2020) and Marlit Lindner, Johannes Schult, and Richard Mayer (2022) found that adding representational pictures to science and mathematics assessment items and tasks decreased the intrinsic load while adding decorative pictures did not. Figure 7.3 (page 112) illustrates the difference between the two.

Accommodations also decrease cognitive load. Accommodations are designed to reduce *construct-irrelevant factors* or elements of assessments that have nothing to do with the content actually being assessed. As Jamal Abedi, Yu Zhang, Susan Rowe, and Hansol Lee (2020) explained:

> An accommodation is effective if it makes assessments more accessible to the recipients by controlling for construct-irrelevant factors. For example, an effective accommodation for ELL [English language learner] students makes assessment more linguistically accessible by reducing the level of unnecessary linguistic complexity as a construct-irrelevant factor. Accommodations—such as a glossary of uncommon or difficult vocabulary, native language assessment, or customized dictionaries—can be quite helpful and effective for ELLs. (p. 42)

Text-Only	Decorative Picture	Representative Picture
A rectangular pool is being filled with water. At 1:23 p.m., the pool has 32 inches of water in it. By 1:48 p.m., the water is 37 inches deep. How much does the water increase every minute? a. $\frac{1}{8}$ inch b. $\frac{1}{5}$ inch c. $\frac{1}{2}$ inch d. 1 inch	A rectangular pool is being filled with water. At 1:23 p.m., the pool has 32 inches of water in it. By 1:48 p.m., the water is 37 inches deep.  How much does the water increase every minute? a. $\frac{1}{8}$ inch b. $\frac{1}{5}$ inch c. $\frac{1}{2}$ inch d. 1 inch	A rectangular pool is being filled with water. At 1:23 p.m., the pool has 32 inches of water in it. By 1:48 p.m., the water is 37 inches deep. 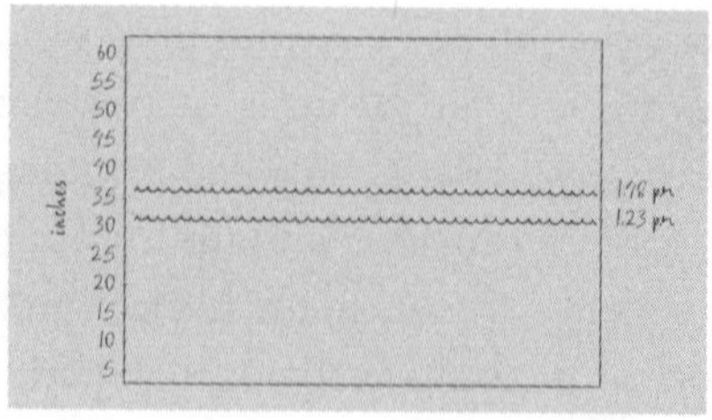 How much does the water increase every minute? a. $\frac{1}{8}$ inch b. $\frac{1}{5}$ inch c. $\frac{1}{2}$ inch d. 1 inch

Figure 7.3: Examples of decorative and representational pictures.

Another way to reduce the cognitive load of items (and to prepare students for the types of items they will likely see on large-scale assessments) is to repeatedly use the same item structures that large-scale assessment items typically follow when designing classroom assessments. These *frames* can be used to help students practice with and even generate assessment items similar to those they will encounter on large-scale assessments (Marzano, Dodson, Simms, & Wipf, 2022). This reduces cognitive load:

> Unfamiliarity with an assessment and the anxiety and confusion that could result are artificial impediments to students' ability to demonstrate their true level of knowledge and skill in the domain being assessed. Providing all students with a baseline of exposure to and practice with an assessment and its various item formats could improve scores *and* enhance the validity of score interpretations by raising scores that would otherwise be inaccurately low indicators of students' abilities. (Marzano et al., 2022, p. 164)

And finally, but perhaps most importantly, each assessment item should clearly address a specific level of the proficiency scale. As shown in figure 7.4, it should be clear to both teacher and students which level of the scale each assessment item addresses.

In some cases, as Bob (2010a) explained, teachers might "want to use or have to use assessments that were not designed with the scale in mind." He elaborated, "This should not be considered a problem. A teacher simply has to interpret these other assessments in terms of the scale" (p. 51). The easiest way to do this is to align the assessment items with the scale levels (as shown in figure 7.4) and proceed to score the assessment using the proficiency scale.

Score	Description	Assessment Items
4.0 Complex	Use the writing process to compose a text about the solution to a problem.	Write a text using the writing process to address the problem of inadequate recycling facilities on campus.
3.0 Target	Use the writing process (prewriting, drafting, revising, editing, and publishing) to create texts.	Write a text using the writing process. Save copies at each stage of the writing process, using Track Changes to show revisions and edits to your first draft.
2.0 Simpler	Understand vocabulary such as *prewriting*, *drafting*, *revising*, *editing*, and *publishing*. List activities associated with each phase of the writing process. Produce artifacts that show their use of each phase of the writing process.	Generate a description and visual for each vocabulary term. Which of the following is NOT a phase of the writing process? a. Prewriting b. Drafting c. Revising d. Researching Which phase of the writing process involves reviewing and refining a draft for grammar, punctuation, spelling, and style? a. Prewriting b. Drafting c. Revising d. Publishing
1.0	With help, some of the content.	
0.0	With help, none of the content.	

Figure 7.4: Aligning assessment items to a proficiency scale.

Parallel Assessments

Finally, when designing assessment events, it is important to ensure that they are parallel. As Bob explained, "Parallel assessments measure the same topic and have items that are at the same levels of difficulty" (Marzano, 2018, p. 33). The most common pitfall here occurs if a teacher designs an assessment that only measures one level of a proficiency scale; for example, if an assessment opportunity only involves level 2.0 items or tasks. If the highest available score on that assessment is a 2.0, then the teacher can't use those scores in a series of formative scores because there's no way of knowing if the student's actual score was a 3.0 or even a 4.0. Therefore, the assessment process works best when all assessment opportunities provide students with the option to demonstrate performance on all levels of the proficiency scale.

However, Bob and colleagues have highlighted at least one situation in which a teacher might assess only one level: "when a teacher is convinced that a student has demonstrated proficiency at a particular score level on a scale" (Marzano et al., 2019, p. 72). If a teacher wanted to verify that a student had achieved the 3.0 level of the scale, let's say, that teacher might design a short interview with the student to gather data to that end. This is an acceptable use of a single-level assessment, but in general, assessments that allow students to demonstrate the full range of what they know for a particular scale are more useful for teachers.

ASSESSMENT SCORING

In the same way that a teacher considers all of a student's formative scores when computing a summative score, the teacher should consider all of a student's responses to assessment items or tasks when computing a score for that particular assessment opportunity. The goal of scoring an assessment is to assign a score that most accurately represents the student's knowledge and skill of the learning target as demonstrated *at that point in time*. Sometimes this is a straightforward process. If a student got all the 2.0 items correct and none of the 3.0 or 4.0 items correct, their score should probably be a 2.0. If they got all the 2.0 and 3.0 items correct, but none of the 4.0 items, their score should probably be a 3.0. As mentioned in chapter 5 (page 69), half-point scores can add precision. If a student answered all the 2.0 items and some of the 3.0 items correctly, then their score could be a 2.5. If they answered all the 3.0 items and some of the 4.0 items correctly, then their score could be a 3.5. Figure 7.5 gives additional guidance for using half-point scores.

Score	Description
4.0	All of the more complex content
3.5	Some of the more complex content
3.0	All of the target content
2.5	Some of the target content
2.0	All of the simpler content
1.5	Some of the simpler content
1.0	With help, some of the target content
0.5	With help, some of the simpler content
0.0	With help, none of the content

Source: Adapted from Marzano, 2010a, p. 48.

Figure 7.5: Descriptors for half-point scores.

As shown in figure 7.5, half-point scores allow a teacher to acknowledge that a student knows some of the next level of content, but not all of it. This works well, as long as students' patterns of responses are neat and tidy. However, teachers should be aware that this is not always the case and they may sometimes need to address aberrant response patterns on assessments.

Aberrant Patterns

Sometimes student responses at various score levels don't quite make sense: "Aberrant patterns occur when a student's collection of responses to items at different levels do not make sense" (Marzano & Abbott, 2022, p. 27). For example, a student might answer easier items (that correspond to the simpler content on the proficiency scale) incorrectly, but answer target-content items correctly. This is counterintuitive; how could a student demonstrate competence on the target learning but not on the simpler content?

Aberrant patterns are typically the result of error in an assessment opportunity; the student might have been tired or careless, or the assessment task or item might not have been designed very well. Whatever the cause of an aberrant pattern of student responses or performance, the teacher can respond by simply collecting more information from the student about what they know and are able to do. If the teacher is unsure about whether a student understands or can do a specific level of content, they simply present additional opportunities for students to demonstrate their understanding or skill.

Mixed Scores and Zeros

There are two things you should never do when scoring assessments using proficiency scales. First, do not mix in scores or grades for behavior, attendance, effort, group work, participation, or anything else that isn't related to the topic being scored. A proficiency scale score should express a student's current level of knowledge or skill for the specific learning target stated in the proficiency scale. If a student behaves poorly in class, is absent, or does not exhibit appropriate effort or collaboration, those challenges must be addressed and can be scored (using proficiency scales for the self-system and metacognitive skills mentioned in chapters 1, page 15, and 2, page 33), but not at the expense of accurately reporting a student's current status and growth on, say, the science topic of matter and energy. As stated previously, if you want to assign a score for something other than the topic at hand, create a proficiency scale for it and assign a separate score.

Second, do not assign zeros for incomplete or missing assignments. A zero on the proficiency scale indicates that, even with help, a student cannot demonstrate understanding or skill with any of the content. Unless you're sure that is the case, don't use zero. Use *I* for incomplete, or *M* for missing, or another meaningful indicator, but don't confound the meaning of 0.0.

Again, missing or incomplete assignments are an issue and should be addressed, but in a different way than a total lack of knowledge or skill (0.0) with specific content would be addressed.

FEEDBACK

Much has been said about the importance of feedback. Perhaps the easiest and most impactful way to share feedback with students is to share their formative scores with them. Ryan and Deci (2020) noted that:

> Feedback about performance can have varied functional significance, or meaning, to the recipient. Feedback can have informational significance if it is efficacy relevant (i.e., provides inputs that help the person improve or highlight areas of competence). Informational inputs tend to enhance intrinsic motivation and internalization. (p. 6)

Formative scores—and the information a proficiency scale provides to students about what to work on next—is exactly this kind of efficacy-relevant feedback. Bob (2010) suggested having students track their formative scores on a chart or graph so they can visually see their progress and growth in learning over time.

Teachers can also ask students to articulate the score they think they have achieved on a proficiency scale. If you're familiar with the work of John Hattie (2009, 2012, 2015, 2023) and his rank-ordered lists of factors related to student achievement (based on his syntheses of meta-analyses), you'll recognize student self-reported grades as a frequent flier near the top of his lists. When students estimate their score on a particular learning goal or topic, it positively and significantly impacts their achievement. Bob (2006) recommended that teachers "ask students to score themselves. . . . the students' self-assigned scores might be compared with those assigned by the teacher. Any discrepancies might be the subject of discussion between the teacher and the students" (p. 88). Ernesto Panadero and Anastasiya Lipnevich (2022) pointed out some of the perceived challenges of self-assessment and strongly recommended that educators pursue it despite those challenges:

> Humans are imperfect self-assessors in general as demonstrated by the vast research into cognitive biases (i.e., Tversky & Kahneman, 1974), and the extent of bias is greater in learners who are novices. Therefore, should researchers and instructors have no hope in their quest to examine and develop excellent self-assessors? Our answer is a categorical "No!": effective and deliberate self-assessment should remain as one of the ultimate goals of instructional feedback because self-assessment increases academic performance (Brown & Harris, 2013), self-regulated learning, and self-efficacy (Panadero et al., 2017). (p. 7)

Sharing proficiency scales with students, helping them to understand the score levels, and asking them to score themselves is a simple way for teachers to leverage the power of student self-assessment.

GRADING AND REPORTING

The purpose of grading and reporting is to accurately represent a student's current status *and* growth on specific topics. Overall or omnibus grades (including letter grades) are not very helpful for this purpose because they are typically calculated by averaging (or otherwise quantitatively combining) scores from various assignments on various topics to arrive at a single number or letter that represents a student's performance in a broad content area (mathematics, science, social studies, English language arts, and so on). They provide no information about a student's specific strengths and growth areas within each content area. Rather, report cards that show—for each topic—where a student started, where they were expected to be by the end of a grading period (because some topics are not fully covered within a grading period), and where they actually were by the end of the grading period present the clearest picture to students and their parents or guardians of their achievement on the guaranteed topics of the school or district curriculum. As early as 2000, Bob advocated for report cards that showed this using bar charts for each measured topic. As shown in figure 7.6 (page 116), each topic would have a horizontal bar with dark and light shading. The dark shading shows the

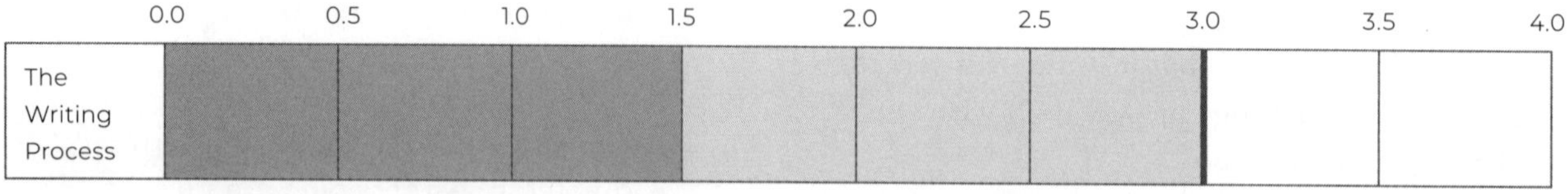

Figure 7.6: Bar chart showing a student's status and growth on a topic.

student's score at the beginning of the grading period; the light shading shows their score at the end of the grading period. The difference between the two shows the students' growth. And the bold line indicates the expected score for the end of the grading period.

In chapter 5 (page 69), we discussed the idea of a supplemental measurement topic—a topic that teachers can fill with whatever content they feel is important for their students to learn but is not articulated in the school's guaranteed curriculum. A teacher might include one or multiple additional topics within this supplemental measurement topic. When collecting assessment scores for these supplemental topics, the teacher would simply keep track of them across a grading period and then average them to compute a summative "supplemental topic" score. As Bob (2018) explained, "Since the supplemental category includes multiple topics, the best way to summarize the scores in the supplemental measurement topic is to simply compute their average" (p. 105). A learning trend only applies to a series of scores when those scores are all on the same topic. Since the supplemental topic can include multiple topics, averaging is a more appropriate approach to synthesize those scores into a summative supplemental topic score.

SUMMARY

In this chapter, we discussed the important measurement role of the teacher. Large-scale assessments do not typically give useful feedback for specific students and specific topics. Although all assessments contain error, an approach to classroom assessment that utilizes proficiency scales to collect series of formative scores can mitigate that error and provide teachers with patterns of evidence useful for determining summative scores for topics. When designing and scoring assessments, teachers can create opportunities for students to demonstrate what they know and are able to do in ways that provide valuable feedback and more accurate grading and reporting of their current status and growth. In addition to their important self-regulatory and measurement roles, teachers are responsible for instruction. In the next chapter, which concludes part 2, we explore that instructional role.

CHAPTER 8

INSTRUCTION

Instruction is the process of teaching and learning. It is the core of education, and it plays a vital role in shaping students' knowledge, skills, and values. Effective instruction develops from a deep understanding of how students learn and how to create a learning environment conducive to student success. In this chapter, we begin by exploring the nature of effective instruction, from the perspective of instructional models. Then we explore three factors that have strong influences on instruction: planning, technology, and review.

INSTRUCTIONAL MODELS

An *instructional model* is a structure that links teaching strategies together in a way that helps educators identify which strategies are most likely to work in which situations. Not all strategies are guaranteed to work in all situations, as the following history illustrates. In 2003, Bob and his colleagues Debra Pickering and Jane E. Pollock published a book called *Classroom Instruction That Works*, in which they reviewed nine categories of research-based instructional strategies. In that work—and more explicitly in a 2009 article called "Setting the Record Straight on 'High-Yield' Strategies"—Bob explained that the research-based strategies highlighted in *Classroom Instruction That Works* and similar books have a high probability of increasing student achievement. But he discouraged educators from referring to them as "high-yield strategies":

> The term "high yield" encourages educators to assume that strategies identified in the research are guaranteed to work. . . . educators must always look to whether a particular strategy is producing the desired results as opposed to simply assuming that if a strategy is being used, positive results will ensue. (Marzano, 2009b, pp. 34–35)

Bob reemphasized this point in both *The Art and Science of Teaching* (2007) and *The New Art and Science of Teaching* (2017), which presented instructional models. Instructional models are an important part of any discussion of instruction because they clearly articulate the parameters in which strategies are most likely to work, and they help educators select strategies to use in specific situations.

For example, in *The New Art and Science of Teaching* framework (Marzano, 2017), there are three categories: feedback, content, and context. The strategies in the feedback category are those most likely to be productive in feedback situations (such as after an assessment), those in the content category are most likely to be helpful when students are interacting with content (such as during learning tasks), and those in the context category are most likely to create a positive context for learning (such as those that promote student engagement).

Another reason that an instructional model is an essential part of Bob's approach to instruction is the same reason that proficiency scales are an essential part of Bob's approach to curriculum: clarity. An instructional model clearly defines what a school, district, or state means by "effective instruction." This clarity is important for teacher growth, as it provides a menu of growth goals for teachers (as discussed in chapter 6, page 91) and a framework for teacher evaluation (which we discuss in chapter 11, page 141). There are two other similarities between proficiency scales and an instructional model: unidimensionality and scoring scales.

A Viable Set of Unidimensional Elements

Each element of an instructional model should be unidimensional. That is, it should refer to just one element of effective teaching. Because teaching is a complex endeavor, this means that most good instructional models have a lot of elements. For example, Bob's 2017 *The New Art and Science of Teaching* model has forty-three elements, the Marzano Academies model (Marzano & Abbott, 2022) has forty-nine elements, the Westminster Instructional Model (used by Westminster Public Schools [2023] in Colorado) has sixty elements, and Charlotte Danielson's 2007 Framework for Teaching has a whopping seventy-six elements. Many schools adopt a preexisting framework (such as *The New Art and Science of Teaching* or Danielson's Framework for Teaching), but others, such as Westminster Public Schools, create their own, often drawing from preexisting frameworks. If a school chooses to create their own framework, there are several points to be aware of.

First, a school's instructional model does not necessarily have to include every single element of the instructional model it draws from. Like curriculum, an instructional model should be viable. If there are too many elements in an instructional model, it's unfeasible to collect data, compile formative scores, and track current summative scores for each element in a timely, efficient manner. Therefore, limit the number of elements while still ensuring that the selected elements adequately represent all the important aspects of the model you're working from. For example, in Bob's *The New Art and Science of Teaching* model, there are forty-three elements sorted into ten design areas; you'd probably want to ensure that your set of elements for effective teaching includes representation from all ten design areas.

Additionally, the elements should represent, at minimum, the following four domains of teacher professional practice. This list is from Bob and Michael Toth's 2013 book, *Teacher Evaluation That Makes a Difference*, but these domains are similar to those in Charlotte Danielson's and other models.

- Classroom strategies and behaviors
- Planning and preparing
- Reflecting on teaching
- Collegiality and professionalism

All four domains might not feature equally; a school or district might decide to have more topics around classroom strategies and behaviors and fewer for the other areas. But it is important to acknowledge that effective teaching involves more than just classroom strategies.

A Scoring Scale for Each Element

Second, each element of an instructional model should be accompanied by a scale for measuring current status and growth. *The New Art and Science of Teaching* model uses the scale in figure 8.1. In their 2021 book, *Improving Teaching Development and Evaluation*, Bob, Cameron L. Rains, and Philip B. Warrick provided scoring scales and student evidence for all forty-three elements of *The New Art and Science of Teaching* model.

4 Innovating	I adapt behaviors and create new strategies for unique student needs and situations.
3 Applying	I use the strategies and behaviors associated with this element, and I monitor the extent to which my actions affect students.
2 Developing	I use the strategies and behaviors associated with this element, but I do not monitor the effect on students.
1 Beginning	I use the strategies and behaviors associated with this element incorrectly or with parts missing.
0 Not Using	I am unaware of strategies and behaviors associated with this element.

Source: Marzano, 2017, p. 104.

Figure 8.1: Developmental scale for elements.

As shown in figure 8.1, the scale has an internal logic to it. If you're not using an element, your score is 0 (not using) for that element. If you try to use an element but don't get it quite right (like if you leave out a step or piece), your score is 1 (beginning) for that element. Once you're executing a strategy well, you're at level 2 (developing). The step from level 2 (developing) to level 3 (applying) is—importantly—not determined by what the teacher does, but by how students *respond* to what the teacher does. If most of your students respond in the desired manner to the element, you are at level 3 (applying). For example, if you are working on the element of physical movement, you want your students to engage in the movement activities you use and experience increased energy after movement activities. You might also want them to be able to explain the purpose of movement activities in the classroom. You can collect data about that through class polls, student surveys, counting how many students are engaging in movement activities, and so on. Finally, level 4 (innovating) is achieved when the teacher adapts an element to reach students for whom it isn't yet working. With physical movement, a teacher might have to adjust movement strategies for a differently abled student to participate. Such adjustments would signal use of the element at level 4 (innovating).

In chapter 11 (page 141), we discuss how a principal can use a model of instruction for instructional leadership purposes (such as teacher evaluation and teacher development). Here, we provide this overview of instructional models to emphasize that Bob and others have already defined high-quality instruction in their work. For that reason, this chapter does not attempt to recreate that work. Schools and districts should explore the available instructional models and either adopt one or use elements of multiple models to create one for their specific situation and circumstances. The remainder of this chapter explores three important influences on instruction: planning, technology, and review.

PLANNING

As discussed in chapters 3 and 4 (pages 41 and 47), learning tasks should be carefully matched to learning goals. Students learn declarative knowledge through constructing meaning, organizing, and storing; learning tasks that address these factors include acquisition, organization, analysis, and utilization tasks. Students learn procedural knowledge through modeling, shaping, and internalizing; learning tasks that address these factors include acquisition, execution, and utilization tasks. The planning process involves identifying whether each element of a proficiency scale is declarative or procedural knowledge, and which learning tasks are most appropriate for it. For example, consider the proficiency scale in figure 8.2 (page 120).

4.0 Complex	Use the writing process to compose a text about the solution to a problem.
3.0 Target	Use the writing process (prewriting, drafting, revising, editing, and publishing) to create texts.
2.0 Simpler	Understand vocabulary such as *prewriting, drafting, revising, editing,* and *publishing.* List activities associated with each phase of the writing process. Produce artifacts that show their use of each phase of the writing process.
1.0	With help, some of the content.
0.0	Even with help, none of the content.

Figure 8.2: Sample proficiency scale.

The target at the 3.0 level of this scale is procedural knowledge. Specifically, it is a macroprocess that students should learn to the level of controlled processing; skills can be learned to automaticity, but macroprocesses will always require thought as they are being executed.

There are three elements of simpler content articulated in this scale. The first two are declarative knowledge; they are things students need to know. The third element is procedural; students must execute each phase of the writing process to produce each artifact. This analysis of the target and simpler content is the first step in effective planning because the nature of each element on the proficiency scale determines the learning tasks best suited to that item. Figure 8.3 shows specific learning tasks that a teacher might plan for each of the elements on this proficiency scale.

Level	Learning Target	Learning Tasks
4.0 Complex	Use the writing process to compose a text about the solution to a problem.	Utilization: Use the writing process to compose a text about the solution to a problem.
3.0 Target	Use the writing process (prewriting, drafting, revising, editing, and publishing) to create texts.	Execution: Use the writing process to write a text about a topic of your choice.
2.0 Simpler	Understand vocabulary such as *prewriting, drafting, revising, editing,* and *publishing.*	Acquisition: Write a description and draw a picture to illustrate each term. Organization: Draw a concept map to show how these terms are related to terms you already know.
	List activities associated with each phase of the writing process.	Acquisition: Use the internet to identify at least two activities associated with each phase of the writing process. Organization: Draw a diagram to show how those activities are related to each other and to the writing process sequence. Analysis: Construct an argument about which phases of the writing process are most important.
	Produce artifacts that show their use of each phase of the writing process.	Acquisition: Identify one activity for each phase of the writing process. Acquisition: Find an example of effective execution of each activity you identified. Execution: Complete the activity you identified for each phase of the writing process.

Figure 8.3: Proficiency scale with learning tasks.

The complex element at the 4.0 level is already stated as a task; students who demonstrate proficiency with the target element can move directly to working on the complex task (or a similar complex task of their own design).

Notice in figure 8.3 that the teacher has clearly defined what types of learning tasks students will engage in for each element. For the vocabulary, acquisition and organization tasks are planned. The teacher has decided that students will go one cognitive level deeper (analysis) with the second simpler element. These are the kinds of decisions teachers should make during planning. Once teachers define the types of learning tasks they will use for each element of the proficiency scale, they can decide what technology resources they might use to support or enhance each task.

TECHNOLOGY

Technology has drastically impacted and (especially with the advent of generative AI) will continue to revolutionize the instructional role of the teacher. However, I want to proceed carefully here, because technostress is real. As Christopher Califf and Stoney Brooks (2020) explained:

> Technostress is an overarching process that includes technology-related stressors (i.e., techno-stressors), psychological strain, and workplace outcomes, such as organizational commitment and turnover intention. . . . Users may encounter several techno-stressors related to unfamiliarity with new technology and constant technological updates, as well as feeling overwhelmed by the copious amounts of information induced by technology. (pp. 1–2)

Teachers are particularly at risk for technostress because they are often at the forefront of technology implementation and use in education. Again, Califf and Brooks (2020) explained:

> Our results reveal that K–12 teachers are experiencing high levels of techno-overload, and that such overload is significantly related to burnout. Teachers who exhibit techno-overload feel as though the technology they use for work is contributing to longer working days and a fundamental change in work habits (Ragu-Nathan et al., 2008). This corroborates findings that technology is profoundly changing and transforming education, and in particular, is fundamentally altering the way teachers carry out their job tasks. (p. 10)

Therefore, I want to begin our discussion of technology as an instructional tool with one of my favorite quotes from the OECD (2015): "Technology can amplify great teaching, but great technology cannot replace poor teaching" (p. 4).

Above all, technology is a tool. The word is closely related to the word *technique* (from the same Greek root, τέχνη [tékhnē, "art"]); it's one way to get things done, but not the only way. Looking at the review of meta-analyses since 2015 on technology in education in table 8.1 (page 122), it is clear that while technology can be helpful and effective when used appropriately, it's not a panacea.

Good teaching without technology is better than poor teaching with technology. In support of this idea, Brandon Olszewski and Helen Crompton (2020) stated that "the effect of educational technology is not necessarily determined by the level of hardware access, but instead, by what students and teachers do with the technology available" (p. 7). In their report on student effort in learning with technology, titled "Quality Beats Frequency," Tim Fütterer, Katharina Scheiter, Xian Cheng, and Kathleen Stürmer (2022) noted, "the findings of this study support the assumption that the quality of technology integration (that is, the extent to which lessons with tablet computers are perceived as more cognitively activating) is important for successful learning with technology" (p. 15).

Teachers should always be able to explain why they are using technology in an instructional situation; if the technology isn't enhancing learning, they should reconsider its use. This is the same approach teachers should take with all instructional strategies and tools: if they aren't producing the desired student outcomes, teachers either need to re-examine how they are using them

TABLE 8.1: Meta-Analyses on Technology in Education

Citation	Relationship of Interest	Number of Studies or Effects	Effect Size	Notes
Caskurlu, Maeda, Richardson, & Lv, 2020	Impact on learning of an actual human teacher designing and facilitating an online course ("teaching presence")	Twenty-three studies	0.60	Studies in this meta-analysis were with graduate and undergraduate students.
Castro-Alonso, Wong, Adesope, & Paas, 2021	Effect of multimedia pedagogical agents (on-screen characters) on learning	Thirty-two effect sizes	0.20	Two-dimensional agents (0.38) are better than three-dimensional agents (0.11); more elaborate characters are not necessarily better (because they can be distracting).
Garzón, Kinshuk, Baldiris, Gutiérrez, & Pavón, 2020	Impact of augmented reality on learning outcomes	Forty-six studies	0.72	Augmented reality works best with collaborative learning (0.85).
Hew, Bai, Dawson, & Lo, 2021	Impact of flipped classroom on student outcomes	495 studies total Cognitive outcomes (seventeen meta-analyses) Behavioral outcomes (four meta-analyses) Perceptual outcomes (five meta-analyses)	Cognitive outcomes 0.19–1.13 Behavioral outcomes 1.40–3.12 Perceptual outcomes 0.05–1.62	Cognitive outcomes are "domain-specific knowledge of a subject." Behavioral outcomes are "learners' motor skills or competences in performing a task." Perceptual outcomes are "learner satisfaction."
Hillmayr, Ziernwald, Reinhold, Hofer, & Reiss, 2020	Impact of technology on learning in secondary grades (mathematics and science)	Ninety-two studies	0.65	Teacher training makes a difference (0.84). Using technology as a supplement (not a replacement) for other instructional strategies is best (0.64).
Howard & Gutworth, 2020	Impact of virtual reality training on social skills	Twenty-three studies	0.69	Knowledge-based instruction is best (0.76).
Noetel et al., 2022	Impact of multimedia design on learning	1,189 studies	0.99 effect of captioning videos for second-language learning	Contiguity, or putting related material close together on screen is effective (0.74). Using digital cues to draw attention to important information is effective (0.43). Hearing text with visuals is better than seeing text next to visuals (0.38).

Citation	Relationship of Interest	Number of Studies or Effects	Effect Size	Notes
Spanjers et al., 2015	Impact of blended learning on achievement	Twenty-four studies	0.34	Blended learning that involves quizzes works better than with no quizzes.
Villena-Taranilla, Tirado-Olivares, Cózar-Gutiérrez, & González-Calero, 2022	Impact of virtual reality training on K–6 learning outcomes	Twenty-one studies	0.64	Immersive virtual reality is best (1.11). Short interventions (less than two hours) are best (0.72).

or switch to a different approach. As Rick DuFour and Bob put it in 2011, "Instruction is a means to an end—student learning—and thus the ultimate test of effective instruction is actual evidence that students have learned" (p. 142). Technology does not possess inherent educational value; its value depends entirely on how it is used.

Once teachers have planned the learning tasks they will use during instruction and matched technology resources that will support or enhance instruction, instruction occurs. As mentioned at the beginning of this chapter, there are a multitude of instructional models that clearly define the elements of good instruction, and I will not attempt to reiterate that work here. However, there is one element of good instruction that an overwhelming body of research supports and I will conclude this chapter with it: review.

REVIEW

Review is probably the most egregiously underutilized strategy in education. As Bob said in 2017, "Teachers typically move through content with little time or resources to continually make additions and corrections to old content while processing new content" (p. 64). And yet, it is the key to lasting learning. As Bob and Kosena explained in 2022:

> During recall, students don't just pull up stored information in a verbatim fashion. Instead, recall involves reassembling information from permanent [or long-term] memory into working memory. Each time students do this reassembling, it provides an opportunity for them to reshape and improve their understanding of the content recalled. . . . If students are not asked to recall content, that content will fade relatively quickly and they will not be able to use it. (p. 71)

There is one particular review strategy that I want to focus on here: retrieval practice. According to Pooja Agarwal, Ludmila Nunes, and Janell Blunt (2021), retrieval practice is "the act of recalling previously learned information" (p. 1409). It is also referred to as *practice testing*, and its positive impacts are sometimes called the *testing effect*. Lukas Sotola and Marcus Crede (2021) explained further:

> When people are tested on certain material, they are forced to summon it from memory in order to produce a correct answer—this is termed retrieval. On the other hand, when people merely study the content by, for example, reading their notes repeatedly, they are only passively absorbing the content, which does not include the process of retrieval. (p. 408)

There is a rich history and hundreds of studies showing the learning benefits of retrieval practice. As early as 1906, Edward Thorndike commented, "the active recall of a fact from within is, as a rule, better than its impression from without" (p. 123). In 1909, Edwina Abbott kicked off over a century of research on retrieval practice with her seminal study on the topic. In 1939, Herbert Spitzer conducted a study of 3,605 sixth graders from ninety-one different schools; he found that practice testing benefited both high-performing and low-performing students. In 2010, Andrew Butler found that retrieval practice improved students' performance on both the content they were tested on and related content.

In addition to these individual studies, there have been three major meta-analyses since 2014 on the effects of practice testing. Table 8.2 summarizes their findings.

As noted, the meta-analysis by Olusola Adesope, Dominic Trevisan, and Narayankripa Sundararajan (2017) examined the conditions under which retrieval practice enhances learning. Specifically, they found the following.

- Multiple-choice practice tests (0.70) work better than short-answer practice tests (0.48).
- Allowing more than a day between retrieval practice and a final test works best (0.82, compared to 0.56 for less than one day).
- Feedback was not an important moderator; the presence or absence of feedback on the practice test did not affect student results.
- Retrieval practice works best with secondary students (0.83) compared to primary (0.64) and postsecondary (0.60) students.

Given the nature and strength of these combined findings, I strongly recommend that every educator at least try retrieval practice as a review strategy in their classroom. There is strong research evidence that it produces positive learning outcomes in a wide variety of formats for a wide variety of learners in a wide variety of cultures.

TABLE 8.2: Meta-Analyses on Retrieval Effect

Meta-Analysis	Number of Studies	Number of Effect Sizes	Number of Participants	Average Effect Size	Notes
Rowland, 2014	61	159	Not reported	0.50	This meta-analysis examined the effects of practice testing versus restudy. Studies in the meta-analysis spanned from 1975 to 2013.
Adesope et al., 2017	118	272	15,427	0.61	This meta-analysis examined the conditions under which retrieval practice enhances learning.
Sotola & Crede, 2021	48	52	7,864	0.42	This meta-analysis examined the effect of practice quizzes on final class grades.

SUMMARY

In this chapter, we discussed the importance of a model of instruction and explored three elements that influence instruction: planning, technology, and review. Planning is the process of defining the nature of each element on a proficiency scale and identifying appropriate learning tasks to learn that knowledge or skill. Technology is a tool that can enhance and support learning tasks. And review, especially retrieval practice, is a high-probability strategy with over one hundred years of research supporting its effectiveness.

PART III
PRINCIPALS

As noted in the introduction, the goal of this book is to provide a comprehensive picture of how various educational pieces fit together. Given my analysis of Bob's work and research since 2020, I have chosen to assert that the three most important educational roles are students, teachers, and principals. I have not included district leaders for three reasons.

First, I have not fully examined the literature from this period related to the district's important roles. In his 2009 book with Timothy Waters, *District Leadership That Works*, Bob explained how important districts are to the educational endeavor. Bob and Waters synthesized data from 2,714 districts, 4,500 ratings of superintendent leaders, and 3.4 million student achievement scores and found a 0.24 correlation between district leadership and student achievement. They identified five district-level responsibilities with a statistically significant correlation to students' academic achievement:

1. Ensuring collaborative goal setting
2. Establishing non-negotiable goals for achievement and instruction
3. Creating broad alignment with and support of district goals
4. Monitoring achievement and instruction goals
5. Allocating resources to support the goals for achievement and instruction (Marzano & Waters, 2009, p. 6)

This is helpful, but the discussion of how these responsibilities are achieved draws from and must be informed by business and organizational research as much as—if not more than—educational research. For example, Bob's High Reliability Schools framework is a model for how to effectively manage educational organizations (Marzano, Warrick, & Simms, 2014). It involves organizing, prioritizing, and measuring the impact of initiatives and programs. HRS was born out of the business and organizational literature on high reliability organizations such as nuclear power plants, air traffic control centers, and military operations (Weick & Sutcliffe, 2007; Weick, Sutcliffe, & Obstfeld, 1999). Since I have not included the business and organizational literature in my current review of research, I have not addressed district roles in this book.

Second, and related to the first reason, teachers do not typically have a formal role in decision making at the district level. Teacher concerns are largely educational, while district concerns are largely organizational. Since my audience here is teachers, I believe that the roles of the district, while very important, are tangential to the focus of this book, and I have not included them here.

Third, please recall the analogy I presented in the introduction between education and medicine. I likened the systems of education (curriculum, instruction, assessment, grading, and so on) to the systems of the human body (circulatory, respiratory, skeletal, muscular, nervous, and so on). And I likened the roles of education (students, teachers, principals) to the structures of the human body (head, torso, limbs). If I add the district to this analogy, I would align it with the environment that the body exists within; it impacts the body, but is not the body itself. In the same way that we draw a line between studying bodies (biology) and studying the environments within which those bodies exist (ecology), I am drawing a line between the educational body (students, teachers, principals) and the educational environment (districts). There is much to say about the district and its important role in the educational endeavor; I am simply not saying it here.

Part three of this book examines the roles of the principal or school leader. For teachers, the intent of this part is to help you more fully understand the role of a school leader so that you can more effectively partner with them. The principal's roles are important, but they cannot function effectively apart from you. A good school leader (as we will see in this part) makes school leadership a collaborative endeavor. In a high-functioning school, teachers lead as much or more than the principal. Therefore, the goal of this part is to help teachers better understand, appreciate, and collaborate with their principals and school leaders.

In 2005, Bob and his colleagues Timothy Waters and Brian McNulty synthesized sixty-nine studies involving 2,802 schools, 1.4 million students, and 14,000 teachers. They found the correlation between school leadership and student achievement to be 0.25. More recently, Huang Wu and Jianping Shen (2022) performed a second-order meta-analysis (a meta-analysis of meta-analyses) of twelve meta-analyses with eighteen overall effect sizes. They likewise found that principal leadership has a statistically significant positive relationship with student achievement ($d = 0.34$). There have been other second-order meta-analyses on the impact of principal leadership (Hattie, 2009; Tan, Gao, & Shi, 2022), but I highlight the work of Wu and Shen (2022) because they noted an interesting finding:

> There was . . . not enough evidence to claim that a specific leadership model or practice

is more effective than others in improving student achievement. For instance, there seems to be a belief in the field over the years that instructional leadership has a greater effect than transformational leadership on student achievement (Liebowitz & Porter, 2019), but our analyses failed to support this claim. . . . No one leadership practice is consistently associated with higher effect size estimates. (p. 13)

Therefore, instead of focusing on one leadership strategy or practice, Wu and Shen (2022) recommended "integrated leadership":

> Foremost, in efforts to promote school improvement, we, together with many other scholars, would encourage [educators] to view principal leadership as an integrated leadership of multiple approaches and practices (Leithwood & Sun, 2012; Shen et al., 2019; Witzier et al., 2003). Integrated leadership implies that school leaders need to engage in a wide range of leadership practices rather than focusing only on some of them. (p. 13)

This finding aligns with possibly the greatest challenge of school leadership: principals must lead in many different ways in many different areas.

In 2021, Jason Grissom, Anna Egalite, and Constance Lindsay synthesized research on the roles of the principal in a report called *How Principals Affect Students and Schools: A Systematic Synthesis of Two Decades of Research*. Their report is part of a multidecade effort by the Wallace Foundation to investigate school leadership practices linked to student achievement (previous reports include Leithwood et al., 2004 and Louis et al., 2010). Grissom and colleagues (2021) found that "the size of principal effects is nearly as large as estimates of individual teacher effects on student learning" (p. 39). They elaborated:

> The magnitude of principal effects uncovered by our systematic review of the most rigorous studies is substantively important. The math gains from replacing a below-average principal with an above-average one—again, 0.18 standard deviations—would be larger than approximately 70 percent of the effects (on math achievement) of various educational interventions in 747 studies compiled by Kraft (2020). Reading gains would be larger than about 50 percent. (p. 39)

These are exciting research findings, but the authors caution against interpreting them to mean that *either teachers or principals* have a greater impact on student achievement.

> Should we conclude from this comparison that it is almost as important for an individual student to have an effective principal as it is to have an effective teacher? We should not—but the question may be incomplete. . . .
>
> Principals' effects on student achievement are mostly indirect, coming largely through their efforts to recruit, develop, support, and retain a talented teaching staff and create conditions for them to deliver strong instruction. . . .
>
> For the individual student, teacher effectiveness is central. At the same time, a student learns more in a school with an effective principal in part because the principal makes it more likely the student is exposed to effective teachers. (p. 39)

As educators know from experience, the roles of the teacher and principal are intertwined in such a way that the whole is more than the sum of its parts; effective collaboration between teachers and principals results in greater student achievement than either could accomplish by themselves.

In addition to synthesizing the overall effects of principals on student achievement, Grissom and colleagues (2021) also identified three categories of skills required for effective school leadership.

1. **Instructional:** "Supporting and leading the school's instructional program" (p. 54)
2. **People:** "Develop[ing] and interact[ing] with people in and around their school" (p. 56)
3. **Organizational:** "Manag[ing] a complex organization" (p. 57)

Taking the last first, we use these three categories to structure part 3; chapter 9 (page 129) will focus on organizational leadership, chapter 10 (page 135) on people leadership, and chapter 11 (page 141) on instructional leadership.

CHAPTER 9

ORGANIZATIONAL LEADERSHIP

Schools are complex organizations that require effective leadership to succeed. In this way, they are similar to organizations outside the educational field; successfully running either a school or a business requires a leadership approach that involves creating a safe environment, managing budgets and resources, hiring and managing personnel, maintaining facilities, and using data to inform action, among other things. Grissom and colleagues (2021) called these activities "a general class of management skills that transcend schools. That is, they would be relevant to leading other kinds of organizations, such as private businesses or nonprofits" (p. 57). As stated here and previously, education has benefited from business and organizational research and theory regarding leadership. In the introduction to this book (page 1), I reviewed one of the central ideas drawn from business and organizational research: continuous improvement.

While some might think that effective leadership requires a specific type of person, Bob and colleagues (2018) highlighted that effective leadership is less about a person and far more about a process: "Effective leadership is not a function of having a specific personality type or a certain demeanor; it is a function of informed action aimed at continuous improvement" (p. 24). Continuous improvement places organizational leadership activities within "iterative, structured cycles of data analysis to solve problems and test new solutions" (Bush-Mecenas, 2022, p. 462). That is, continuous improvement requires the continuous collection and analysis of data regarding specific problems so that those problems can be solved. There are a number of frameworks for continuous improvement; here we review the one that Bob has proposed: High Reliability Schools.

In 2014, Bob and colleagues proposed an approach to continuous school improvement called High Reliability Schools. It presents a five-level hierarchy of factors that are necessary for school improvement and student success.

1. **Safe, supportive, and collaborative culture:** This level focuses on creating a school environment where all students and staff feel safe, respected, and valued.
2. **Effective teaching in every classroom:** This level focuses on ensuring that all students have access to high-quality instruction.
3. **Guaranteed and viable curriculum:** This level focuses on developing and implementing a curriculum aligned with state and national standards and that ensures that all students have the opportunity to learn what they need to succeed.
4. **Standards-referenced reporting:** This level focuses on using data to track student progress and identify students who need additional support.
5. **Competency-based education:** This level focuses on designing and implementing educational systems that ensure all students master the essential skills and knowledge they need for success.

School leaders can use the HRS framework for two important continuous improvement activities: prioritization and measurement.

PRIORITIZATION

Relative to prioritization, educators cannot do everything. There are far more excellent programs, practices, and initiatives available than any one school could possibly implement. School leaders must do two things: (1) identify the programs, practices, and initiatives that are being used (or considered) to improve their school, and (2) rank those programs, practices, and initiatives in order of importance. The HRS levels offer one way to rank order programs, practices, and initiatives and they have an intuitive logic to them. For example, culture is at level 1 because a safe, supportive, and collaborative culture is a prerequisite for the success of initiatives related to instruction, curriculum, grading and reporting, and competency-based education. But it is not enough by itself. Instruction (level 2) precedes curriculum (level 3) because, as Bob and colleagues (2018) explained, "an effective teacher can overcome a weak curriculum, whereas a strong curriculum cannot overcome a weak teacher" (p. 32). Levels 4 and 5 require accurately tracking individual student achievement on specific topics of the curriculum. Doing this requires clarity on the specific topics of the curriculum (level 3). The power of the HRS framework then, is not necessarily in the exact nature of its levels (although they are based on decades of research; Marzano et al., 2018, 2024), but in the idea that the levels have a logical relationship that allows school leaders to prioritize the work of school improvement.

For teachers, this means partnering with your principal and other school leaders to identify those programs, practices, and initiatives being used to improve your school and then organizing them into the levels of the HRS (or other logical) framework. Additionally, it means that when leaders bring new initiatives, programs, or practices to teachers (or vice versa), conversations should ensue regarding how important the new activity is relative to those currently in place, and if they determine it is important, where it fits in the hierarchy. For example, if a new initiative regarding grading (HRS level 4) is proposed, and a school is still working to build a safe, supportive, and collaborative culture (HRS level 1) and effective instruction in every classroom (HRS level 2), principals and teachers may want to consider two questions. First, will the new activity succeed before work on levels 1 and 2 is further along? And second, does the new activity merit repurposing resources that are currently being expended on activities related to levels 1 and 2?

As explained in the introduction (page 1), available research and theory should inform these conversations about the relative priority of various activities. It behooves schools to consider programs, practices, and initiatives that have a strong research base. For example, a school might be considering offering an early college high school program. According to Mengli Song, Kristina Zeiser, Drew Atchison, and

Iliana Brodziak de los Reyes (2021), early college high school is a specific kind of dual-enrollment program. It was created as part of a 2002 collaborative initiative by the Bill and Melinda Gates Foundation, the Carnegie Corporation of New York, the Ford Foundation, and the W. K. Kellogg Foundation. Julie Edmunds, Faith Unlu, Jane Furey, Elizabeth Glennie, and Nina Arshavsky (2020) explained:

> The early college model is a new model of schooling that combines the high school and college experiences, explicitly focusing on practices and structures that are intended to increase students' success in college while also shortening the amount of time that students spend in the educational system. Essentially, the early college model is a test case of whether we can restructure the educational system in a way that embeds attainment of postsecondary credentials into high school. (p. 273)

And it seems to be working well. In a study of ten early college programs in five states (North Carolina, Ohio, South Carolina, Texas, and Utah) involving 2,458 students, Song and colleagues (2021) found that early college students earned postsecondary degrees at a higher rate than control students. Specifically, by the end of the sixth year after expected high school graduation, 45.4 percent of the early college students had earned a postsecondary degree in comparison to only 33.5 percent of the control group.

But a robust research-and-evidence base is not enough to justify adopting a specific program, such as early college high school. As explained in the introduction (page 1), context is a critical factor in the effectiveness of a program. If a high school already has a strong culture, effective instruction, clearly articulated curriculum, accurate and specific grading and reporting practices, and is promoting students based on their mastery of the content, early college high school might be an excellent way for that school to extend opportunities for students while they are still in high school. But if a high school is still working to ensure effective instruction in every classroom or clearly articulate the specific topics of their curriculum, adding an early college high school program might cause more problems than it solves. It might draw resources (time, energy, money) away from activities that have a greater impact for more students.

In sum, using a hierarchy of factors—such as the HRS framework—to organize and prioritize school programs, practices, and initiatives can help principals and teachers identify and pursue an appropriate number of activities that are most appropriate for the school's current context and development as an organization.

MEASUREMENT

Measurement systems in an organization allow leaders to identify activities that are or are not resulting in the desired outcomes and make adjustments accordingly. To know if a program, practice, or initiative is working, educators must collect and analyze data regarding that activity. This is the second way that principals and teachers can use the HRS framework for continuous improvement, and it involves two types of metrics: leading indicators and lagging indicators.

Leading Indicators

The HRS framework presents a set of leading indicators for each level. The term *leading indicator* comes from business and economics literature; a leading indicator is a measurable factor associated with a specific outcome. In other words, it is a condition that has already demonstrated leading to a desired state. For example, one of the leading indicators for HRS level 1—a safe, supportive, and collaborative culture—is "teachers have formal roles in the decision-making process regarding school initiatives" (Marzano et al., 2014, p. 15). Past research has shown that when teachers have formal roles in the decision-making process regarding school initiatives, school culture improves (Marzano et al., 2005). Therefore, it makes sense that schools and districts would seek to achieve a school where teachers have formal roles in the decision-making process regarding school initiatives if they want to improve their school culture. Table 9.1 (page 132) shows the leading indicators for all five HRS levels.

TABLE 9.1: Leading Indicators for HRS Levels

Level	Leading Indicators
Level 1: Safe, Supportive, and Collaborative Culture	1.1—The faculty and staff perceive the school environment as safe, supportive, and orderly. 1.2—Students, parents, and the community perceive the school environment as safe, supportive, and orderly. 1.3—Teachers have formal roles in the decision-making process regarding school initiatives. 1.4—Collaborative teams regularly interact to address common issues regarding curriculum, assessment, instruction, and the achievement of all students. 1.5—Teachers and staff have formal ways to provide input regarding the optimal functioning of the school. 1.6—Students, parents, and the community have formal ways to provide input regarding the optimal functioning of the school. 1.7—The school acknowledges the success of the whole school as well as individuals within the school. 1.8—The school manages its fiscal, operational, and technological resources in a way that directly supports teachers.
Level 2: Effective Teaching in Every Classroom	2.1—The school communicates a clear vision as to how teachers should address instruction. 2.2—The school supports teachers to continually enhance their pedagogical skills through reflection and professional growth plans. 2.3—The school is aware of and monitors predominant instructional practices. 2.4—The school provides teachers with clear, ongoing evaluations of their pedagogical strengths and weaknesses that are based on multiple sources of data and are consistent with student achievement data. 2.5—The school provides teachers with job-embedded professional development that is directly related to their instructional growth goals. 2.6—Teachers have opportunities to observe and discuss effective teaching.
Level 3: Guaranteed and Viable Curriculum	3.1—The school curriculum and accompanying assessments adhere to state and district standards. 3.2—The school curriculum is focused enough that teachers can adequately address it in the time they have available. 3.3—All students have the opportunity to learn the critical content of the curriculum. 3.4—The school establishes clear and measurable goals that focus on critical needs regarding improving overall student achievement at the school level. 3.5—The school analyzes, interprets, and uses data to regularly monitor progress toward school achievement goals. 3.6—The school establishes appropriate school- and classroom-level programs and practices to help students meet individual achievement goals when data indicate interventions are needed.
Level 4: Standards-Referenced Reporting	4.1—The school establishes clear and measurable goals focused on critical needs regarding improving achievement of individual students. 4.2—The school analyzes, interprets, and uses data to regularly monitor progress toward achievement goals for individual students.
Level 5: Competency-Based Education	5.1—Students move on to the next level of the curriculum for any subject area only after they have demonstrated competence at the previous level. 5.2—The school schedule accommodates students moving at a pace appropriate to their situation and needs. 5.3—The school affords students who have demonstrated competency levels greater than those articulated in the system immediate opportunities to begin work on advanced content or career paths of interest.

Source: Marzano et al., 2018, pp. 31–32.

The leading indicators for a level are conditions shown to support the focus of that level. At HRS levels 1 and 2, the leading indicators have an indirect relationship with student achievement outcomes. That is, the leading indicators at levels 1 and 2 have a positive relationship with culture and instruction, which in turn have the potential to impact student achievement. Levels 3, 4, and 5 focus more directly on student achievement, so the leading indicators at those levels have a more direct relationship with student achievement. This is an important idea to keep in mind when considering organizational leadership: not all activities have a direct relationship to student achievement, and that is fine. In the same way that students often need to work on simpler content before working on target content, schools may need to work on foundational structures (culture, instruction, curriculum) before they work on target structures (student achievement).

As explained in the previous section, school leaders choose the programs, practices, or initiatives that they think will lead to the condition articulated by the leading indicator. There are many options, and these activities might be those already in place in a school or new activities that the school adopts. For example, for the leading indicator about teacher roles in the decision-making process, a school leader might use committees, town hall–style meetings, focus groups, or other structures for teachers to give formal input.

Lagging Indicators

How do you know if the program, practice, or initiative you put in place is producing the conditions stated in a leading indicator? You collect and analyze data on *lagging indicators*. A lagging indicator improves if the condition is in place, and suffers if the condition is not in place. It is called "lagging" because it changes after a program, practice, or initiative is put in place. If a school implements committees for teacher input on decisions, they might collect lagging indicator data by asking for teachers' perception of their input level on a specific decision made using the committee structure. If most or all of the teachers report they had sufficient input, that indicates that the committee structure is helping the school achieve the desired state of the leading indicator. But if most of the teachers say they did not, or if the number of teachers saying they did declines over time, the committee structure may not be working and the school would likely want to try something else.

In the HRS framework, Bob and colleagues (2014, 2018) do not provide specific lagging indicators for schools. That is because lagging indicators need to be appropriate to the program, practice, or initiative a school is using. Because schools have an almost unlimited number of programs, practices, or initiatives to choose from for each leading indicator, the lagging indicators cannot be prescribed. To put it succinctly, the leading indicators are research-based, and the lagging indicators are context-based. For a particular school, a particular type of data might be most appropriate. If teacher surveys do not work (for whatever reason) as a data collection device for a school, the school might instead collect data by recording who gave input and what the input was for each decision made with teacher input. If those data show that an increasing number of teachers give input on a decision over time, that lagging indicator would also support the idea that the school is improving on the leading indicator or condition that all teachers have formal roles in the decision-making process.

SUMMARY

In this chapter, we explored organizational leadership in the context of Bob's HRS framework. We discussed how a school can use the HRS framework as a tool to prioritize the programs, practices, and initiatives it engages in, and as a measurement tool to determine whether those programs, practices, and initiatives are achieving the desired outcomes. We discussed leading and lagging indicators and how a school can use them for clarity about what conditions to aim for, and to inform when changes and adjustments are needed. In the next chapter, we take a closer look at HRS level 1—safe, supportive, and collaborative culture—by examining the second category of skills related to the role of the principal: people leadership.

CHAPTER 10

PEOPLE LEADERSHIP

Schools are fundamentally people organizations. As DuFour and Bob wrote in 2011, "school improvement means people improvement" (p. 15) and "schools can only be as good as the people within them" (p. 20). Because of this people-centered dynamic of education, people leadership is a critical role of school principals (Jacobson et al., 2007). Safe, supportive, and collaborative cultures with strong relationships and high trust can lead to a number of positive outcomes, including teacher collective efficacy, targeted student support, and collaboration between all members of the community. As Bob and colleagues (2024) stated, "A culture that supports agency and collaboration likewise empowers students and teachers to grow both individually and collectively" (p. 10).

How can teachers and principals partner to build a safe, supportive, and collaborative school culture? In this chapter, we will first discuss how cultivating trust and autonomy can contribute to a safe and orderly environment. Then, we will examine the function of collaborative teams, which are the building blocks of a professional learning community. Finally, we will address communication with parents and how it facilitates their positive involvement in the school community.

TRUST AND AUTONOMY

Trust is essential for education. Research by Curt Adams (2013) and Melinda Moye, Alan Henkin, and Robert Egley (2005) has shown that collective trust (trust among principals, teachers, and students) is associated with higher academic performance and greater teacher empowerment. Teachers who feel empowered and trusted by their principals are more likely to have positive attitudes toward their students (Price, 2015). Trust is typically a prerequisite for any collaborative efforts, and Hollingworth and colleagues (2018) found that trust was higher in schools where teachers had *defined autonomy*—clearly articulated boundaries within which their decisions would be honored.

We discussed autonomy in chapter 2 (page 33); according to self-determination theory, autonomy—along with competence and relatedness—is a necessary element for healthy development (Ryan & Deci, 2000, 2017, 2020). To provide teachers with autonomy, principals need to put structures in place that clearly demarcate what decisions teachers can make on their own and what outcomes they are responsible for. One of the best known structures for creating defined autonomy is the professional learning community, or PLC. Table 10.1 shows several ways of describing the term *professional learning community.*

Professional learning communities vary in their design and success depending on the school context, and principals play an important role in this variation. Research on PLCs has found the following.

- Liz Hollingworth (2012) found that the success of PLCs largely depends on the relationship between teachers and school leaders.
- Goly Brown (2015) found that PLCs contribute to a positive school community. However, Jessica Rigby, Christine Andrews-Larson, and I-Chien Chen (2020) pointed out that school leaders sometimes influence PLCs to focus on standardized test preparation instead of instruction.
- In some contexts, principals use PLCs as a school reform strategy. Kristin Huggins, James Scheurich, and James Morgan (2011) explored the role of principal leadership in guiding the PLC in one low-achieving school.
- Roger Goddard, Linda Skrla, and Serena Salloum (2017) found that PLCs can increase collective efficacy and help close racial achievement gaps.

In sum, principals play a key role in the formation, direction, and success of professional learning communities as a structure for educator collaboration. Not all PLCs are productive, and the principal plays a major role in determining their efficacy. A high-functioning professional learning community is a structure that principals and teachers can use to provide defined autonomy to teachers and teacher teams, thus promoting a climate of trust and safety. Next, we discuss the building blocks of a professional learning community: collaborative teams.

TABLE 10.1: Descriptions of *Professional Learning Community*

Source	Description
Hord, 1997	A professional learning community is a group of teachers who work together to improve their teaching and student learning. They do this by looking at what is happening in their school, identifying areas for improvement, and then making changes to their curriculum, instruction, or relationships with other community members. They then assess the results of their changes to see if they have been effective.
Stoll, Bolam, McMahon, Wallace, & Thomas, 2006	A PLC is a group of people who regularly meet to share and discuss their work in a way that is thoughtful, critical, and supportive. They are open to learning from each other and changing their practices based on what they learn. The group is inclusive of everyone, regardless of their background or experience.
Fulton & Britton, 2011	PLCs are a way for teachers to come together to share ideas, collaborate on lessons, and learn from each other. The goal is to help teachers become more effective in the classroom and to improve student outcomes.
DuFour, DuFour, Eaker, Many, & Mattos, 2016	PLCs are a process of continuous improvement for educators. By working together and sharing ideas, educators can learn from each other and develop new and better ways to teach. This, in turn, leads to improved student learning.

Adapted from Marzano et al., 2016.

COLLABORATION

Collaboration is a process in which two or more people work together to achieve a common goal (Hord, 1986). When well implemented in schools, it allows teachers to share ideas, learn from each other, and support each other. However, collaboration is more than just staff cooperation. It requires teachers to be willing to share resources, responsibilities, and accountability.

According to Rick DuFour, Rebecca DuFour, Robert Eaker, Thomas Many, and Mike Mattos (2016), the building blocks of a professional learning community are *collaborative teams*. They explained, "It is difficult to overstate the importance of collaborative teams in the improvement process. It is even more important, however, to emphasize that collaboration does not lead to improved results unless people are focused on the right work" (p. 12). In alignment with the High Reliability Schools framework outlined in chapter 9 (page 129), I would suggest that there are four major focuses for collaborative teams that constitute "the right work."

1. **Instruction:** Effective teaching in every classroom (HRS level 2)
2. **Curriculum:** Guaranteed and viable curriculum (HRS level 3)
3. **Measurement:** Standards-referenced reporting (HRS level 4)
4. **Mastery:** Competency-based education (HRS level 5)

We have already discussed three of these areas: instruction in chapter 8 (page 117), curriculum in chapter 5 (page 69), and measurement in chapter 7 (page 103). In this chapter, we discuss how teacher teams might focus on mastery by using grouping structures that allow each student to receive the instruction they need when they need it. Teams' capacity to focus on higher levels of the HRS framework is determined by their successful implementation of the leading indicators at lower levels. A collaborative team must lay the foundation of high-quality initial instruction (using an instructional model), curriculum (using proficiency scales), and measurement (using a series of formative scores from classroom assessments) to facilitate their work at the mastery level.

Ability Grouping

In their 2016 study, Saiying Steenbergen-Hu, Matthew C. Makel, and Paula Olszewski-Kubilius (2016) reported results from a second-order meta-analysis that examined the impact of grouping same-ability students together on student achievement. They synthesized thirteen meta-analyses on ability grouping (including 172 studies) and found:

> Students benefited, at least to a small degree, from within-class grouping, cross-grade subject grouping, and special grouping for the gifted. . . . *Overall, high-, medium-, and low-ability students benefited equally from ability grouping.* The effects of within-class and cross-grade subject grouping are especially noteworthy given that research has consistently shown benefits for these types of acceleration. . . . Overall, these findings provide support for using ability grouping to meet the learning needs of students. (p. 889; emphasis added)

The authors described three key features of *ability grouping*:

> a. It involves placing students into different classrooms or small groups based on their initial achievement skill levels, readiness, or abilities;
>
> b. the main purpose of such placement is to create a more homogeneous learning environment so that teachers can provide instruction better matched to students' needs and so that students can benefit from interactions with their comparable academic peers; and
>
> c. such placements are not permanent school administrative arrangements that lead to restrictions on students' graduation, destination, or career paths. (pp. 850–851)

As noted in point b, the goal of ability grouping is to better match instruction to students' needs. While there are many ways to identify student needs, collaborative teams with their curriculum clearly articulated in proficiency scales (as described in chapter 5, page 69) are uniquely positioned to pinpoint and address specific student needs for specific topics of the curriculum. For example, a group of three ELA teachers might bring the distribution of their students' current summative scores for the writing process proficiency scale, as shown in figure 10.1 (page 138), to a collaborative team meeting.

Knowing what each student needs to do next to achieve mastery or progress beyond it provides the team a variety of grouping and intervention options. Students working on level 4.0 content likely need time—with teacher guidance and coaching available—to progress

		TEACHER A	TEACHER B	TEACHER C
4.0 Complex	Use the writing process to compose a text about the solution to a problem.	Seven students	Three students	Three students
3.0 Target	Use the writing process (prewriting, drafting, revising, editing, and publishing) to create texts.	Eleven students	Nine students	Sixteen students
2.0 Simpler	Understand vocabulary such as *prewriting, drafting, revising, editing,* and *publishing.* List activities associated with each phase of the writing process. Produce artifacts that show their use of each phase of the writing process.	Five students	Fourteen students	Six students
1.0	With help, some of the content.	Three students	No students	One student
0.0	Even with help, none of the content.	No students	No students	No students

Figure 10.1: Writing process proficiency scale with student summative score distribution.

on their utilization tasks. Students who have mastered the 3.0 content could have the choice to either undertake a 4.0 knowledge utilization task for this topic or to accept a 3.0 score on this topic and use their time to work on a different topic. Students at the score 2.0 and 1.0 levels need further instruction, practice, and feedback to reach proficiency at the 3.0 level.

Teachers A, B, and C could approach ability grouping for this distribution of students in a variety of ways, depending on their context and constraints (such as time, space, schedule, and so on). For example, if the three teachers had a common time when each of them taught ELA, teacher A might work with the twenty-five students who need to progress from the 2.0 level to the 3.0 level. During that same time, teacher B might work with the thirteen students working on knowledge utilization tasks and the four students currently at the 1.0 level; this would allow her to provide targeted and specific support to the four students at the 1.0 level, while also providing intermittent coaching and guidance for the thirteen students at the 4.0 level. Teacher C might work with the thirty-six students at the 3.0 level, helping them to decide whether to pursue a 4.0 task for the writing process, or to work on a different topic (and facilitating work on both). This is just one example of how the team might approach grouping in this situation; there are many other options and teacher teams are best positioned to design this type of ability grouping structure.

Co-Teaching

As you consider grouping structures to help students work toward and beyond mastery of specific curricular topics, consider the possibility of co-teaching. *Co-teaching* means there is more than one educator in a classroom. As Marzano and colleagues (2017) noted, "the premise behind team teaching . . . is there are more teachers available in the same room to address the different levels of student needs" (Marzano, Norford, et al., 2017, p. 144). In the example above, an extra teacher could join the 3.0 group to increase the level of support for students as they select their next learning opportunity (either a 4.0 task for the writing process or working on a different topic).

Schools may want to take advantage of the benefits of co-teaching but may not have the fiscal resources to provide an additional teacher in every classroom that needs support. For such cases, Steven Hemelt, Helen Ladd, and Calen Clifton (2021) highlighted the positive impact of teaching assistants (TAs):

> We find evidence that TAs have positive effects on student test scores in reading and math, with the largest, consistent, and most robust effects in reading. As we illustrated above, the effects of TAs in that subject are sufficiently large to show that hiring TAs can be a cost-effective way to improve test scores in reading. In addition, we find that TAs have larger positive effects

> on the academic performance of students of color and suggestive evidence that the effects are higher in high-poverty districts than in other types of districts. Finally, we also find evidence that TAs help to boost school-level proficiency rates, particularly among non-White students and those in high-poverty districts. (p. 299)

Simon Andersen, Louise Beuchert, Helena Nielsen, and Mette Thomsen (2018) conducted a study of teaching assistants in Denmark. They also found positive effects of TAs, particularly on reading scores, and explained that teaching assistants were most effective when they were "part of a professional team who share responsibility for a classroom rather than help with practical tasks" (p. 35). In sum, collaborative teams can (and probably should) include more than just teachers. Teaching assistants, counselors, media center staff, paraprofessionals, and literacy and special education specialists are valuable teammates and can expand co-teaching possibilities that are unavailable to teams comprised only of classroom teachers.

COMMUNICATION

Effective communication supports the development of interpersonal relationships within a school and allows principals to more efficiently implement initiatives, programs, and practices (Hollingworth et al., 2018). Principals regularly communicate with a variety of stakeholders, including teachers, staff, students, parents, and the community. It is important for principals to communicate clearly and concisely, and to be able to listen to and understand the perspectives of others. Research has shown that effective communication can lead to a number of positive outcomes, including the following.

- Shared expectations, which lead to increased teacher satisfactionand school commitment (Price, 2012)
- Increased parental involvement, which leads to increased student achievement (Gordon & Louis, 2009)

We will discuss the first item, shared expectations, in more depth in chapter 11 (page 141). Here, we finish our discussion of people leadership by focusing on the communication role of the principal with parents, and how teachers can best partner with principals to cultivate parent involvement that leads to higher levels of student academic achievement.

Contrary to expectations, parents' greatest potential to impact student achievement *is not* helping students with their homework. Rather, a parent's greatest impact on the achievement of their student lies in their expectations for that student. In a meta-analysis of 169 studies on the impact of parental expectations on academic achievement, Martin Pinquart and Markus Ebeling (2020) found correlations between parental expectations and student achievement ($r = 0.30$). Based on these findings, they observed that "transmission of positive parental achievement-related expectations and the promotion of a positive academic self-concept seem to be more promising than parental attempts to directly influence the achievement of their children, such as checking homework" (p. 477). That is, one of the more impactful things that parents can do is to expect their children to do well in school.

As principals and teachers communicate with parents, it is beneficial to keep this fact in mind. Many parents have limited resources, and educators can help parents understand where their time and energy are best spent relative to school. To that end, a study by Carly Robinson, Raj Chande, Simon Burgess, and Todd Rogers (2022) reminded school and district leaders to be selective about where they ask parents to be involved:

> Parent engagement interventions are not costless. Successfully directing parental investments toward some parent engagement behaviors can crowd out other, possibly beneficial, behaviors. Parents have limited time, attention, and resources to invest in their child's education, so there can be opportunity costs to shifting parental effort. (p. 171)

Given the research results from Pinquart and Ebeling (2020), it makes sense that schools would strive to focus parental involvement on activities that cultivate high educational expectations, such as goal setting, tracking progress, and celebrating success.

Educators at schools who have articulated their curriculum as proficiency scales can use proficiency scales as the foundation of this type of communication. As Bob (2019) stated, "To be successful, students must understand what they are expected to achieve and how to get there. The best vehicle for delivering that knowledge is a proficiency scale" (p. 7). This applies to parents, too. A proficiency scale clearly articulates the target learning expectation for their student (3.0 level), the required steps to get there (2.0 level), and ways to demonstrate performance above and beyond the target learning (4.0 level). It communicates a more specific and powerful level of expectation when a parent asks, "What level are you at on the Writing Process proficiency scale?" as opposed to "How are you doing in writing?" And celebrations become more meaningful when a student says, "I just moved to score 3.0 on the Writing Process proficiency scale!" rather than "I got a B in writing." A proficiency scale provides a common language for principals, teachers, students, and parents to use to articulate expectations, set goals, track progress, and celebrate success and invites parents into the learning process with greater clarity and more potential to leverage their expectations for greater student achievement.

SUMMARY

In this chapter, we explored the people leadership aspects of the principal's role and ways that teachers can partner with the principal to enhance the culture of the school. First, we reviewed the role of defined autonomy in building and sustaining high levels of trust and discussed how the professional learning community structure can support defined autonomy. Second, we discussed collaboration and collaborative teams. We highlighted the importance of educator teams focusing on the right work, provided four HRS-aligned focuses for collaborative teams, and took a closer look at how educators can collaboratively use ability grouping and co-teaching to help students reach mastery on learning targets. Finally, we addressed the importance of communication to the principal's role, and how both teachers and principals can leverage proficiency scales as a communication tool to facilitate parents' high expectations for their students. In the next and final chapter, we turn to what is often considered the most important role of the principal: instructional leadership.

CHAPTER 11

INSTRUCTIONAL LEADERSHIP

Good instructional leaders can help teachers teach better and students learn more. But not all instruction-related leadership activities are created equal. The most effective instructional leadership focuses on activities that help teachers improve their classroom teaching (May & Supovitz, 2011). Grissom and colleagues (2021) grouped such activities into three categories:

1. Teacher evaluation
2. Professional learning
3. Data-driven improvement

In this chapter, we explore each of these areas, highlighting how principals and teachers can partner to enhance teaching and learning through instructional leadership.

Notably, activities in each of these areas require an instructional model, a concept reviewed in chapter 8 (page 117). Recall that an effective instructional model should do the following.

1. Clearly define what a school, district, or state means by "effective instruction"
2. Contain unidimensional elements (usually a lot of them, because teaching is complex)
3. Be accompanied by a set of scoring scales that describe levels of performance for each element

Bob and colleagues (2021) explained:

> An instructional model . . . is foundational to developing teacher expertise. A teacher must have a model of instruction if he or she is to set meaningful goals, focus on those goals, and adjust over time based on feedback aligned to his or her goals. (p. 15)

Because we are examining instructional models from a principal's perspective in this chapter, I have an additional suggestion about articulating an instructional model: Different roles within the school may require different instructional models, because expertise might look different for a classroom teacher, special education teacher, school counselor or psychologist, and so on. To illustrate this point, research by Evelyn Johnson, Angela Crawford, Yuzhu Zheng, and Laura Moylan (2021) compared special education teachers' evaluation scores using two different systems: Danielson's Framework for Teaching and the authors' (2018) own Recognizing Effective Special Education Teachers (RESET) models. They found that special education teachers consistently scored higher on the RESET model than they did on the Framework for Teaching model. In an extreme example, one teacher received opposite scores on each indicator; the RESET model rated her at a high level of proficiency, while the Framework for Teaching model rated her at a below basic level of proficiency on the same indicator. In sum, if the expectations differ, each role should have its own set of topics for effective teaching.

As we discuss teacher evaluation, professional learning, and data-driven improvement (for both teachers and students), it will become clear how foundational an instructional model is for the exercise of instructional leadership.

TEACHER EVALUATION

While principals have several roles relative to teacher evaluation, one of the most important is building teacher buy-in. Research shows that teachers who perceive the evaluation system as legitimate are more likely to grow and improve their instructional practice (Kim, Sun, & Youngs, 2019). Unfortunately, most teacher evaluation systems rely heavily on classroom observations, which have a somewhat dubious reputation.

Observations

While classroom observations are extremely common, there may be better ways of assessing teaching. First, classroom observations are cumbersome. I have yet to meet an administrator who doesn't feel, at least in part, that observations are a chore, something that they must do, but it would be nice not to have to do it. Second, classroom observations are not terribly reliable; they are rife with error—classification error, scoring error, issues with sample size, misuse of protocols (see chapter 4 of *Improving Teacher Development and Evaluation* [Marzano et al., 2021] for details). After all, an observation is simply an assessment event, and as we know by now, all assessments contain error.

Going a step further, Lukas Begrich, Susanne Kuger, Eckhard Klieme, and Mareike Kunter (2021) found that—in some ways—long observations by trained raters were no better than short observations by untrained raters. Using a psychological paradigm called "thin slices" (which goes back to the work of Nalini Ambady and Robert Rosenthal in 1993), they measured instructional quality using judgments based on thirty-second first impressions. Of course, administrators should not really use thirty-second observations for coaching or evaluating. However, these thin-slices judgments by untrained raters were surprisingly consistent and surprisingly accurate for classroom management and classroom support skills. Relative to consistency, Begrich and colleagues (2021) found that "observations of 30 [seconds] leave different raters who have no experience with judging instructional features with quite similar impressions" (p. 11). Relative to accuracy, they reported the following:

> We examined whether the thin slices ratings show an overlap with the ratings of instructional quality features given by trained raters who had watched the full lessons. . . . for classroom management and constructive support [giving supportive feedback], we found significant correlations with systematic ratings related to the respective dimension across both studies. . . . These results suggest that judgements of classroom management and constructive support given by untrained raters having observed lessons for 30 [seconds] are, to some extent, not only equivalent to judgements of trained raters having observed the full lessons but also similarly differentiated regarding these components of instructional quality. (p. 11)

This is very early-stage research on the use of this thin-slices paradigm for observations, but the results are, at minimum, thought-provoking. If principals and teachers were to use some sort of a thin-slice approach to generate formative scores for teachers, they would need to ensure that those scores were (1) open to adjustment based on additional data (either collected by the leader or submitted by the teacher) and (2) only one data point in a robust series of data points collected using a variety of assessment methods.

Measurement Process

Given the unreliable nature of classroom observations, Bob and colleagues (2021) recommended a teacher evaluation system that "only requires a few actual observations and relies heavily on nonobservational evidence submitted by teachers" (p. 76). At its core, that process is very similar to the process for measuring student learning presented in chapter 7 (page 103). Table 11.1 compares the measurement-of-student-learning process presented in chapter 7 with my summary of Bob's measurement-of-teacher-expertise process. My summary is a simplified version of Bob's process; for a more detailed and nuanced explanation, please see chapters 5–6 of *Improving Teacher Development and Evaluation* (Marzano et al., 2021).

As shown in table 11.1, the first step in measuring teacher expertise is for teachers to select growth goals from the instructional model. Bob recommends that teachers identify these growth goals by self-evaluating on the instructional model. That is, teachers use the scale for each element to record what they think their current level of performance is with that element. Then, teachers select goals (generally three per year) from among those elements with low scores. Teachers share those growth goals with their principal; when the principal comes to observe the teacher, they look specifically at the teacher's performance in growth goal areas. This allows the principal to focus an observation on specific strategies that the teacher is deliberately practicing, and allows feedback conversations to center on those elements of the instructional model that are of greatest interest to the teacher.

In the same way that a proficiency scale provides a common language and scoring scale for students, teachers, and parents, an instructional model with scoring scales provides a common language of instruction between principals and teachers. If a principal and teacher disagree about a teacher's current score on a particular element, each can present data to support their perspective. For example, a teacher believes he is at level 3 (applying) of the scale for the element of examining similarities and differences, and the principal believes he is at level 2 (developing) for that element. To support his self-evaluation, the teacher might provide evidence (in the form of a student survey or exit ticket) that most of his students understand the similarities and differences between two elements compared during a lesson and can explain how comparison activities deepen their knowledge. In light of this additional evidence, the principal might agree that the teacher is at level 3 (applying) for that element.

Which brings up the third part of the measurement process for teacher expertise: never trust a single observation. A classroom observation is essentially an assessment event, and all assessments contain error. If a particular

TABLE 11.1: Comparison of Measurement Processes for Student Learning and Teacher Expertise

Measurement of Student Learning	Measurement of Teacher Expertise
1. Assess students on topics they've had an opportunity to learn.	1. Observe teachers on elements they have identified as growth goals.
2. Use proficiency scales to score students accurately.	2. Use instructional model scales to score teachers accurately.
3. Never trust a single assessment.	3. Never trust a single observation.
4. Determine summative scores by considering patterns in formative scores for specific topics.	4. Determine summative scores by considering patterns in formative scores for specific elements.

element isn't observed during an observation, or if the teacher disagrees with the principal's assessment of an element, it is simply an opportunity to seek more evidence and reevaluate.

Finally, teachers' summative scores for each element can be determined by using a pattern of formative scores. For example, across a school year, suppose that a teacher received the following pattern of scores for the element of examining similarities and differences.

- September 5 observation: 2
- October 19 artifact: 3
- December 12 observation: 2
- February 14 student surveys: 3
- March 3 observation: 3

It is reasonable to assert that the teacher's summative score on this element is likely a 3 (applying), given this pattern of scores. To sum up, this measurement process is designed to generate a robust and defensible score that can be used to give a teacher feedback on their growth and development for a specific aspect of effective teaching.

Student Surveys

As we conclude this section on teacher evaluation, recall that Bob's approach to teacher evaluation relies heavily on nonobservational evidence; in the previous section I mentioned several examples of nonobservational evidence, such as exit tickets, artifacts, class polls, and student surveys. In 2016, Bob and colleagues stated that "direct feedback from students can be a powerful tool in transforming teacher development. Feedback includes not only achievement data but also the opinions and impressions of students, such as those gathered through student surveys" (p. 95). Additionally, the Bill and Melinda Gates Foundation's (2012) Measures of Effective Teaching (MET) project found that:

> Teachers' student survey results are predictive of student achievement gains. Students know an effective classroom when they experience one. . . . Further, the MET project finds student surveys produce more consistent results than classroom observations or achievement gain measures. . . . Even a high-quality observation system entails at most a handful of classroom visits, while student surveys aggregate the impressions of many individuals who've spent many hours with a teacher. (p. 2)

When implemented within a system of formative scoring based on a set of topics for effective teaching, student surveys and nontraditional types of observation (along with other assessment approaches) can provide reasonable options for data collection.

If a teacher and principal agreed to use surveys for data collection, they might employ the following process.

1. Identify the specific element of the instructional model for which student surveys will collect data.
2. Develop a survey that asks students questions about (a) the teacher's use of the element, (b) their response to the teacher's use of the element, and (c) the extent to which they found the use of the element adapted to their unique needs and situations.
3. Administer the survey to students anonymously to ensure they feel comfortable giving honest feedback.
4. Analyze the survey results.
    a. Consider responses about the teacher's use of the element first, to determine whether the teacher is at least at level 2 (developing). If responses indicate that the teacher is not using the element correctly, then the teacher's score is likely level 1 (beginning).
    b. Then consider responses about the use of the element, to determine whether the teacher is at least at level 3 (developing).
    c. Finally, consider responses about the extent to which students found use of the element adapted to their unique needs and situations, to determine whether the teacher is at level 4 (innovating).

Notice that the items on the survey align with the levels of the scale in the same way that a student assessment would have items aligned to each level of the proficiency scale. Additionally, note the protocol used to analyze the surveys: first, evaluators seek evidence for level 2 (developing) performance. If evidence for level 2 (developing) performance is present, then evaluators seek evidence for level 3 (applying) and level 4 (innovating). If evidence for level 2 (developing) performance is not present, they assign a score of 1 (beginning). Bob and colleagues (2021) recommend the use of a similar protocol across teacher evaluation activities, including observations and other data collection activities.

PROFESSIONAL LEARNING

Professional learning, which includes traditional professional development, feedback, and coaching, is essential for teacher growth and student achievement. High-performing schools invest in professional learning opportunities that focus on teaching and help teachers improve their skills (Shin, Slater, & Backhoff, 2013). When professional learning opportunities align with school goals and the schoolwide instructional program, student achievement and growth are higher (Newmann et al., 2001).

Principals can play an important role in improving student achievement by coaching teachers. However, it is important to note that coaching needs to be done in a thoughtful and systematic way, and it should be part of a broader instructional leadership strategy. For example, Jason Grissom, Susanna Loeb, and Benjamin Master (2013) collected data from a hundred principals in Miami-Dade County Public Schools. They sought to identify which leadership strategies and behaviors had the greatest impact on school performance. They found that principals' time is best used to coach teachers, rather than on classroom walkthroughs. Simply visiting classrooms didn't improve outcomes, but meeting with teachers to discuss their strengths and goals, while providing feedback and support, did.

As with teacher evaluation, coaching and feedback activities between principals and teachers should be grounded in an instructional model (Kraft & Gilmour, 2016) that provides a common language for discussing instruction and a common scale for measuring instructional growth. While much coaching and feedback can occur within the teacher evaluation structures outlined in the previous section, there are other structures that can be very useful for instruction-focused professional learning. One of those structures is known as instructional rounds.

Instructional Rounds

Bob has recommended instructional rounds since at least 2011. Instructional rounds in education were adapted in the early 2000s from the practice of medical rounds (Teitel, 2009), in which doctors and other healthcare professionals visit patients in a hospital to assess their condition and develop treatment plans. The approach is straightforward and consists of four steps.

1. **Select a focus for the instructional rounds.** This could be one or more elements that the group will seek to observe. Group members can observe other elements too, but all members of the group will look for the focus elements.
2. **Visit the classroom or watch a video of a highly effective teacher.** Use student growth and achievement data to identify highly effective teachers to observe during rounds. The visit or video should last about fifteen to twenty minutes.
3. **Debrief the observation.** Teachers discuss what they saw and heard. The group could use a simple set of questions to guide the debrief, such as the following.
    a. What did I see that I would like to try in my own practice?
    b. What did I see that I don't understand?
    c. What did I see that validates my current practice?
4. **Commit to action.** Each member of the instructional round should write down what they will do as a result of the experience. The leader of the round should follow up with each member of the group to find out how the action went and provide further support if needed.

Note in step 2 that instructional rounds do not need to take place live in a classroom; video footage of a highly effective teacher (if captured with an appropriately wide-angle lens) can be just as effective as live observations, and far easier to use asynchronously. Teams of teachers might develop the habit of conducting a video-based instructional round at the beginning of each of their regular meetings. Alternatively, if teachers have common planning time to meet in collaborative teams, they could use a portion of that time to observe a colleague in their building. Instructional rounds need not be overformal or time-consuming. Leveraging video—and the proliferation of smartphones to capture it—as a professional learning strategy is both efficient and cost effective. The use of video for professional learning is also the basis of video self-reflection.

Video Self-Reflection

In a video self-reflection, teachers record themselves teaching and then watch the recording with a coaching partner to evaluate and reflect on their performance. Allison Kretlow and Christina Bartholomew (2010) found that video self-reflection was a fruitful technique for coaches to provide feedback to teachers, as well as allowing teachers opportunities to reflect on their practice.

As with instructional rounds, video self-reflections should have a focus; preferably the teacher has identified one or more growth goal elements of the instructional model to be the focus of the video self-reflection. The teacher then records about twenty minutes of a lesson in which they demonstrate one or more of the focus elements. The teacher and coaching partner then watch the video together. Using the scales of the instructional model, each one scores the focus elements. They then compare their scores and share the evidence they used to assign each score. If discrepancies exist between the scores each assigned, they might rewatch portions of the video and discuss what they see and hear that led to the score they assigned.

Alternatively, if a teacher has not yet set growth goals, the focus of a video reflection might involve watching for "specific strategies that the teacher is using correctly and effectively, strategies that the teacher is attempting to use but is executing incorrectly or with parts missing, and strategies that a teacher could have used but did not" (Marzano & Simms, 2013, pp. 28–29). This could lead to a conversation where the coaching partner helps the teacher score themselves on the instructional model scales and select growth goal elements.

Ultimately, the goal of video self-reflection is nonevaluative; by examining their instruction and discussing it with a trusted other, teachers have opportunities to notice and process elements of their practice of which they might otherwise be unaware. By correcting errors or seeking to develop elements that are missing from their practice, teachers can increase their effectiveness and the growth of students in their classroom.

DATA-DRIVEN IMPROVEMENT

Effective principals use data in many ways. One of the most important—as described in chapter 9 (page 129)—is to measure the outcomes of school improvement programs, practices, and initiatives. Data can also help principals build buy-in among parents, students, and other community members. But the most important use of data may be to monitor student progress and ensure that students who need extra support to achieve the target learning goals receive it (Elfers & Stritikus, 2014; Shin et al., 2013). To that end, I would argue that data-driven improvement should start with two questions for teachers and two questions for principals. First, every teacher should be able to answer two questions for each student under their purview.

1. What is the student's current status for each topic in the guaranteed curriculum?
2. What is the student's growth rate for each topic in the guaranteed curriculum?

And every principal should be able to answer two questions for each teacher under their purview.

1. What is the teacher's current status for each element in the instructional model?
2. What is the teacher's growth rate for each element in the instructional model?

Current status is the current summative score (generated using a series of formative scores) on a topic or element. *Growth rate* is a number that expresses how quickly the student or teacher is progressing on a topic or element; it could be expressed as "score levels grown" divided by "weeks addressed" or a similar metric.

Teachers and principals should also identify the target status and target growth rates for various checkpoints during the school year. For example, by the end of the first trimester (twelve weeks), a student might be expected (depending on the nature of the content and how it is taught) to be at the 3.0 level for four of the twelve topics in a particular content area and grade level. Additionally, that student might be expected to demonstrate a growth rate of at least two score levels per topic over the twelve-week period (a total of eight score levels). Consider the student whose scores are shown in figure 11.1.

Regarding current status, this student has not achieved score 3.0 for two of the four topics addressed in the first trimester. Regarding growth rate, the student has grown eight score levels in twelve weeks across the four topics. Looking at these data, principals and teachers might conclude that this student is learning at an appropriate pace, but needs to reallocate their learning time to those topics for which they have not yet achieved proficiency. Additionally, in the next trimester, this student will need to move at a faster pace in order to achieve proficiency on the two topics remaining from trimester 1 and all four topics that will be addressed in trimester 2. However, if assessment data at the beginning of trimester 2 show that the student's beginning score on any of topics 5–8 is higher than 1.0, his trimester 2 pace requirements may change. The same analysis and conclusions are applicable to teacher evaluation data, although pace and status targets may be calculated differently, given differing expectations for teacher development and growth rates.

This type of data analysis allows teachers and principals to follow the learning of each student carefully and brings clarity to the intervention endeavor. Some students may be learning at an appropriate pace, but not allocating their time to the topics that need their attention most. Other students might be achieving proficiency on the topics addressed, but started with such high scores that they are not progressing at an appropriate pace. Still other students may be missing both status and pace targets. Depending on a student's (or a teacher's) status and pace profile, intervention should probably look different as it is tailored to their specific needs.

Additionally, data such as these can help teachers and principals identify specific classes that need additional support. Research by Thamar Voss, Lisa Zachrich, Benjamin Fauth, and Jörg Wittwer (2022) found:

> Measuring the teaching quality in one of a teacher's classes does not necessarily make it possible to accurately predict the teaching quality in another of the same teacher's classes. This applies both to classes taught by the same teacher in different subjects as well as to classes taught by the same teacher in the same subject. (p. 6)

As table 11.2 (page 148) shows, Voss and colleagues measured how much of the variance in four elements (cognitive activation, student support, classroom disturbances, and monitoring) was due to the teacher versus other factors. Class A and class B are two different classes taught by the same teacher.

As table 11.2 indicates, the teacher is not the only factor influencing what happens in the classroom. As every teacher knows, the students in a class exert a lot of influence on what happens in that class. Students are not widgets, and teachers are not assembly-line workers; we should never treat them as such. Therefore, in many circumstances, it may be more appropriate to talk about *classes* that need additional support rather than *teachers* who need additional support. The type of data analysis and data-driven improvement described in this section makes those conclusions available to teachers and principals.

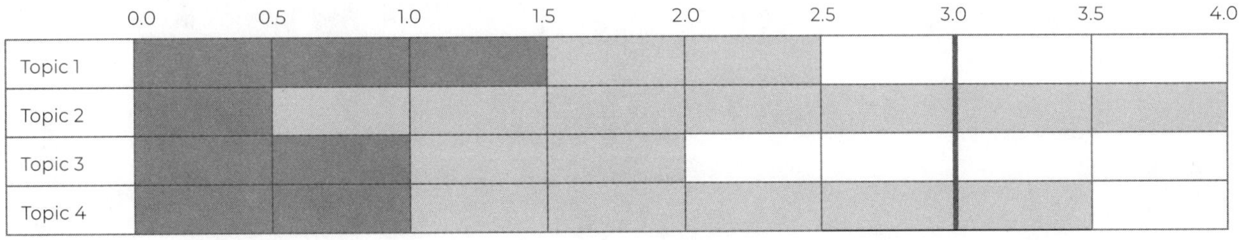

Figure 11.1: Student scores on four topics after the first trimester.

TABLE 11.2: Proportion of Variance of Classroom Elements Due to the Teacher

Element	Proportion of the Variance Due to the Teacher in Class A	Proportion of the Variance Due to the Teacher in Class B
Cognitive Activation	61 percent	52 percent
Student Support	57 percent	35 percent
Classroom Disturbances	51 percent	45 percent
Monitoring	77 percent	74 percent

SUMMARY

In this chapter, we examined three elements of instructional leadership, all of which require using an instructional model. First, we discussed how principals and teachers can partner to create teacher evaluation systems that are reliable, valid, and accurate. Many of the same principles that apply to measuring student learning also apply to measuring teacher growth and development. Next, we reviewed strategies for job-embedded professional learning, including instructional rounds and video self-reflection. Finally, we discussed how teachers and principals can use proficiency scales and an instructional model to collect and analyze data about student and teacher status and growth. Such analysis allows educators to draw conclusions about the specific interventions needed by specific individuals, and to see patterns of need at both the student and classroom levels.

In this part, we examined three critical roles of the principal, and explored ways that teachers and principals can partner to build strong organizations with healthy cultures that emphasize high-quality instruction and student learning. The teacher-principal partnership is likely the most important one in education; by understanding the roles of the principal and partnering to support and sustain those roles, educators can ensure that the educational body functions in a fully abled manner.

EPILOGUE

Education is a complex system. There is no one-size-fits-all solution, and what works for one student or school may not work for another. However, by understanding the key elements of education and how they interact, we can increase our chances of success. Over the last eleven chapters, I have presented the following structure based on my synthesis of Bob's fifty years of work in the field and my examination of the extant educational research.

- Students
  - » Self-System
  - » Metacognitive System
  - » Knowledge System
  - » Cognitive System
- Teachers
  - » Self-Regulation
  - » Measurement
  - » Instruction
- Principals
  - » Organizational Leadership
  - » People Leadership
  - » Instructional Leadership

As explained in the introduction, I liken the systems of education to the systems of the human body. In the same way that the circulatory, respiratory, skeletal, muscular, nervous, endocrine, digestive, immune, and other biological systems work in interconnected ways to make a body function, I believe the systems of education work in interconnected ways to make education function. I also liken students, teachers, and principals to the head, torso, and limbs of the body, and the district to the environment the body lives within.

The metaphor helps me organize my thinking about the important roles in education and how those roles interact with the important systems in education. As I look forward in education, I desire for educators to be increasingly respected as professionals and for the educational field to be increasingly respected as a research- and evidence-based field. As is likely obvious from the content of this book, I lean toward the science side of "the art and science of teaching." I think that educational research has great potential to inform and refine the educational practice of my colleagues in schools, but I find the bridge between educational research and practice to still be somewhat flimsy, despite the best efforts of many (including Bob Marzano) to strengthen and expand it. Therefore, my hope for this book is that it furthers the goal of helping educators turn research into practice and my hope for you is that you will embrace action research. As you seek strategies and solutions to test in your classroom and school, I hope that this book serves as a resource to help you to more easily find the strategy or solution you're looking for.

REFERENCES AND RESOURCES

Abbott, E. E. (1909). On the analysis of the factor of recall in the learning process. *The Psychological Review: Monograph Supplements, 11*(1), 159–177. https://doi.org/10.1037/h0093018

Abedi, J., Zhang, Y., Rowe, S. E., & Lee, H. (2020). Examining effectiveness and validity of accommodations for English language learners in mathematics: An evidence-based computer accommodation decision system. *Educational Measurement: Issues and Practice, 39*(4), 41–52. https://doi.org/10.1111/emip.12328

Adams, C. M. (2013). Collective trust: A social indicator of instructional capacity. *Journal of Educational Administration, 51*(3), 363–382.

Adesope, O. O., Trevisan, D. A., & Sundararajan, N. (2017). Rethinking the use of tests: A meta-analysis of practice testing. *Review of Educational Research, 87*(3), 659–701. https://doi.org/10.3102/0034654316689306

Agarwal, P. K., Nunes, L. D., & Blunt, J. R. (2021). Retrieval practice consistently benefits student learning: A systematic review of applied research in schools and classrooms. *Educational Psychology Review, 33*(4), 1409–1453. https://doi.org/10.1007/s10648-021-09595-9

Agnoli, S., Mancini, G., Pozzoli, T., Baldaro, B., Russo, P. M., & Surcinelli, P. (2012). The interaction between emotional intelligence and cognitive ability in predicting scholastic performance in school-aged children. *Personality and Individual Differences, 53*(5), 660–665. https://doi.org/10.1016/j.paid.2012.05.020

Akin, U., Aydın, İ., Erdoğan, Ç., & Demirkasimoğlu, N. (2014). Emotional labor and burnout among Turkish primary school teachers. *The Australian Educational Researcher, 41*(2), 155–169. https://doi.org/10.1007/s13384-013-0138-4

Allen, K.-A., Gray, D. L., Baumeister, R. F., & Leary, M. R. (2022). The need to belong: A deep dive into the origins, implications, and future of a foundational construct. *Educational Psychology Review, 34*(2), 1133–1156. https://doi.org/10.1007/s10648-021-09633-6

Alliance for Excellent Education. (2014, July). *On the path to equity: Improving the effectiveness of beginning teachers.* Washington, DC: Author. Accessed at https://all4ed.org/wp-content/uploads/2014/07/PathToEquity.pdf on July 13, 2023.

Ambady, N., & Rosenthal, R. (1993). Half a minute: Predicting teacher evaluations from thin slices of nonverbal behavior and physical attractiveness. *Journal of Personality and Social Psychology, 64*(3), 431–441. https://doi.org/10.1037/0022-3514.64.3.431

American Psychological Association. (n.d.). *Teacher stress module transcript.* Washington, DC: Author. Accessed at https://www.apa.org/education/k12/teacher-stress.pdf on July 12, 2023.

Anderman, E. M. (2020). Achievement motivation theory: Balancing precision and utility. *Contemporary Educational Psychology, 61,* Article 101864. https://doi.org/10.1016/j.cedpsych.2020.101864

Andersen, S. C., Beuchert, L., Nielsen, H. S., & Thomsen, M. K. (2018). The effect of teacher's aides in the classroom: Evidence from a randomized trial. *Journal of the European Economic Association, 18*(1), 469–505. https://doi.org/10.1093/jeea/jvy048

Anderson, J. R. (1982). Acquisition of cognitive skill. *Psychological Review, 89*(4), 369–406.

Anderson, J. R. (1983). *The architecture of cognition.* Cambridge, MA: Harvard University Press.

Anderson, J. R. (1995). *Learning and memory: An integrated approach.* New York: Wiley.

Anderson, J. R., Reder, L. M., & Simon, H. A. (1996). Situated learning and education. *Educational Researcher, 25*(4), 5–11.

Anderson, J. R., Reder, L. M., & Simon, H. A. (2000). *Applications and misapplications of cognitive psychology to mathematics education* [Unpublished paper]. Carnegie Mellon University, Department of Psychology, Pittsburgh, PA.

Anderson, L. W., & Krathwohl, D. (Eds.). (2001). *A taxonomy for learning, teaching, and assessing: A revision of Bloom's taxonomy of educational objectives.* Boston: Allyn & Bacon.

Araiza-Alba, P., Keane, T., Chen, W. S., & Kaufman, J. (2021). Immersive virtual reality as a tool to learn problem-solving skills. *Computers & Education, 164*, Article 104121. https://doi.org/10.1016/j.compedu.2020.104121

Argelagós, E., & Pifarré, M. (2012). Improving information problem solving skills in secondary education through embedded instruction. *Computers in Human Behavior, 28*(2), 515–526. https://doi.org/10.1016/j.chb.2011.10.024

Aronson, J., & Steele, C. M. (2005). Stereotypes and the fragility of academic competence, motivation, and self-concept. In A. J. Elliot & C. S. Dweck (Eds.), *Handbook of competence and motivation* (pp. 436–456). New York: Guilford.

Ashman, G., Kalyuga, S., & Sweller, J. (2020). Problem-solving or explicit instruction: Which should go first when element interactivity is high? *Educational Psychology Review, 32*(1), 229–247. https://doi.org/10.1007/s10648-019-09500-5

Auwarter, A. E., & Aruguete, M. S. (2008). Effects of student gender and socioeconomic status on teacher perceptions. *The Journal of Educational Research, 101*(4), 242–246. https://doi.org/10.3200/JOER.101.4.243-246

Babad, E. (2009). *The social psychology of the classroom.* New York: Routledge.

Baddeley, A. D. (1992). Working memory. *Science, 255*, 556–559. https://doi.org/10.1126/science.1736359

Bae, C. L., DeBusk-Lane, M. L., & Lester, A. M. (2020). Engagement profiles of elementary students in urban schools. *Contemporary Educational Psychology, 62*, Article 101880. https://doi.org/10.1016/j.cedpsych.2020.101880

Bandura, A. (1997). *Self-efficacy: The exercise of control.* New York: W. H. Freeman.

Bandura, A. (2001). Social cognitive theory: An agentic perspective. *Annual Review of Psychology, 52*, 1–26. https://doi.org/10.1146/annurev.psych.52.1.1

Bardach, L., Klassen, R. M., & Perry, N. E. (2022). Teachers' psychological characteristics: Do they matter for teacher effectiveness, teachers' well-being, retention, and interpersonal relations? An integrative review. *Educational Psychology Review, 34*(1), 259–300. https://doi.org/10.1007/s10648-021-09614-9

Baumeister, R. F., Vohs, K. D., & Tice, D. M. (2007). The strength model of self-control. *Current Directions in Psychological Science, 16*(6), 351–355. https://doi.org/10.1111/j.1467-8721.2007.00534.x

Begrich, L., Kuger, S., Klieme, E., & Kunter, M. (2021). At a first glance—How reliable and valid is the thin slices technique to assess instructional quality? *Learning and Instruction, 74,* Article 101466. https://doi.org/10.1016/j.learninstruc.2021.101466

Belfield, C. R., & Bailey, T. R. (2019). The labor market value of higher education: Now and in the future. In M. B. Paulsen & L. W. Perna (Eds.), *Higher education: Handbook of theory and research* (Vol. 34, pp. 373–414). New York: Springer.

Bellamy, G. T., Crawford, L., Marshall, L. H., & Coulter, G. A. (2005). The fail-safe schools challenge: Leadership possibilities from high reliability organizations. *Educational Administration Quarterly, 41*(3), 383-412.

Bennett, A. A., Bakker, A. B., & Field, J. G. (2018). Recovery from work-related effort: A meta-analysis. *Journal of Organizational Behavior, 39*(3), 262–275. https://doi.org/10.1002/job.2217

Bergdahl, N., Nouri, J., Fors, U., & Knutsson, O. (2020). Engagement, disengagement and performance when learning with technologies in upper secondary school. *Computers & Education, 149,* Article 103783. https://doi.org/10.1016/j.compedu.2019.103783

Bernacki, M. L., Greene, M. J., & Lobczowski, N. G. (2021). A systematic review of research on personalized learning: Personalized by whom, to what, how, and for what purpose(s)? *Educational Psychology Review, 33*(4), 1675–1715. https://doi.org/10.1007/s10648-021-09615-8

Bers, M. U. (2018). *Coding as a playground: Programming and computational thinking in the early childhood classroom.* New York: Routledge.

Bill & Melinda Gates Foundation. (2012, September). *Asking students about teaching: Student perception surveys and their implementation.* Seattle, WA: Author. Accessed at https://usprogram.gatesfoundation.org/news-and-insights/usp-resource-center/resources/asking-students-about-teaching-student-perception-surveys-and-their-implementation on July 12, 2023.

Bitler, M., Corcoran, S. P., Domina, T., & Penner, E. K. (2021). Teacher effects on student achievement and height: A cautionary tale. *Journal of Research on Educational Effectiveness, 14*(4), 900–924. https://doi.org/10.1080/19345747.2021.1917025

Bjork, R. A., Dunlosky, J., & Kornell, N. (2013). Self-regulated learning: Beliefs, techniques, and illusions. *Annual Review of Psychology, 64,* 417–444. https://doi.org/10.1146/annurev-psych-113011-143823

Black, P., & Wiliam, D. (1998). Assessment and classroom learning. *Assessment in Education: Principles, Policy & Practice, 5*(1), 7–74. http://dx.doi.org/10.1080/0969595980050102

Blanchard, M. R., Southerland, S. A., Osborne, J. W., Sampson, V. D., Annetta, L. A., & Granger, E. M. (2010). Is inquiry possible in light of accountability?: A quantitative comparison of the relative effectiveness of guided inquiry and verification laboratory instruction. *Science Education, 94*(4), 577–616. https://doi.org/10.1002/sce.20390

Blazar, D., & Archer, C. (2020). Teaching to support students with diverse academic needs. *Educational Researcher, 49*(5), 297–311. https://doi.org/10.3102/0013189X20931226

Blazar, D., Heller, B., Kane, T., Polikoff, M., Staiger, D. O., Carrell, S., et al. (2019). *Learning by the book: Comparing math achievement growth by textbook in six Common Core states.* Cambridge, MA: Center for Education Policy Research.

Boekaerts, M., & Corno, L. (2005). Self-regulation in the classroom: A perspective on assessment and intervention. *Applied Psychology, 54*(2), 199–231. https://doi.org/10.1111/j.1464-0597.2005.00205.x

Bong, M. (2009). Age-related differences in achievement goal differentiation. *Journal of Educational Psychology, 101*(4), 879–896. https://doi.org/10.1037/a0015945

Boogren, T. H. (2018). *Take time for you: Self-care action plans for educators.* Bloomington, IN: Solution Tree Press.

Borman, G. D., Choi, Y., & Hall, G. J. (2021). The impacts of a brief middle-school self-affirmation intervention help propel African American and Latino students through high school. *Journal of Educational Psychology, 113*(3), 605–620. https://doi.org/10.1037/edu0000570

Borman, G. D., Pyne, J., Rozek, C. S., & Schmidt, A. (2022). A replicable identity-based intervention reduces the Black-White suspension gap at scale. *American Educational Research Journal, 59*(2), 284–314. https://doi.org/10.3102/00028312211042251

Borman, G. D., Rozek, C. S., Pyne, J., & Hanselman, P. (2019). Reappraising academic and social adversity improves middle school students' academic achievement, behavior, and well-being. *Proceedings of the National Academy of Sciences, 116*(33), 16286–16291. https://doi.org/10.1073/pnas.1820317116

Bowman, L. L., Levine, L. E., Waite, B. M., & Gendron, M. (2010). Can students really multitask? An experimental study of instant messaging while reading. *Computers & Education, 54*(4), 927–931. https://doi.org/10.1016/j.compedu.2009.09.024

Brandt, R. (1995). Overview: What to do with those new standards. *Educational Leadership, 52*(6), 5.

Brante, E. W., & Strømsø, H. I. (2018). Sourcing in text comprehension: A review of interventions targeting sourcing skills. *Educational Psychology Review, 30*(3), 773–799. https://doi.org/10.1007/s10648-017-9421-7

Bray, B., & McClaskey, K. (2014). *Make learning personal: The what, who, wow, where, and why.* Thousand Oaks, CA: Corwin Press.

Breakstone, J., Smith, M., Wineburg, S., Rapaport, A., Carle, J., Garland, M. et al. (2021). Students' civic online reasoning: A national portrait. *Educational Researcher, 50*(8), 505–515. https://doi.org/10.3102/0013189X211017495

Brophy, J. E., & Good, T. L. (1974). *Teacher-student relationships: Causes and consequences.* New York: Holt, Rinehart & Winston.

Brotheridge, C. M., & Lee, R. T. (2002). Testing a conservation of resources model of the dynamics of emotional labor. *Journal of Occupational Health Psychology, 7*(1), 57–67. https://doi.org/10.1037/1076-8998.7.1.57

Brown III, G. (2015). What's the difference? Principal practices that support the achievement of low-income students in demographically diverse schools. *Academy of Educational Leadership Journal, 19*(2), 11–31.

Burić, I., Kim, L. E., & Hodis, F. (2021). Emotional labor profiles among teachers: Associations with positive affective, motivational, and well-being factors. *Journal of Educational Psychology, 113*(6), 1227–1243. https://doi.org/10.1037/edu0000654

Burkam, D. T., LoGerfo, L., Ready, D., & Lee, V. E. (2007). The differential effects of repeating kindergarten. *Journal of Education for Students Placed at Risk, 12*(2), 103–136. https://doi.org/10.1080/10824660701261052

Bush-Mecenas, S. (2022). "The business of teaching and learning": Institutionalizing equity in educational organizations through continuous improvement. *American Educational Research Journal, 59*(3), 461–499. https://doi.org/10.3102/00028312221074404

Butler, A. C. (2010). Repeated testing produces superior transfer of learning relative to repeated studying. *Journal of Experimental Psychology: Learning, Memory, and Cognition, 36*(5), 1118–1133. https://doi.org/10.1037/a0019902

Butler, R. (2007). Teachers' achievement goal orientations and associations with teachers' help seeking: Examination of a novel approach to teacher motivation. *Journal of Educational Psychology, 99*(2), 241–252. https://doi.org/10.1037/0022-0663.99.2.241

Butler, R. (2012). Striving to connect: Extending an achievement goal approach to teacher motivation to include relational goals for teaching. *Journal of Educational Psychology, 104*(3), 726–742. https://doi .org/10.1037/a0028613

Califf, C. B., & Brooks, S. (2020). An empirical study of techno-stressors, literacy facilitation, burnout, and turnover intention as experienced by K–12 teachers. *Computers & Education, 157,* Article 103971. https:// doi.org/10.1016/j.compedu.2020.103971

Camacho-Morles, J., Slemp, G. R., Pekrun, R., Loderer, K., Hou, H., & Oades, L. G. (2021). Activity achievement emotions and academic performance: A meta-analysis. *Educational Psychology Review, 33*(3). 1051–1095. https://doi.org/10.1007/s10648-020-09585-3

Carnevale, A. P., Rose, S. J., & Cheah, B. (2011). *The college payoff: Education, occupations, life-time earnings.* Washington, DC: Center on Education and the Workforce. Accessed at http://cew.georgetown.edu /collegepayoff/ on July 12, 2023.

Carnevale, A. P., Smith, N., & Strohl, J. (2013). *Recovery: Job growth and education requirements through 2020.* Washington, DC: Center on Education and the Workforce. Accessed at https://repository.library .georgetown.edu/bitstream/handle/10822/559311/Recovery2020.FR.Web.pdf on July 12, 2023.

Carpenter, S. K., Endres, T., & Hui, L. (2020). Students' use of retrieval in self-regulated learning: Implications for monitoring and regulating effortful learning experiences. *Educational Psychology Review, 32*(4), 1029–1054. https://doi.org/10.1007/s10648-020-09562-w

Carr, A., & Marzouq, S. (2012). The 2 × 2 achievement goal framework in primary school: Do young children pursue mastery-avoidance goals? *The Psychology of Education Review, 36*(2), 3–8. https://doi.org/10.53841 /bpsper.2011.36.2.3

Caskurlu, S., Maeda, Y., Richardson, J. C., & Lv, J. (2020). A meta-analysis addressing the relationship between teaching presence and students' satisfaction and learning. *Computers & Education, 157,* Article 103966. https://doi.org/10.1016/j.compedu.2020.103966

Castro-Alonso, J. C., Wong, R. M., Adesope, O. O., & Paas, F. (2021). Effectiveness of multimedia pedagogical agents predicted by diverse theories: A meta-analysis. *Educational Psychology Review, 33*(3), 989–1015. https://doi.org/10.1007/s10648-020-09587-1

Chen, G., Chan, C. K. K., Chan, K. K. H., Clarke, S. N., & Resnick, L. B. (2020). Efficacy of video-based teacher professional development for increasing classroom discourse and student learning. *Journal of the Learning Sciences, 29*(4–5), 642–680. https://doi.org/10.1080/10508406.2020.1783269

Chen, G., Lo, C. K., & Hu, L. (2020). Sustaining online academic discussions: Identifying the characteristics of messages that receive responses. *Computers & Education, 156,* Article 103938. https://doi.org/10.1016 /j.compedu.2020.103938

Chen, O., Paas, F., & Sweller, J. (2021). Spacing and interleaving effects require distinct theoretical bases: A systematic review testing the cognitive load and discriminative-contrast hypotheses. *Educational Psychology Review, 33*(4), 1499–1522. https://doi.org/10.1007/s10648-021-09613-w

Chetty, R., Friedman, J. N., & Rockoff, J. E. (2014). Measuring the impacts of teachers II: Teacher value-added and student outcomes in adulthood. *American Economic Review, 104*(9), 2633–2679. http://dx.doi .org/10.1257/aer.104.9.2633

Cheung, F. Y. L., & Lun, V. M.-C. (2015). Relation between emotional labor and organizational citizenship behavior: An investigation among Chinese teaching professionals. *The Journal of General Psychology, 142*(4), 253–272. https://doi.org/10.1080/00221309.2015.1091764

Chin, J. M.-C. (2007). Meta-analysis of transformational school leadership effects on school outcomes in Taiwan and the USA. *Asia Pacific Education Review, 8*(2), 166–177.

Chin, M. J., Quinn, D. M., Dhaliwal, T. K., & Lovison, V. S. (2020). Bias in the air: A nationwide exploration of teachers' implicit racial attitudes, aggregate bias, and student outcomes. *Educational Researcher, 49*(8), 566–578. https://doi.org/10.3102/0013189X20937240

Christodoulou, S. A., & Diakidoy, I.-A. N. (2020). The contribution of argument knowledge to the comprehension and critical evaluation of argumentative text. *Contemporary Educational Psychology, 63*, Article 101903. https://doi.org/10.1016/j.cedpsych.2020.101903

Ciani, K. D., & Sheldon, K. M. (2010). Evaluating the mastery-avoidance goal construct: A study of elite college baseball players. *Psychology of Sport and Exercise, 11*(2), 127–132. https://doi.org/10.1016/j.psychsport.2009.04.005

Cohen, J. (1988). *Statistical power analysis for the behavioral sciences.* Mahwah, NJ: Erlbaum.

Collaborative for Academic, Social, and Emotional Learning. (2005). *Safe and sound: An educational leader's guide to evidence-based social and emotional learning programs—Illinois edition.* Chicago: Author.

Copur-Gencturk, Y., Cimpian, J. R., Lubienski, S. T., & Thacker, I. (2020). Teachers' bias against the mathematical ability of female, Black, and Hispanic students. *Educational Researcher, 49*(1), 30–43. https://doi.org/10.3102/0013189X19890577

Corcoran, R. P., Cheung, A. C. K., Kim, E., & Xie, C. (2018). Effective universal school-based social and emotional learning programs for improving academic achievement: A systematic review and meta-analysis of 50 years of research. *Educational Research Review, 25*, 56–72. https://doi.org/10.1016/j.edurev.2017.12.001

Costa, A. L., & Kallick, B. (2009). *Habits of mind across the curriculum: Practical and creative strategies for teachers.* Alexandria, VA: ASCD.

Cragg, L., & Gilmore, C. (2014). Skills underlying mathematics: The role of executive function in the development of mathematics proficiency. *Trends in Neuroscience and Education, 3*(2), 63–68. https://doi.org/10.1016/j.tine.2013.12.001

Creemers, B., & Kyriakides, L. (2008). *The dynamics of educational effectiveness: A contribution to policy, practice, and theory in contemporary schools.* New York: Routledge. https://doi.org/10.4324/9780203939185

Cropley, M., & Zijlstra, F. R. H. (2011). Work and rumination. In J. Langan-Fox & C. L. Cooper (Eds.), *Handbook of stress in the occupations.* Cheltenham, United Kingdom: Edward Elgar Publishing. https://doi.org/10.4337/9780857931153.00061

Csikszentmihalyi, M., Abuhamdeh, S., & Nakamura, J. (2014). Flow. In M. Csikszentmihalyi, *Flow and the foundations of positive psychology: The collected works of Mihaly Csikszentmihalyi* (pp. 227–238). New York: Springer.

Currey, M. (2013). *Daily rituals: How artists work.* New York: Knopf.

Currey, M. (2019). *Daily rituals: Women at work.* New York: Knopf.

Danielson, C. (2007). *Enhancing professional practice: A framework for teaching* (2nd ed.). Alexandria, VA: ASCD.

Danielson, C. (2008). *The handbook for enhancing professional practice: Using the framework for teaching in your school.* Alexandria, VA: ASCD.

DeCuir-Gunby, J. T., & Bindra, V. G. (2022). How does teacher bias influence students?: An introduction to the special issue on teachers' implicit attitudes, instructional practices, and student outcomes. *Learning and Instruction, 78*, Article 101523. https://doi.org/10.1016/j.learninstruc.2021.101523

De La Paz, S., & Felton, M. K. (2010). Reading and writing from multiple source documents in history: Effects of strategy instruction with low to average high school writers. *Contemporary Educational Psychology, 35*(3), 174–192. https://doi.org/10.1016/j.cedpsych.2010.03.001

Demetriou, H., & Wilson, E. (2009). Synthesising affect and cognition in teaching and learning. *Social Psychology of Education, 12*(2), 213–232. https://doi.org/10.1007/s11218-008-9075-x

Denessen, E., Hornstra, L., van den Bergh, L., & Bijlstra, G. (2022). Implicit measures of teachers' attitudes and stereotypes, and their effects on teacher practice and student outcomes: A review. *Learning and Instruction, 78*, Article 101437. https://doi.org/10.1016/j.learninstruc.2020.101437

DiCerbo, K. (2020). Assessment for learning with diverse learners in a digital world. *Educational Measurement: Issues and Practice, 39*(3), 90–93. https://doi.org/10.1111/emip.12374

Dicke, A.-L., Rubach, C., Safavian, N., Karabenick, S. A., & Eccles, J. S. (2021). Less direct than you thought: Do teachers transmit math value to students through their cognitive support for understanding? *Learning and Instruction, 76*, Article 101521. https://doi.org/10.1016/j.learninstruc.2021.101521

Dignath, C., Buettner, G., & Langfeldt, H.-P. (2008). How can primary school students learn self-regulated learning strategies most effectively?: A meta-analysis on self-regulation training programmes. *Educational Research Review, 3*(2), 101–129. https://doi.org/10.1016/j.edurev.2008.02.003

Dignath, C., & Büttner, G. (2008). Components of fostering self-regulated learning among students: A meta-analysis on intervention studies at primary and secondary school level. *Metacognition and Learning, 3*(3), 231–264. https://doi.org/10.1007/s11409-008-9029-x

Dignath, C., & Veenman, M. V. J. (2021). The role of direct strategy instruction and indirect activation of self-regulated learning—Evidence from classroom observation studies. *Educational Psychology Review, 33*(2), 489–533. https://doi.org/10.1007/s10648-020-09534-0

Di Leo, I., & Muis, K. R. (2020). Confused, now what? A Cognitive-Emotional Strategy Training (CEST) intervention for elementary students during mathematics problem solving. *Contemporary Educational Psychology, 62*, Article 101879. https://doi.org/10.1016/j.cedpsych.2020.101879

Di Leo, I., Muis, K. R., Singh, C. A., & Psaradellis, C. (2019). Curiosity. . . confusion? Frustration! The role and sequencing of emotions during mathematics problem solving. *Contemporary Educational Psychology, 58*, 121–137. https://doi.org/10.1016/j.cedpsych.2019.03.001

Dishon, G., & Kafai, Y. B. (2020). Making more of games: Cultivating perspective-taking through game design. *Computers & Education, 148*, Article 103810. https://doi.org/10.1016/j.compedu.2020.103810

D'Mello, S., & Graesser, A. (2012). Dynamics of affective states during complex learning. *Learning and Instruction, 22*(2), 145–157. https://doi.org/10.1016/j.learninstruc.2011.10.001

Dodson, C. W. (2019). *The critical concepts in social studies.* Centennial, CO: Marzano Resources. Accessed at https://www.marzanoresources.com/critical-concepts-social-studies.html on July 13, 2023.

Donaldson, J. P., & Allen-Handy, A. (2020). The nature and power of conceptualizations of learning. *Educational Psychology Review, 32*(2), 545–570. https://doi.org/10.1007/s10648-019-09503-2

Donker, M. H., van Vemde, L., Hessen, D. J., van Gog, T., & Mainhard, T. (2021). Observational, student, and teacher perspectives on interpersonal teacher behavior: Shared and unique associations with teacher and student emotions. *Learning and Instruction, 73*, Article 101414. https://doi.org/10.1016/j.learninstruc.2020.101414

Dönmez, O., & Akbulut, Y. (2021). Timing and relevance of secondary tasks impact multitasking performance. *Computers & Education, 161*, Article 104078. https://doi.org/10.1016/j.compedu.2020.104078

Downs, A. (1957). *An economic theory of democracy.* New York: Harper.

Duckworth, A. L., Quirk, A., Gallop, R., Hoyle, R. H., Kelly, D. R., & Matthews, M. D. (2019). Cognitive and noncognitive predictors of success. *Proceedings of the National Academy of Sciences, 116*(47), 23499–23504. http://dx.doi.org/10.1073/pnas.1910510116

Duckworth, A. L., Taxer, J. L., Eskreis-Winkler, L., Galla, B. M., & Gross, J. J. (2019). Self-control and academic achievement. *Annual Review of Psychology, 70*, 373–399. https://doi.org/10.1146/annurev-psych-010418-103230

DuFour, R., DuFour, R., Eaker, R., Many, T. & Mattos, M. (2016). *Learning by doing: A handbook for Professional Learning Communities at Work* (3rd ed.). Bloomington, IN: Solution Tree Press.

DuFour, R., & Marzano, R. J. (2011). *Leaders of learning: How district, school, and classroom leaders improve student achievement.* Bloomington, IN: Solution Tree Press.

Duijzer, C., Van den Heuvel-Panhuizen, M., Veldhuis, M., Doorman, M., & Leseman, P. (2019). Embodied learning environments for graphing motion: A systematic literature review. *Educational Psychology Review, 31*(3), 597–629. https://doi.org/10.1007/s10648-019-09471-7

Dumas, D., McNeish, D., & Greene, J. A. (2020). Dynamic measurement: A theoretical-psychometric paradigm for modern educational psychology. *Educational Psychologist, 55*(2), 88–105. https://doi.org/10.1080/00461520.2020.1744150

Dunlosky, J., Rawson, K. A., Marsh, E. J., Nathan, M. J., & Willingham, D. T. (2013). Improving students' learning with effective learning techniques: Promising directions from cognitive and educational psychology. *Psychological Science in the Public Interest, 14*(1), 4–58. https://doi.org/10.1177/1529100612453266

Durlak, J. A., Domitrovich, C. E., Weissberg, R. P., & Gullotta, T. P. (2015). *Handbook of social and emotional learning: Research and practice* (1st ed.). New York: Guilford Press.

Durlak, J. A., Weissberg, R. P., Dymnicki, A. B., Taylor, R. D., & Schellinger, K. B. (2011). The impact of enhancing students' social and emotional learning: A meta-analysis of school-based universal interventions. *Child Development, 82*(1), 405–432. https://doi.org/10.1111/j.1467-8624.2010.01564.x

Dweck, C. S. (2006). *Mindset: The new psychology of success.* New York: Random House.

Eaker, R., & Marzano, R. J. (Eds.). (2020). *Professional Learning Communities at Work and High Reliability Schools: Cultures of continuous learning.* Bloomington, IN: Solution Tree Press.

Ebbinghaus, H. (1885). *Memory: A contribution to experimental psychology* (H. A. Ruger & C. E. Bussenius, Trans.). New York: Teachers College.

Eccles (Parsons), J. S., Adler, T. F., Futterman, R., Goff, S. B., Kaczala, C. M., Meece, J. L. et al. (1983). Expectancies, values, and academic behaviors. In J. T. Spence (Ed.), *Achievement and achievement motives: Psychological and sociological approaches* (pp. 75–146). San Francisco: W. H. Freeman.

Eccles, J. S., & Wigfield, A. (2020). From expectancy-value theory to situated expectancy-value theory: A developmental, social cognitive, and sociocultural perspective on motivation. *Contemporary Educational Psychology, 61*, Article 101859. https://doi.org/10.1016/j.cedpsych.2020.101859

Edmunds, J. A., Unlu, F., Furey, J., Glennie, E., & Arshavsky, N. (2020). What happens when you combine high school and college? The impact of the early college model on postsecondary performance and completion. *Educational Evaluation and Policy Analysis, 42*(2), 257–278. https://doi .org/10.3102/0162373720912249

Eduvate Rhode Island. (n.d.). *Creating a shared understanding of personalized learning for Rhode Island.* Accessed at http://eduvateri.org/wp-content/uploads/2016/09/Personalized_Learning_Paper_Final.pdf on July 13, 2023.

Efklides, A. (2011). Interactions of metacognition with motivation and affect in self-regulated learning: The MASRL model. *Educational Psychologist, 46*(1), 6–25. https://doi.org/10.1080/00461520.2011.538645

Elfers, A. M., & Stritikus, T. (2014). How school and district leaders support classroom teachers' work with English language learners. *Educational Administration Quarterly, 50*(2), 305–344.

Endedijk, H. M., Breeman, L. D., van Lissa, C. J., Hendrickx, M. M. H. G., den Boer, L., & Mainhard, T. (2022). The teacher's invisible hand: A meta-analysis of the relevance of teacher-student relationship quality for peer relationships and the contribution of student behavior. *Review of Educational Research, 92*(3), 370–412. https://doi.org/10.3102/00346543211051428

Engels, M. C., Spilt, J., Denies, K., & Verschueren, K. (2021). The role of affective teacher-student relationships in adolescents' school engagement and achievement trajectories. *Learning and Instruction, 75*, Article 101485. https://doi.org/10.1016/j.learninstruc.2021.101485

Ferguson, R. F. (2003). Teachers' perceptions and expectations and the Black-White test score gap. *Urban Education, 38*(4), 460–507. https://doi.org/10.1177/0042085903038004006

Fiorella, L. (2020). The science of habit and its implications for student learning and well-being. *Educational Psychology Review, 32*(3), 603–625. https://doi.org/10.1007/s10648-020-09525-1

Fitts, P. M., & Posner, M. I. (1967). *Human performance.* Belmont, CA: Brooks Cole.

Fjørtoft, H. (2020). Multimodal digital classroom assessments. *Computers & Education, 152*, Article 103892. https://doi.org/10.1016/j.compedu.2020.103892

Forsblom, L., Pekrun, R., Loderer, K., & Peixoto, F. (2022). Cognitive appraisals, achievement emotions, and students' math achievement: A longitudinal analysis. *Journal of Educational Psychology, 114*(2), 346–367. https://doi.org/10.1037/edu0000671

Frenzel, A. C., Goetz, T., Stephens, E. J., & Jacob, B. (2009). Antecedents and effects of teachers' emotional experiences: An integrated perspective and empirical test. In P. A. Schutz & M. Zembylas (Eds.), *Advances in teacher emotion research: The impact on teachers' lives* (pp. 129–151). New York: Springer. https://doi. org/10.1007/978-1-4419-0564-2_7

Fries, L., Son, J. Y., Givvin, K. B., & Stigler, J. W. (2021). Practicing connections: A framework to guide instructional design for developing understanding in complex domains. *Educational Psychology Review, 33*(2), 739–762. https://doi.org/10.1007/s10648-020-09561-x

Fulton, K., & Britton, T. (2011). *STEM teachers in professional learning communities: From good teachers to great teaching.* Washington, DC: National Commission on Teaching and America's Future.

Fütterer, T., Scheiter, K., Cheng, X., & Stürmer, K. (2022). Quality beats frequency? Investigating students' effort in learning when introducing technology in classrooms. *Contemporary Educational Psychology, 69*, Article 102042. https://doi.org/10.1016/j.cedpsych.2022.102042

Galla, B. M., & Duckworth, A. L. (2015). More than resisting temptation: Beneficial habits mediate the relationship between self-control and positive life outcomes. *Journal of Personality and Social Psychology, 109*(3), 508–525. https://doi.org/10.1037/pspp0000026

Garzón, J., Kinshuk, Baldiris, S., Gutiérrez, J., & Pavón, J. (2020). How do pedagogical approaches affect the impact of augmented reality on education? A meta-analysis and research synthesis. *Educational Research Review, 31*, Article 100334. https://doi.org/10.1016/j.edurev.2020.100334

Gaspard, H., & Lauermann, F. (2021). Emotionally and motivationally supportive classrooms: A state-trait analysis of lesson- and classroom-specific variation in teacher- and student-reported teacher enthusiasm and student engagement. *Learning and Instruction, 75*, Article 101494. https://doi.org/10.1016/j.learninstruc.2021.101494

Gawronski, B., & Bodenhausen, G. V. (2006). Associative and propositional processes in evaluation: An integrative review of implicit and explicit attitude change. *Psychological Bulletin, 132*(5), 692–731. https://doi.org/10.1037/0033-2909.132.5.692

Gerbeth, S., Stamouli, E., & Mulder, R. H. (2022). The relationships between emotional competence and team learning behaviours. *Educational Research Review, 36*. https://doi.org/10.1016/j.edurev.2022.100439

Gicheva, D. (2022). Teachers' working hours during the COVID-19 pandemic. *Educational Researcher, 51*(1), 85–87.

Gill, A., Trask-Kerr, K., & Vella-Brodrick, D. (2021). Systematic review of adolescent conceptions of success: Implications for wellbeing and positive education. *Educational Psychology Review, 33*(4), 1553–1582. https://doi.org/10.1007/s10648-021-09605-w

Gjicali, K., Finn, B. M., & Hebert, D. (2020). Effects of belief generation on social exploration, culturally-appropriate actions, and cross-cultural concept learning in a game-based social simulation. *Computers & Education, 156*, Article 103959. https://doi.org/10.1016/j.compedu.2020.103959

Glass, G. V. (1976). Primary, secondary, and meta-analysis of research. *Educational Researcher, 5*(10), 3–8. https://doi.org/10.2307/1174772

Gluschkoff, K., Elovainio, M., Kinnunen, U., Mullola, S., Hintsanen, M., Keltikangas-Järvinen, L., et al. (2016). Work stress, poor recovery and burnout in teachers. *Occupational Medicine, 66*(7), 564–570. https://doi.org/10.1093/occmed/kqw086

Goddard, R. D., Skrla, L., & Salloum, S. J. (2017). The role of collective efficacy in closing student achievement gaps: A mixed methods study of school leadership for excellence and equity. *Journal of Education for Students Placed at Risk, 22*(4), 220–236

Goldberg, P., Sümer, Ö., Stürmer, K., Wagner, W., Göllner, R., Gerjets, P., et al. (2021). Attentive or not? Toward a machine learning approach to assessing students' visible engagement in classroom instruction. *Educational Psychology Review, 33*(1). 27–49. https://doi.org/10.1007/s10648-019-09514-z

Goodfellow, S., & Nowicki, S., Jr. (2009). Social adjustment, academic adjustment, and the ability to identify emotion in facial expressions of 7-year-old children. *The Journal of Genetic Psychology: Research and Theory on Human Development, 170*(3), 234–243. https://doi.org/10.1080/00221320903218281

Google. (2023). *Bard* (September 27 version) [Large language model]. Accessed at http://bard.google.com on October 14, 2023.

Gordon, M. F., & Louis, K. S. (2009). Linking parent and community involvement with student achievement: Comparing principal and teacher perceptions of stakeholder influence. *American Journal of Education, 116*(1), 1–31.

Graham, S. (2020). An attributional theory of motivation. *Contemporary Educational Psychology, 61*, Article 101861. https://doi.org/10.1016/j.cedpsych.2020.101861

Graham, S., Kiuhara, S. A., & MacKay, M. (2020). The effects of writing on learning in science, social studies, and mathematics: A meta-analysis. *Review of Educational Research, 90*(2), 179–226. https://doi.org/10.3102/0034654320914744

Grandey, A. A. (2000). Emotional regulation in the workplace: A new way to conceptualize emotional labor. *Journal of Occupational Health Psychology, 5*(1), 95–110. https://doi.org/10.1037/1076-8998.5.1.95

Grandey, A. A. (2003). When "the show must go on": Surface acting and deep acting as determinants of emotional exhaustion and peer-rated service delivery. *Academy of Management Journal, 46*(1), 86–96.

Grandey, A. A., & Gabriel, A. S. (2015). Emotional labor at a crossroads: Where do we go from here? *Annual Review of Organizational Psychology and Organizational Behavior, 2*, 323–349. https://doi.org/10.1146/annurev-orgpsych-032414-111400

Grassinger, R., Scheunpflug, A., Zeinz, H., & Dresel, M. (2018). Smart is who makes lots of errors? The relevance of adaptive reactions to errors and a positive error climate for academic achievement. *High Ability Studies, 29*(1), 37–49. https://doi.org/10.1080/13598139.2018.1459294

Greene, J. A., Copeland, D. Z., & Deekens, V. M. (2021). A model of technology incidental learning effects. *Educational Psychology Review, 33*(3). 883–913. https://doi.org/10.1007/s10648-020-09575-5

Grissom, J. A., Egalite, A. J., & Lindsay, C. A. (2021). *How principals affect students and schools: A systematic synthesis of two decades of research.* New York: The Wallace Foundation.

Grissom, J. A., Loeb, S., & Master, B. K. (2013). Effective instructional time use for school leaders. *Educational Researcher, 42*(8), 433–444.

Grosse, C. S., & Renkl, A. (2007). Finding and fixing errors in worked examples: Can this foster learning outcomes? *Learning and Instruction, 17*(6), 612–634. https://doi.org/10.1016/j.learninstruc.2007.09.008

Hachfeld, A., Anders, Y., Schroeder, S., Stanat, P., & Kunter, M. (2010). Does immigration background matter? How teachers' predictions of students' performance relate to student background. *International Journal of Educational Research, 49*(2–3), 78–91. https://doi.org/10.1016/j.ijer.2010.09.002

Hadwin, A. F., Järvelä, S., & Miller, M. (2011). Self-regulated, co-regulated, and socially shared regulation of learning. In B. J. Zimmerman & D. H. Schunk (Eds.), *Handbook of self-regulation of learning and performance* (pp. 65–84). New York: Routledge.

Hagan, C. A., Halberstadt, A. G., Cooke, A. N., & Garner, P. W. (2020). Teachers' beliefs about children's anger and skill in recognizing children's anger expressions. *Frontiers in Psychology, 11*, 474. https://doi.org/10.3389/fpsyg.2020.00474

Hagenauer, G., Hascher, T., & Volet, S. E. (2015). Teacher emotions in the classroom: Associations with students' engagement, classroom discipline and the interpersonal teacher-student relationship. *European Journal of Psychology of Education, 30*(4), 385–403. https://doi.org/10.1007/s10212-015-0250-0

Halberstadt, A. G., Castro, V. L., Chu, Q., Lozada, F. T., & Sims, C. M. (2018). Preservice teachers' racialized emotion recognition, anger bias, and hostility attributions. *Contemporary Educational Psychology, 54*, 125–138. https://doi.org/10.1016/j.cedpsych.2018.06.004

Hattan, C., & Alexander, P. A. (2021). The effects of knowledge activation training on rural middle-school students' expository text comprehension: A mixed-models study. *Journal of Educational Psychology, 113*(5), 879–897. http://dx.doi.org/10.1037/edu0000623

Hattie, J. (2009). *Visible learning: A synthesis of over 800 meta-analyses relating to achievement.* New York: Routledge.

Hattie, J. (2012). *Visible learning for teachers: Maximizing impact on learning.* New York: Routledge.

Hattie, J. (2015). The applicability of Visible Learning to higher education. *Scholarship of Teaching and Learning in Psychology, 1*(1), 79–91. https://doi.org/10.1037/stl0000021

Hattie, J. (2023). *Visible learning: The sequel. A synthesis of over 2,100 meta-analyses relating to achievement.* New York: Routledge.

Hattie, J., Hodis, F. A., & Kang, S. H. K. (2020). Theories of motivation: Integration and ways forward. *Contemporary Educational Psychology, 61,* Article 101865. https://doi.org/10.1016/j.cedpsych.2020.101865

Haynes, M. (2014). *On the path to equity: Improving the effectiveness of beginning teachers.* Accessed at https://all4ed.org/reports-factsheets/path-to-equity/ on October 23, 2023.

Heflebower, T., Hoegh, J. K., & Warrick, P. (2014). *A school leader's guide to standards-based grading.* Bloomington, IN: Marzano Resources.

Hemelt, S. W., Ladd, H. F., & Clifton, C. R. (2021). Do teacher assistants improve student outcomes? Evidence from school funding cutbacks in North Carolina. *Educational Evaluation and Policy Analysis, 43*(2), 280–304. https://doi.org/10.3102/0162373721990361

Hendriks, M. A., & Scheerens, J. (2013). School leadership effects revisited: A review of empirical studies guided by indirect-effect models. *School Leadership & Management, 33*(4), 373–394. https://doi.org/10.1080/13632434.2013.813458

Herman, K. C., Reinke, W. M., Dong, N., & Bradshaw, C. P. (2022). Can effective classroom behavior management increase student achievement in middle school? Findings from a group randomized trial. *Journal of Educational Psychology, 114*(1), 144–160. http://dx.doi.org/10.1037/edu0000641

Hew, K. F., Bai, S., Dawson, P., & Lo, C. K. (2021). Meta-analyses of flipped classroom studies: A review of methodology. *Educational Research Review, 33,* Article 100393. https://doi.org/10.1016/j.edurev.2021.100393

Hillmayr, D., Ziernwald, L., Reinhold, F., Hofer, S. I., & Reiss, K. M. (2020). The potential of digital tools to enhance mathematics and science learning in secondary schools: A context-specific meta-analysis. *Computers & Education, 153,* Article 103897. https://doi.org/10.1016/j.compedu.2020.103897

Hochschild, A. R. (1983). *The managed heart: Commercialization of human feeling.* Oakland: University of California Press.

Hofmann, W., Baumeister, R. F., Förster, G., & Vohs, K. D. (2012). Everyday temptations: An experience sampling study of desire, conflict, and self-control. *Journal of Personality and Social Psychology, 102*(6), 1318–1335. https://doi.org/10.1037/a0026545

Hollingworth, L. (2012). Why leadership matters: Empowering teachers to implement formative assessment. *Journal of Educational Administration, 50*(3), 365–379.

Hollingworth, L., Olsen, D., Asikin-Garmager, A., & Cunningham, K. M. W. (2018). Initiating conversations and opening doors: How principals establish a positive building culture to sustain school improvement efforts. *Educational Management Administration & Leadership, 46*(6), 1014–1034.

Holmes, J., Guy, J., Kievit, R. A., Bryant, A., Mareva, S., CALM Team, et al. (2021). Cognitive dimensions of learning in children with problems in attention, learning, and memory. *Journal of Educational Psychology, 113*(7), 1454–1480. https://doi.org/10.1037/edu0000644

Hord, S. M. (1986). A synthesis of research on organizational collaboration. *Educational Leadership, 43*(5), 22–26.

Hord, S. M. (1997). *Professional learning communities: Communities of continuous inquiry and improvement.* Austin, TX: Southwest Educational Development Laboratory.

Howard, M. C., & Gutworth, M. B. (2020). A meta-analysis of virtual reality training programs for social skill development. *Computers & Education, 144*, Article 103707. https://doi.org/10.1016/j.compedu.2019.103707

Howe, C., Hennessy, S., Mercer, N., Vrikki, M., & Wheatley, L. (2019). Teacher-student dialogue during classroom teaching: Does it really impact on student outcomes? *Journal of the Learning Sciences, 28*(4–5), 462–512. https://doi.org/10.1080/10508406.2019.1573730

Hu, L., Chen, G., Li, P., & Huang, J. (2021). Multimedia effect in problem solving: A meta-analysis. *Educational Psychology Review, 33*(4), 1717–1747. https://doi.org/10.1007/s10648-021-09610-z

Huggins, K. S., Scheurich, J. J., & Morgan, J. R. (2011). Professional learning communities as a leadership strategy to drive math success in an urban high school serving diverse, low-income students: A case study. *Journal of Education for Students Placed at Risk, 16*(2), 67–88.

Hughes, J. N., Gleason, K. A., & Zhang, D. (2005). Relation influences on teachers' perceptions of academic competence in academically at-risk minority and majority first grade students. *Journal of School Psychology, 43*(4), 303–320. https://doi.org/10.1016/j.jsp.2005.07.001

Hülsheger, U. R., Lang, J. W. B., & Maier, G. W. (2010). Emotional labor, strain, and performance: Testing reciprocal relationships in a longitudinal panel study. *Journal of Occupational Health Psychology, 15*(4), 505–521. https://doi.org/10.1037/a0021003

Hülsheger, U. R., & Schewe, A. F. (2011). On the costs and benefits of emotional labor: A meta-analysis of three decades of research. *Journal of Occupational Health Psychology, 16*(3), 361–389. https://doi.org/10.1037/a0022876

Husén, T. (Ed.). (1967a). *International study of achievement in mathematics* (Vol. 1). New York: Wiley.

Husén, T. (Ed.). (1967b). *International study of achievement in mathematics* (Vol. 2). New York: Wiley.

Hussar, B., Zhang, J., Hein, S., Wang, K., Roberts, A., Cui, J., et al. (2020). *The condition of education 2020* (NCES 2020–144). U.S. Department of Education. Accessed at https://nces.ed.gov/pubsearch/pubsinfo.asp?pubid=2020144 on July 13, 2023.

Iancu, A. E., Rusu, A., Măroiu, C., Păcurar, R., & Maricuţoiu, L. P. (2018). The effectiveness of interventions aimed at reducing teacher burnout: A meta-analysis. *Educational Psychology Review, 30*(2), 373–396. https://doi.org/10.1007/s10648-017-9420-8

İnan-Kaya, G., & Rubie-Davies, C. M. (2022). Teacher classroom interactions and behaviours: Indications of bias. *Learning and Instruction, 78*, Article 101516. https://doi.org/10.1016/j.learninstruc.2021.101516

Izard, C., Fine, S., Schultz, D., Mostow, A., Ackerman, B., & Youngstrom, E. (2001). Emotion knowledge as a predictor of social behavior and academic competence in children at risk. *Psychological Science, 12*(1), 18–23. https://doi.org/10.1111/1467-9280.00304

Jacobson, M. J., Markauskaite, L., Portolese, A., Kapur, M., Lai, P. K., & Roberts, G. (2017). Designs for learning about climate change as a complex system. *Learning and Instruction, 52*, 1–14. https://doi.org/10.1016/j.learninstruc.2017.03.007

Jacobson, S. L., Brooks, S., Giles, C., Johnson, L., & Ylimaki, R. (2007). Successful leadership in three high-poverty urban elementary schools. *Leadership and Policy in Schools, 6*(4), 291–317.

Järvelä, S. (2006). Personalised learning? New insights into fostering learning capacity. *Personalising education* (pp. 31–46). Paris: OECD.

Johnson, E. S., Crawford, A. R., Zheng, Y., & Moylan, L. A. (2021). Does special educator effectiveness vary depending on the observation instrument used? *Educational Measurement: Issues and Practice, 40*(1), 36–43. https://doi.org/10.1111/emip.12394

Johnson, E. S., Zheng, Y., Crawford, A. R., & Moylan, L. A. (2018). Developing an explicit instruction special education teacher observation rubric. *The Journal of Special Education*, *53*(1), 28–40. https://doi.org/10.1177/0022466918796224

Jonsson, B., Wiklund-Hörnqvist, C., Stenlund, T., Andersson, M., & Nyberg, L. (2021). A learning method for all: The testing effect is independent of cognitive ability. *Journal of Educational Psychology*, *113*(5), 972–985. http://dx.doi.org/10.1037/edu0000627

Junker, R., Donker, M. H., & Mainhard, T. (2021). Potential classroom stressors of teachers: An audiovisual and physiological approach. *Learning and Instruction*, *75*, Article 101495. https://doi.org/10.1016/j.learninstruc.2021.101495

Junker, R., & Holodynski, M. (2022). Teaching versus watching? Using video feedback to counter teacher stress. *Teacher Development*, *26*(4), 472–491. https://doi.org/10.1080/13664530.2022.2089221

Kammerer, Y., Meier, N., & Stahl, E. (2016). Fostering secondary-school students' intertext model formation when reading a set of websites: The effectiveness of source prompts. *Computers & Education*, *102*, 52–64. http://dx.doi.org/10.1016/j.compedu.2016.07.001

Kane, T. J., McCaffrey, D. F., Miller, T., & Staiger, D. O. (2013). *Have we identified effective teachers?* Seattle, WA: Bill & Melinda Gates Foundation. Accessed at https://usprogram.gatesfoundation.org/-/media/dataimport/resources/pdf/2016/12/met-validating-using-random-assignment-research-paper.pdf on July 13, 2023.

Kapur, M. (2008). Productive failure. *Cognition and Instruction*, *26*(3), 379–424. https://doi.org/10.1080/07370000802212669

Kapur, M. (2012). Productive failure in learning the concept of variance. *Instructional Science*, *40*(4), 651–672.

Kapur, M. (2014). Productive failure in learning math. *Cognitive Science*, *38*(5), 1008–1022. https://doi.org/10.1111/cogs.12107

Kapur, M., & Bielaczyc, K. (2012). Designing for productive failure. *Journal of the Learning Sciences*, *21*(1), 45–83. https://doi.org/10.1080/10508406.2011.591717

Karadağ, E. (2020). The effect of educational leadership on students' achievement: A cross-cultural meta-analysis research on studies between 2008 and 2018. *Asia Pacific Education Review*, *21*(1), 49–64. https://doi.org/10.1007/s12564-019-09612-1

Karadağ, E., Bektaş, F., Çoğaltay, N., & Yalçın, M. (2015). The effect of educational leadership on students' achievement: A meta-analysis study. *Asia Pacific Education Review*, *16*(1), 79–93. https://doi.org/10.1007/s12564-015-9357-x

Khoury, C. (2014). *The effect of co-teaching on the academic achievement outcomes of students with disabilities: A meta-analytic synthesis* [Doctoral dissertation, University of North Texas]. UNT Doctoral Dissertations. Accessed at https://digital.library.unt.edu/ark:/67531/metadc699966/m2/1/high_res_d/dissertation.pdf on November 15, 2023.

Kim, H. Y., LaRusso, M. D., Hsin, L. B., Harbaugh, A. G., Selman, R. L., & Snow, C. E. (2018). Social perspective-taking performance: Construct, measurement, and relations with academic performance and engagement. *Journal of Applied Developmental Psychology*, *57*, 24–41. https://doi.org/10.1016/j.appdev.2018.05.005

Kim, J., Sun, M., & Youngs, P. (2019). Developing the "will": The relationship between teachers' perceived policy legitimacy and instructional improvement. *Teachers College Record*, *121*(3).

King-Sears, M. E., Stefanidis, A., Berkeley, S., & Strogilos, V. (2021). Does co-teaching improve academic achievement for students with disabilities? A meta-analysis. *Educational Research Review, 34*, Article 100405. https://doi.org/10.1016/j.edurev.2021.100405

Kingsley, T. L., Cassady, J. C., & Tancock, S. M. (2015). Successfully promoting 21st century online research skills: Interventions in 5th-grade classrooms. *Reading Horizons, 54*(2), 91–134.

Klingbeil, D. A., & Renshaw, T. L. (2018). Mindfulness-based interventions for teachers: A meta-analysis of the emerging evidence base. *School Psychology Quarterly, 33*(4), 501–511. https://doi.org/10.1037/spq0000291

Kraft, M. A. (2020). Interpreting effect sizes of education interventions. *Educational Researcher, 49*(4), 241–253. https://doi.org/10.3102/0013189X20912798

Kraft, M. A., & Gilmour, A. F. (2016). Can principals promote teacher development as evaluators? A case study of principals' views and experiences. *Educational Administration Quarterly, 52*(5), 711–753.

Krämer, S., Möller, J., & Zimmermann, F. (2021). Inclusive education of students with general learning difficulties: A meta-analysis. *Review of Educational Research, 91*(3), 432–478. https://doi.org/10.3102/0034654321998072

Kraushar, J. M., & Novak, D. C. (2010). Examining the affects of student multitasking with laptops during the lecture. *Journal of Information Systems Education, 21*(2), 241–251.

Kretlow, A. G., & Bartholomew, C. C. (2010). Using coaching to improve the fidelity of evidence-based practices: A review of studies. *Teacher Education and Special Education, 33*(4), 279–299.

Krou, M. R., Fong, C. J., & Hoff, M. A. (2021). Achievement motivation and academic dishonesty: A meta-analytic investigation. *Educational Psychology Review, 33*(2), 427–458. https://doi.org/10.1007/s10648-020-09557-7

Kuhn, D. (2022). Metacognition matters in many ways. *Educational Psychologist, 57*(2), 73–86. https://doi.org/10.1080/00461520.2021.1988603

Kunter, M., Klusmann, U., Baumert, J., Richter, D., Voss, T., & Hachfeld, A. (2013). Professional competence of teachers: Effects on instructional quality and student development. *Journal of Educational Psychology, 105*(3), 805–820. https://doi.org/10.1037/a0032583

Kuo, Y.-L., Casillas, A., Allen, J., & Robbins, S. (2021). The moderating effects of psychosocial factors on achievement gains: A longitudinal study. *Journal of Educational Psychology, 113*(1), 138–156. http://dx.doi.org/10.1037/edu0000471

Lai, P. K., Portolese, A., & Jacobson, M. J. (2017). Does sequence matter? Productive failure and designing online authentic learning for process engineering. *British Journal of Educational Technology, 48*(6), 1217–1227. https://doi.org/10.1111/bjet.12492

Lally, P., van Jaarsveld, C. H. M., Potts, H. W. W., & Wardle, J. (2010). How are habits formed: Modeling habit formation in the real world. *European Journal of Social Psychology, 40*(6), 998–1009. https://doi.org/10.1002/ejsp.674

Landl, E. (2020). Alignment challenges within the context of federal peer review. *Educational Measurement: Issues and Practice, 39*(2), 23–27. https://doi.org/10.1111/emip.12330

Lauermann, F., & Butler, R. (2021). The elusive links between teachers' teaching-related emotions, motivations, and self-regulation and students' educational outcomes. *Educational Psychologist, 56*(4), 243–249. https://doi.org/10.1080/00461520.2021.1991800

Lazarides, R., Fauth, B., Gaspard, H., & Göllner, R. (2021). Teacher self-efficacy and enthusiasm: Relations to changes in student-perceived teaching quality at the beginning of secondary education. *Learning and Instruction, 73*, Article 101435. https://doi.org/10.1016/j.learninstruc.2020.101435

Lazarides, R., & Schiefele, U. (2021). The relative strength of relations between different facets of teacher motivation and core dimensions of teaching quality in mathematics—A multilevel analysis. *Learning and Instruction, 76*, Article 101489. https://doi.org/10.1016/j.learninstruc.2021.101489

Lazarides, R., & Watt, H. M. G. (2015). Girls' and boys' perceived mathematics teacher beliefs, classroom learning environments and mathematical career intentions. *Contemporary Educational Psychology, 41*, 51–61. https://doi:10.1016/j.cedpsych.2014.11.005

Legette, K. B., Halberstadt, A. G., & Majors, A. T. (2021). Teachers' understanding of racial inequity predicts their perceptions of students' behaviors. *Contemporary Educational Psychology, 67*, Article 102014. https://doi.org/10.1016/j.cedpsych.2021.102014

Leithwood, K., Louis, K. S., Anderson, S., & Wahlstrom, K. (2004). *Review of research: How leadership influences student learning.* New York: Wallace Foundation.

Leithwood, K., & Sun, J. (2012). The nature and effects of transformational school leadership: A meta-analytic review of unpublished research. *Educational Administration Quarterly, 48*(3), 387–423. https://doi.org/10.1177/0013161X11436268

Liebowitz, D. D., & Porter, L. (2019). The effect of principal behaviors on student, teacher, and school outcomes: A systematic review and meta-analysis of the empirical literature. *Review of Educational Research, 89*(5), 785–827. https://doi.org/10.3102/0034654319866133

Lindner, M. A. (2020). Representational and decorative pictures in science and mathematics tests: Do they make a difference? *Learning and Instruction, 68*, Article 101345. https://doi.org/10.1016/j.learninstruc.2020.101345

Lindner, M. A., Schult, J., & Mayer, R. E. (2022). A multimedia effect for multiple-choice and constructed-response test items. *Journal of Educational Psychology, 114*(1), 72–88. https://doi.org/10.1037/edu0000646

Lipsey, M. W., Puzio, K., Yun, C., Hebert, M. A., Steinka-Fry, K., Cole, M. W., et al. (2012, November). *Translating the statistical representation of the effects of education interventions into more readily interpretable forms.* Washington, DC: National Center for Special Education Research.

Lobczowski, N. G. (2020). Bridging gaps and moving forward: Building a new model for socioemotional formation and regulation. *Educational Psychologist, 55*(2), 53–68. https://doi.org/10.1080/00461520.2019.1670064

Locke, E. A., & Latham, G. P. (2013). Goal setting theory: The current state. In E. A. Locke & G. P. Latham (Eds.), *New developments in goal setting and task performance* (pp. 623–630). New York: Routledge. https://doi.org/10.4324/9780203082744

Loderer, K., Pekrun, R., & Lester, J. C. (2020). Beyond cold technology: A systematic review and meta-analysis on emotions in technology-based learning environments. *Learning and Instruction, 70*, Article 101162. https://doi.org/10.1016/j.learninstruc.2018.08.002

Loibl, K., & Rummel, N. (2014a). Knowing what you don't know makes failure productive. *Learning and Instruction, 34*, 74–85. https://doi.org/10.1016/j.learninstruc.2014.08.004

Loibl, K., & Rummel, N. (2014b). The impact of guidance during problem-solving prior to instruction on students' inventions and learning outcomes. *Instructional Science, 42*(3), 305–326.

Lortie-Forgues, H., Sio, U. N., & Inglis, M. (2021). How should educational effects be communicated to teachers? *Educational Researcher, 50*(6), 345–354. https://doi.org/10.3102/0013189X20987856

Losinski, M., Sanders, S., Parks-Ennis, R., Wiseman, N., & Katsiyannis, A. (2019). An investigation of co-teaching to improve academic achievement of students with disabilities: A meta-analysis. *Journal of the American Academy of Special Education Professionals*, 149–170. Accessed at https://www.naset.org/index.php?id=5158 on July 13, 2023.

Louis, K. S., Leithwood, K., Wahlstrom, K. L., & Anderson, S. E. (2010). *Investigating the links to improved student learning: Final report of research findings*. Minneapolis: University of Minnesota, Center for Applied Research and Educational Improvement.

Macedo-Rouet, M., Braasch, J. L. G., Britt, M. A., & Rouet, J.-F. (2013). Teaching fourth and fifth graders to evaluate information sources during text comprehension. *Cognition and Instruction*, *31*(2), 204–226. https://doi.org/10.1080/07370008.2013.769995

Madigan, D. J., & Curran, T. (2021). Does burnout affect academic achievement? A meta-analysis of over 100,000 students. *Educational Psychology Review*, *33*(2), 387–405. https://doi.org/10.1007/s10648-020-09533-1

Marion, S. B., & Thorley, C. (2016). A meta-analytic review of collaborative inhibition and postcollaborative memory: Testing the predictions of the retrieval strategy disruption hypothesis. *Psychological Bulletin*, *142*(11), 1141–1164. https://doi.org/10.1037/bul0000071

Markus, H., & Nurius, P. (1986). Possible selves. *American Psychologist*, *41*(9), 954–969. Accessed at https://web.stanford.edu/~hazelm/publications/1986_Markus%20&%20Nurius_PossibleSelves.pdf on November 2, 2023.

Martin, A. J., Ginns, P., Burns, E. C., Kennett, R., & Pearson, J. (2021). Load reduction instruction in science and students' science engagement and science achievement. *Journal of Educational Psychology*, *113*(6), 1126–1142. http://dx.doi.org/10.1037/edu0000552

Marzano, R. J. (1991). *Cultivating thinking in English and the language arts*. Urbana, IL: National Council of Teachers of English.

Marzano, R. J. (1992). *A different kind of classroom: Teaching with Dimensions of Learning*. Alexandria, VA: ASCD.

Marzano, R. J. (2000). *Transforming classroom grading*. Alexandria, VA: ASCD.

Marzano, R. J. (2001). *Designing a new taxonomy of educational objectives*. Thousand Oaks, CA: Corwin Press.

Marzano, R. J. (2003a). *Classroom management that works: Research-based strategies for every teacher*. Alexandria, VA: ASCD.

Marzano, R. J. (2003b). *What works in schools: Translating research into action*. Alexandria, VA: ASCD.

Marzano, R. J. (2004). *Building background knowledge for academic achievement: Research on what works in schools*. Alexandria, VA: ASCD.

Marzano, R. J. (2006). *Classroom assessment & grading that work*. Alexandria, VA: ASCD.

Marzano, R. J. (2007). *The art and science of teaching: A comprehensive framework for effective instruction*. Alexandria, VA: ASCD.

Marzano, R. J. (2009a). *Designing and teaching learning goals and objectives*. Bloomington, IN: Marzano Resources.

Marzano, R. J. (2009b). Setting the record straight on "high-yield" strategies. *Kappan*, *91*(1), 30–37.

Marzano, R. J. (2010a). *Formative assessment and standards-based grading*. Bloomington, IN: Marzano Resources.

Marzano, R. J. (Ed.). (2010b). *On excellence in teaching*. Bloomington, IN: Solution Tree Press.

Marzano, R. J. (2010c). *Teaching basic and advanced vocabulary: A framework for direct instruction.* Boston: Heinle.

Marzano, R. J. (2012). *Becoming a reflective teacher.* Bloomington, IN: Marzano Resources.

Marzano, R. J. (2013). *Building basic vocabulary: Teacher's guide.* Boston: National Geographic Learning.

Marzano, R. J. (2017). *The new art and science of teaching.* Bloomington, IN: Solution Tree Press.

Marzano, R. J. (2018). *Making classroom assessments reliable and valid.* Bloomington, IN: Solution Tree Press.

Marzano, R. J. (2019a). *The handbook for the new art and science of teaching.* Bloomington, IN: Solution Tree Press.

Marzano, R. J. (2019b). *Understanding rigor in the classroom.* West Palm Beach, FL: Learning Sciences International.

Marzano, R. J. (2020). *Teaching basic, advanced, and academic vocabulary: A comprehensive framework for elementary instruction.* Bloomington, IN: Marzano Resources.

Marzano, R. J., & Abbott, S. D. (2022). *Teaching in a competency-based elementary school.* Bloomington, IN: Marzano Resources.

Marzano, R. J., & Arredondo, D. (1987). *Tactics for thinking: Teacher's manual.* Alexandria, VA: ASCD.

Marzano, R. J., Aschoff, A. S., & Avila, A. (2022). *Teaching in a competency-based secondary school.* Bloomington, IN: Marzano Resources.

Marzano, R. J., Brandt, R. S., Hughes, C. S., Jones, B. F., Presseisen, B. Z., Rankin, S. C., et al. (1988). *Dimensions of thinking: A framework for curriculum and instruction.* Alexandria, VA: ASCD.

Marzano, R. J., & Brown, J. L. (2009). *A handbook for the art and science of teaching.* Alexandria, VA: ASCD.

Marzano, R. J., & DiStefano, P. (1977). *DiComp: A diagnostic approach to teaching written composition.* Indian Rocks Beach, FL: Relevant Productions.

Marzano, R. J., & DiStefano, P. (1981). *The writing process.* New York: D. Van Nostrand.

Marzano, R. J., Dodson, C. W., Simms, J. A., & Wipf, J. P. (2022). *Ethical test preparation in the classroom.* Bloomington, IN: Marzano Resources.

Marzano, R. J., Frontier, T., & Livingston, D. (2011). *Effective supervision: Supporting the art and science of teaching.* Alexandria, VA: ASCD.

Marzano, R. J., Gaddy, B. B., Foseid, M. C., Foseid, M. P., & Marzano, J. S. (2005). *A handbook for classroom management that works.* Alexandria, VA: ASCD.

Marzano, R. J., Hagerty, P. J., Valencia, S. W., & DiStefano, P. P. (1987). *Reading diagnosis and instruction: Theory into practice.* Englewood Cliffs, NJ: Prentice Hall.

Marzano, R. J., & Hardy, P. B. (2023). *Leading a competency-based secondary school.* Bloomington, IN: Marzano Resources.

Marzano, R. J., & Haystead, M. W. (2008). *Making standards useful in the classroom.* Alexandria, VA: ASCD.

Marzano, R. J., & Heflebower, T. (2012). *Teaching and assessing 21st century skills.* Bloomington, IN: Marzano Resources.

Marzano, R. J., Heflebower, T., Hoegh, J. K., Warrick, P., & Grift, G. (2016). *Collaborative teams that transform schools: The next step in PLCs.* Bloomington, IN: Marzano Resources.

Marzano, R. J., & Kendall, J. S. (1996). *A comprehensive guide to designing standards-based districts, schools, and classrooms.* Alexandria, VA: ASCD.

Marzano, R. J., & Kendall, J. S. (1998). *Implementing standards-based education*. Washington, DC: National Education Association.

Marzano, R. J., & Kendall, J. S. (1999). *Essential knowledge: The debate over what American students should know*. Aurora, CO: Mid-continent Regional Educational Laboratory.

Marzano, R. J., & Kendall, J. S. (2007). *The new taxonomy of educational objectives* (2nd ed.). Thousand Oaks, CA: Corwin Press.

Marzano, R. J., & Kendall, J. S. (2008). *Designing and assessing educational objectives: Applying the new taxonomy*. Thousand Oaks, CA: Corwin Press.

Marzano, R. J., & Kosena, B. J. (2022). *Leading a competency-based elementary school*. Bloomington, IN: Marzano Resources.

Marzano, R. J., & Marzano, J. S. (1988). *A cluster approach to elementary vocabulary instruction*. Newark, DE: International Reading Association.

Marzano, R. J., & Marzano, J. S. (2015). *Managing the inner world of teaching: Emotions, interpretations, and actions*. Bloomington, IN: Marzano Resources.

Marzano, R. J., Norford, J. S., Finn, M., & Finn, D. (2017). *A handbook for personalized competency-based education*. Bloomington, IN: Marzano Resources.

Marzano, R. J., Norford, J. S., Paynter, D. E., Pickering, D. J., & Gaddy, B. B. (2001). *A handbook for classroom instruction that works*. Alexandria, VA: ASCD.

Marzano, R. J., Norford, J. S., & Ruyle, M. (2019). *The new art and science of classroom assessment*. Bloomington, IN: Solution Tree Press.

Marzano, R. J., & Paynter, D. E. (1994). *New approaches to literacy: Helping students develop reading and writing skills*. Washington, DC: American Psychological Association.

Marzano, R. J., Paynter, D. E, & Doty, J. K. (2003). *The pathfinder project: Exploring the power of one—Teacher's manual*. Conifer, CO: Pathfinder Education.

Marzano, R. J., & Pickering, D. J. (1997). *Dimensions of learning: Teacher's manual* (2nd ed.). Alexandria, VA: ASCD.

Marzano, R. J., & Pickering, D. J. (2005). *Building academic vocabulary: Teacher's manual*. Alexandria, VA: ASCD.

Marzano, R. J., & Pickering, D. J. (2011). *The highly engaged classroom*. Bloomington, IN: Marzano Resources.

Marzano, R. J., Pickering, D. J., & McTighe, J. (1993). *Assessing student outcomes: Performance assessment using the Dimensions of Learning model*. Alexandria, VA: ASCD.

Marzano, R. J., Pickering, D. J., & Pollock, J. E. (2001). *Classroom instruction that works: Research-based strategies for increasing student achievement*. Alexandria, VA: ASCD.

Marzano, R. J., Rains, C. L., & Warrick, P. B. (with Simms, J. A.). (2021). *Improving teacher development and evaluation: A guide for leaders, coaches, and teachers*. Bloomington, IN: Marzano Resources.

Marzano, R. J., Rogers, K., & Simms, J. A. (2015). *Vocabulary for the new science standards*. Bloomington, IN: Marzano Resources.

Marzano, R. J., Scott, D., Boogren, T. H., & Newcomb, M. L. (2017). *Motivating and inspiring students: Strategies to awaken the learner*. Bloomington, IN: Marzano Resources.

Marzano, R. J., & Simms, J. A. (2013a). *Coaching classroom instruction*. Bloomington, IN: Marzano Resources.

Marzano, R. J., & Simms, J. A. (2013b). *Vocabulary for the Common Core*. Bloomington, IN: Marzano Resources.

Marzano, R. J., & Simms, J. A. (2014). *Questioning sequences in the classroom*. Bloomington, IN: Marzano Resources.

Marzano, R. J., & Toth, M. D. (2013). *Teacher evaluation that makes a difference: A new model for teacher growth and student achievement*. Alexandria, VA: ASCD.

Marzano, R. J., Warrick, P. B., & Acosta, M. I. (2024). *Five big ideas for leading a High Reliability School*. Bloomington, IN: Marzano Resources.

Marzano, R. J., Warrick, P. B., Rains, C. L., & DuFour, R. (2018). *Leading a High Reliability School*. Bloomington, IN: Solution Tree Press.

Marzano, R. J., Warrick, P., & Simms, J. A. (2014). *A handbook for High Reliability Schools: The next step in school reform*. Bloomington, IN: Marzano Resources.

Marzano, R. J., & Waters, T. (2009). *District leadership that works: Striking the right balance*. Bloomington, IN: Solution Tree Press.

Marzano, R. J., Waters, T., & McNulty, B. A. (2005). *School leadership that works: From research to results*. Alexandria, VA: ASCD.

Marzano, R. J., & Yanoski, D. C. (2016). *Proficiency scales for the new science standards: A framework for science instruction and assessment*. Bloomington, IN: Marzano Resources.

Marzano, R. J., Yanoski, D. C., Hoegh, J. K., & Simms, J. A. (2013). *Using Common Core standards to enhance classroom instruction and assessment*. Bloomington, IN: Marzano Resources.

Maslow, A. H. (1943). A theory of human motivation. *Psychological Review*, *50*(4), 370–396.

Maslow, A. H. (1954). *Motivation and personality*. New York: Harper & Row.

Maslow, A. H. (1969). The farther reaches of human nature. *Journal of Transpersonal Psychology*, *1*(1), 1–9.

Maslow, A. H. (1970). *Motivation and personality* (2nd ed.). New York: Harper & Row.

Mason, L., Junyent, A. A., & Tornatora, M. C. (2014). Epistemic evaluation and comprehension of web-source information on controversial science-related topics: Effects of a short-term instructional intervention. *Computers & Education*, *76*, 143–157. https://doi.org/10.1016/j.compedu.2014.03.016

Mathan, S. A., & Koedinger, K. R. (2005). Fostering the intelligent novice: Learning from errors with metacognitive tutoring. *Educational Psychologist*, *40*(4), 257–265. https://doi.org/10.1207/s15326985ep4004_7

Mauss, I. B., & Robinson, M. D. (2009). Measures of emotion: A review. *Cognition and Emotion*, *23*(2), 209–237. https://doi.org/10.1080%2F02699930802204677

May, H., & Supovitz, J. A. (2011). The scope of principal efforts to improve instruction. *Educational Administration Quarterly*, *47*(2), 332–352.

Mayer, R. E. (2008). Applying the science of learning: Evidence-based principles for the design of multimedia instruction. *American Psychologist*, *63*(8), 760–769. https://doi.org/10.1037/0003-066X.63.8.760

Mayer, R. E. (2014a). Incorporating motivation into multimedia learning. *Learning and Instruction*, *29*, 171–173. https://doi.org/10.1016/j.learninstruc.2013.04.003

Mayer, R. E. (Ed.). (2014b). *The Cambridge handbook of multimedia learning* (2nd ed.). Cambridge, United Kingdom: Cambridge University Press.

Mazer, J. P., McKenna-Buchanan, T. P., Quinlan, M. M., & Titsworth, S. (2014). The dark side of emotion in the classroom: Emotional processes as mediators of teacher communication behaviors and student negative emotions. *Communication Education, 63*(3), 149–168. https://doi.org/10.1080/03634523.2014.904047

McKown, C., Gregory, A., & Weinstein, R. S. (2010). Expectations, stereotypes, and self-fulfilling prophecies in classroom and school life. In J. L. Meece & J. S. Eccles (Eds.), *Handbook of research on schools, schooling, and human development* (pp. 349–380). New York: Routledge.

McKown, C., & Weinstein, R. S. (2003). The development and consequences of stereotype consciousness in middle childhood. *Child Development, 74*(2), 498–515.

McKown, C., & Weinstein, R. S. (2008). Teacher expectations, classroom context, and the achievement gap. *Journal of School Psychology, 46*(3), 235–261. https://doi.org/10.1016/j.jsp.2007.05.001

McLean, L., Sparapani, N., Connor, C. M., & Day, S. (2020). Students' problem behaviors and teachers' warmth and demand as predictors of students' classroom instructional experiences in first grade. *Contemporary Educational Psychology, 61*, Article 101863. https://doi.org/10.1016/j.cedpsych.2020.101863

McMahon, M., Forde, C., & Dickson, B. (2015). Reshaping teacher education through the professional continuum. *Educational Review, 67*(2), 158–178. https://doi.org/10.1080/00131911.2013.846298

McManus, J. L., Saucier, D. A., & Reid, J. E. (2021). A meta-analytic review of interventions to improve children's attitudes toward their peers with intellectual disabilities. *Contemporary Educational Psychology, 65*, Article 101948. https://doi.org/10.1016/j.cedpsych.2021.101948

McREL International. (n.d.a). *Content knowledge: Online edition.* Accessed at https://www2.mcrel.org/compendium/ on July 14, 2023.

McREL International. (n.d.b). *Content knowledge—Online edition. The process of this work.* Accessed at https://www2.mcrel.org/compendium/docs/process.asp on July 14, 2023.

Meissel, K., Meyer, F., Yao, E. S., & Rubie-Davies, C. M. (2017). Subjectivity of teacher judgments: Exploring student characteristics that influence teacher judgments of student ability. *Teaching and Teacher Education, 65*, 48–60. https://doi.org/10.1016/j.tate.2017.02.021

Mende, S., Proske, A., & Narciss, S. (2021). Individual preparation for collaborative learning: Systematic review and synthesis. *Educational Psychologist, 56*(1), 29–53. https://doi.org/10.1080/00461520.2020.1828086

Meyer, D. K. (2014). Situating emotions in classroom practices. In R. Pekrun & L. Linnenbrink-Garcia (Eds.), *International handbook of emotions in education* (pp. 458–472). New York: Routledge.

Michaels, S., O'Connor, C., & Resnick, L. B. (2008). Deliberative discourse idealized and realized: Accountable talk in the classroom and in civic life. *Studies in Philosophy and Education, 27*(4), 283–297. https://doi.org/10.1007/s11217-007-9071-1

Miller, G. A. (1956). The magical number seven, plus or minus two: Some limits on our capacity for processing information. *Psychological Review, 63*(2), 81–97. https://doi.org/10.1037/h0043158

Morell, M., Yang, J. S., Gladstone, J. R., Faust, L. T., Ponnock, A. R., Lim, H. J., et al. (2021). Grit: The long and short of it. *Journal of Educational Psychology, 113*(5), 1038–1058. http://dx.doi.org/10.1037/edu0000594

Morris, D. B., Usher, E. L., & Chen, J. A. (2017). Reconceptualizing the sources of teaching self-efficacy: A critical review of emerging literature. *Educational Psychology Review, 29*(4), 795–833.

Morris, E. W., & Perry, B. L. (2016). The punishment gap: School suspension and racial disparities in achievement. *Social Problems, 63*(1), 68–86. https://doi.org/10.1093/socpro/spv026

Moye, M. J., Henkin, A. B., & Egley, R. J. (2005). Teacher-principal relationships: Exploring linkages between empowerment and interpersonal trust. *Journal of Educational Administration, 43*(2/3), 260–277.

Muis, K. R., Psaradellis, C., Lajoie, S. P., Di Leo, I., & Chevrier, M. (2015). The role of epistemic emotions in mathematics problem solving. *Contemporary Educational Psychology, 42*, 172–185. https://doi.org/10.1016/j.cedpsych.2015.06.003

Muntoni, F., & Retelsdorf, J. (2018). Gender-specific teacher expectations in reading—The role of teachers' gender stereotypes. *Contemporary Educational Psychology, 54*, 212–220. https://doi.org/10.1016/j.cedpsych.2018.06.012

Murphy, P. K., Wilkinson, I. A. G., Soter, A. O., Hennessey, M. N., & Alexander, J. F. (2009). Examining the effects of classroom discussion on students' comprehension of text: A meta-analysis. *Journal of Educational Psychology, 101*(3), 740–764. http://dx.doi.org/10.1037/a0015576

Myhill, D., & Jones, S. (2006). "She doesn't shout at no girls": Pupils' perceptions of gender equity in the classroom. *Cambridge Journal of Education, 36*(1), 99–113. https://doi.org/10.1080/03057640500491054

Näring, G., Briët, M., & Brouwers, A. (2006). Beyond demand–control: Emotional labour and symptoms of burnout in teachers. *Work and Stress, 20*(4), 303–315. https://doi.org/10.1080/02678370601065182

National Commission on Excellence in Education. (1983). *A nation at risk: The imperative for educational reform*. Accessed at https://edreform.com/wp-content/uploads/2013/02/A_Nation_At_Risk_1983.pdf on November 7, 2023.

National Education Goals Panel. (1991). *The national education goals report: Building a nation of learners*. Washington, DC: Author.

National Governors Association Center for Best Practices & Council of Chief State School Officers (CCSSO). (2010). *Common Core State Standards for mathematics*. Washington, DC: Authors.

Newmann, F. M., Smith, B., Allensworth, E., & Bryk, A. S. (2001). Instructional program coherence: What it is and why it should guide school improvement policy. *Educational Evaluation and Policy Analysis, 23*(4), 297–321.

Nicholson-Crotty, S., Grissom, J. A., Nicholson-Crotty, J., & Redding, C. (2016). Disentangling the causal mechanisms of representative bureaucracy: Evidence from assignment of students to gifted programs. *Journal of Public Administration Research and Theory, 26*(4), 745–757. https://doi.org/10.1093/jopart/muw024

Noetel, M., Griffith, S., Delaney, O., Harris, N. R., Sanders, T., Parker, P., et al. (2022). Multimedia design for learning: An overview of reviews with meta-meta-analysis. *Review of Educational Research, 92*(3), 413–454. https://doi.org/10.3102/00346543211052329

Nuthall, G. (1999). The way students learn: Acquiring knowledge from an integrated science and social studies unit. *Elementary School Journal, 99*(4), 303–341.

Nuthall, G., & Alton-Lee, A. (1995). Assessing classroom learning: How students use their knowledge and experience to answer classroom achievement test questions in science and social studies. *American Educational Research Journal, 32*(1), 185–223.

Nye, B., Konstantopoulos, S., & Hedges, L. V. (2004). How large are teacher effects? *Educational Evaluation and Policy Analysis, 26*(3), 237–257. https://doi.org/10.3102/01623737026003237

Oakes, J. (2005). *Keeping track: How schools structure inequality* (2nd ed.). New Haven, CT: Yale University Press.

Oliveira, S., Roberto, M. S., Veiga-Simão, A. M., & Marques-Pinto, A. (2021). A meta-analysis of the impact of social and emotional learning interventions on teachers' burnout symptoms. *Educational Psychology Review, 33*(4), 1779–1808. https://doi.org/10.1007/s10648-021-09612-x

Olivier, E., Galand, B., Morin, A. J. S., & Hospel, V. (2021). Need-supportive teaching and student engagement in the classroom: Comparing the additive, synergistic, and global contributions. *Learning and Instruction, 71,* Article 101389. https://doi.org/10.1016/j.learninstruc.2020.101389

Olszewski, B., & Crompton, H. (2020). Educational technology conditions to support the development of digital age skills. *Computers & Education, 150,* Article 103849. http://dx.doi.org/10.1016/j.compedu.2020.103849

Organisation for Economic Co-operation and Development. (2015). *Students, computers and learning. Making the connection.* Paris: Author. https://doi.org/10.1787/9789264239555-en

Ouellette, J. A., & Wood, W. (1998). Habit and intention in everyday life: The multiple processes by which past behavior predicts future behavior. *Psychological Bulletin, 124*(1), 54–74. https://doi.org/10.1037/0033-2909.124.1.54

Page, R. (1987). Teachers' perceptions of students: A link between classrooms, school cultures, and the social order. *Anthropology & Education Quarterly, 18*(2), 77–99.

Paivio, A. (1986). *Mental representations: A dual coding approach.* Oxford, United Kingdom: Oxford University Press.

Panadero, E. (2017). A review of self-regulated learning: Six models and four directions for research. *Frontiers in Psychology, 8.* https://doi.org/10.3389/fpsyg.2017.00422

Panadero, E., & Lipnevich, A. A. (2022). A review of feedback models and typologies: Towards an integrative model of feedback elements. *Educational Research Review, 35,* Article 100416. https://doi.org/10.1016/j.edurev.2021.100416

Papert, S. (1980). *Mindstorms: Children, computers, and powerful ideas.* New York: Basic Books.

Parrisius, C., Gaspard, H., Trautwein, U., & Nagengast, B. (2020). The transmission of values from math teachers to their ninth-grade students: Different mechanisms for different value dimensions? *Contemporary Educational Psychology, 62,* Article 101891. https://doi.org/10.1016/j.cedpsych.2020.101891

Patrick, S., Kennedy, K., & Powell, A. (2013). *Mean what you say: Defining and integrating personalized, blended and competency education.* Vienna, VA: International Association for K–12 Online Learning.

Pekrun, R. (2006). The control-value theory of achievement emotions: Assumptions, corollaries, and implications for educational research and practice. *Educational Psychology Review, 18*(4), 315–341. https://doi.org/10.1007/s10648-006-9029-9

Pekrun, R. (2018). Control-value theory: A social-cognitive approach to achievement emotions. In G. A. D. Liem & D. M. McInerney (Eds.), *Big theories revisited 2.* (pp. 165–192). Charlotte, NC: Information Age.

Pekrun, R. (2021). Self-appraisals and emotions: A generalized control-value approach. In T. Dicke, F. Guay, H. W. Marsh, R. G. Craven, & D. M. McInerney (Eds.), *Self: A multidisciplinary concept* (pp. 1–30). Charlotte, NC: Information Age.

Pellegrino, J. W. (2020). Important considerations for assessment to function in the service of education. *Educational Measurement: Issues and Practice, 39*(3), 81–85. https://doi.org/10.1111/emip.12372

Perry, T., Steele, C., & Hillard, A. (2003). *Young, gifted, and Black: Promoting high achievement among African-American students.* Boston: Beacon Press.

Piaget, J. (1971). *Genetic epistemology* (E. Duckworth, Trans.). New York: Norton.

Pigott, T. D., & Polanin, J. R. (2020). Methodological guidance paper: High-quality meta-analysis in a systematic review. *Review of Educational Research, 90*(1), 24–46. https://doi.org/10.3102/0034654319877153

Pinquart, M., & Ebeling, M. (2020). Parental educational expectations and academic achievement in children and adolescents—A meta-analysis. *Educational Psychology Review, 32*(2), 463–480. https://doi.org/10.1007/s10648-019-09506-z

Pintrich, P. R. (2000). The role of goal orientation in self-regulated learning. In M. Boekaerts, P. R. Pintrich, & M. Zeidner (Eds.), *Handbook of self-regulation* (pp. 451–502). San Diego, CA: Academic Press. https://doi.org/10.1016/B978-012109890-2/50043-3

Polikoff, M. S. (2020). The present and future of alignment. *Educational Measurement: Issues and Practice, 39*(2), 18–20. https://doi.org/10.1111/emip.12333

Porter, A. C. (2002). Measuring the content of instruction: Uses in research and practice. *Educational Researcher, 31*(7), 3–14. https://doi.org/10.3102/0013189X031007003

Porter, A. C., McMaken, J., Hwang, J., & Yang, R. (2011). Common Core Standards: The new U.S. intended curriculum. *Educational Researcher, 40*(3), 103–116. https://doi.10.3102/0013189X11405038

Price, H. E. (2012). Principal-teacher interactions: How affective relationships shape principal and teacher attitudes. *Educational Administration Quarterly, 48*(1), 39–85.

Price, H. E. (2015). Principals' social interactions with teachers: How principal-teacher social relations correlate with teachers' perceptions of student engagement. *Journal of Educational Administration, 53*(1), 116–139.

Pyne, J., & Borman, G. D. (2020). Replicating a scalable intervention that helps students reappraise academic and social adversity during the transition to middle school. *Journal of Research on Educational Effectiveness, 13*(4), 652–678. https://doi.org/10.1080/19345747.2020.1784330

Qin, X., Wormington, S., Guzman-Alvarez, A., & Wang, M.-T. (2021). Why does a growth mindset intervention impact achievement differently across secondary schools? Unpacking the causal mediation mechanism from a national multisite randomized experiment. *Journal of Research on Educational Effectiveness, 14*(3), 617–644. https://doi.org/10.1080/19345747.2021.1894520

Quinn, D. M. (2017). Racial attitudes of preK–12 and postsecondary educators: Descriptive evidence from nationally representative data. *Educational Researcher, 46*(7), 397–411. https://doi.org/10.3102/0013189X17727270

Radkowitsch, A., Vogel, F., & Fischer, F. (2020). Good for learning, bad for motivation? A meta-analysis on the effects of computer-supported collaboration scripts. *International Journal of Computer-Supported Collaborative Learning, 15*(1), 5–47. https://doi.org/10.1007/s11412-020-09316-4

Rankin, J. G. (2016). *First aid for teacher burnout: How you can find peace and success*. New York: Routledge.

Rapanta, C., & Felton, M. K. (2022). Learning to argue through dialogue: A review of instructional approaches. *Educational Psychology Review, 34*(2). 477–509. https://doi.org/10.1007/s10648-021-09637-2

Rau, M. A. (2020). Comparing multiple theories about learning with physical and virtual representations: Conflicting or complementary effects? *Educational Psychology Review, 32*(2), 297–325. https://doi.org/10.1007/s10648-020-09517-1

Ready, D. D., & Chu, E. M. (2015). Sociodemographic inequality in early literacy development: The role of teacher perceptual accuracy. *Early Education and Development, 26*(7), 970–987. https://doi.org/10.1080/10409289.2015.1004516

Ready, D. D., & Wright, D. L. (2011). Accuracy and inaccuracy in teachers' perceptions of young children's cognitive abilities: The role of child background and classroom context. *American Educational Research Journal, 48*(2), 335–360. https://doi.org/10.3102/0002831210374874

Reeve, J., & Cheon, S. H. (2021). Autonomy-supportive teaching: Its malleability, benefits, and potential to improve educational practice. *Educational Psychologist, 56*(1), 54–77. https://doi.org/10.1080/00461520.2020.1862657

Reeve, J., Cheon, S. H., & Jang, H. (2020). How and why students make academic progress: Reconceptualizing the student engagement construct to increase its explanatory power. *Contemporary Educational Psychology, 62*, Article 101899. https://doi.org/10.1016/j.cedpsych.2020.101899

Relkin, E., de Ruiter, L. E., & Bers, M. U. (2021). Learning to code and the acquisition of computational thinking by young children. *Computers & Education, 169*, Article 104222. https://doi.org/10.1016/j.compedu.2021.104222

Reschly, A. L., & Christenson, S. L. (2012). Jingle, jangle, and conceptual haziness: Evolution and future directions of the engagement construct. In S. L. Christenson, A. L. Reschly, & C. Wylie (Eds.), *Handbook of research on student engagement* (pp. 3–19). New York: Springer. https://doi.org/10.1007/978-1-4614-2018-7_1

Resnick, L. B., Asterhan, C. S. C., & Clarke, S. N. (Eds.). (2015). *Socializing intelligence through academic talk and dialogue.* Washington, DC: American Educational Research Association.

Resnick, L. B., Asterhan, C. S., & Clarke, S. N. (2018). Next generation research in dialogic learning. In G. E. Hall, L. F. Quinn, & D. M. Gollnick (Eds.), *The Wiley handbook of teaching and learning* (pp. 323–338). Hoboken, NJ: Wiley.

Resnick, L. B., Michaels, S., & O'Connor, M. C. (2010). How (well-structured) talk builds the mind. In D. D. Preiss & R. J. Sternberg (Eds.), *Innovations in educational psychology* (pp. 163–194). New York: Springer.

Rieger, S., Göllner, R., Spengler, M., Trautwein, U., Nagengast, B., & Roberts, B. W. (2022). The persistence of students' academic effort: The unique and combined effects of conscientiousness and individual interest. *Learning and Instruction, 80*, Article 101613. https://doi.org/10.1016/j.learninstruc.2022.101613

Rigby, J. G., Andrews-Larson, C., & Chen, I. (2020). Learning opportunities for teaching mathematics: A longitudinal case study of school leaders' influence. *Teachers College Record, 122*(7).

Rios, J. A., Ling, G., Pugh, R., Becker, D., & Bacall, A. (2020). Identifying critical 21st-century skills for workplace success: A content analysis of job advertisements. *Educational Researcher, 49*(2), 80–89. https://doi.org/10.3102/0013189X19890600

Robinson, C. D., Chande, R., Burgess, S., & Rogers, T. (2022). Parent engagement interventions are not costless: Opportunity cost and crowd out of parental investment. *Educational Evaluation and Policy Analysis, 44*(1), 170–177. https://doi.org/10.3102/01623737211030492

Robinson, V. M. J., Lloyd, C. A., & Rowe, K. J. (2008). The impact of leadership on student outcomes: An analysis of the differential effects of leadership types. *Educational Administration Quarterly, 44*(5), 635–674. https://doi.org/10.1177/0013161X08321509

Roeser, R. W., Mashburn, A. J., Skinner, E. A., Choles, J. R., Taylor, C., Rickert, N. P., et al. (2022). Mindfulness training improves middle school teachers' occupational health, well-being, and interactions with students in their most stressful classrooms. *Journal of Educational Psychology, 114*(2), 408–425. https://psycnet.apa.org/doi/10.1037/edu0000675

Rohrer, D., Dedrick, R. F., & Hartwig, M. K. (2020). The scarcity of interleaved practice in mathematics textbooks. *Educational Psychology Review, 32*(3), 873–883. https://doi.org/10.1007/s10648-020-09516-2

Roos, A.-L., Goetz, T., Voracek, M., Krannich, M., Bieg, M., Jarrell, A., et al. (2021). Test anxiety and physiological arousal: A systematic review and meta-analysis. *Educational Psychology Review, 33*(2), 579–618. https://doi.org/10.1007/s10648-020-09543-z

Rosenthal, R., & Jacobson, L. (1968). *Pygmalion in the classroom: Teacher expectation and pupils' intellectual development.* New York: Holt, Rinehart & Winston.

Rothman, R. (2013). *Fewer, clearer, higher: How the Common Core State Standards can change classroom practice.* Cambridge, MA: Harvard Education Press.

Rowland, C. A. (2014). The effect of testing versus restudy on retention: A meta-analytic review of the testing effect. *Psychological Bulletin, 140*(6), 1432–1463. https://psycnet.apa.org/doi/10.1037/a0037559

Rowley, S. J., Ross, L., Lozada, F. T., Williams, A., Gale, A., & Kurtz-Costes, B. (2014). Framing Black boys: Parent, teacher, and student narratives of the academic lives of Black boys. In L. S. Liben & R. S. Bigler (Eds.), *Advances in child development and behavior* (Vol. 47, pp. 301–332). New York: Elsevier. https://doi.org/10.1016/bs.acdb.2014.05.003

Rubie-Davies, C. M. (2007). Classroom interactions: Exploring the practices of high- and low-expectation teachers. *British Journal of Educational Psychology, 77*(2), 289–306. https://doi.org/10.1348/000709906X101601

Rubie-Davies, C. M. (2010). Teacher expectations and perceptions of student attributes: Is there a relationship? *British Journal of Educational Psychology, 80*(1), 121–135. https://doi.org/10.1348/000709909X466334

Rubie-Davies, C., Hattie, J., & Hamilton, R. (2006). Expecting the best for students: Teacher expectations and academic outcomes. *British Journal of Educational Psychology, 76*(3), 429–444. https://doi.org/10.1348/000709905X53589

Rubie-Davies, C. M., Peterson, E. R., Sibley, C. G., & Rosenthal, R. (2015). A teacher expectation intervention: Modelling the practices of high expectation teachers. *Contemporary Educational Psychology, 40*, 72–85. https://doi.org/10.1016/j.cedpsych.2014.03.003

Ryan, R. M., & Deci, E. L. (2000). Intrinsic and extrinsic motivations: Classic definitions and new directions. *Contemporary Educational Psychology, 25*(1), 54–67. https://doi.org/10.1006/ceps.1999.1020

Ryan, R. M., & Deci, E. L. (2017). *Self-determination theory: Basic psychological needs in motivation, development, and wellness.* New York: Guilford.

Ryan, R. M., & Deci, E. L. (2020). Intrinsic and extrinsic motivation from a self-determination theory perspective: Definitions, theory, practices, and future directions. *Contemporary Educational Psychology, 61*, Article 101860. https://doi.org/10.1016/j.cedpsych.2020.101860

Scheerens, J., Witziers, B., & Steen, R. (2013). A meta-analysis of school effectiveness studies. *Revista de Educación, 361*, 619–645. https://doi.org/10.4438/1988-592X-RE-2013-361-235

Schiefele, U. (2009). Situational and individual interest. In K. R. Wenzel & A. Wigfield (Eds.), *Handbook of motivation at school* (pp. 197–222). New York: Routledge.

Schmeichel, B. J. (2007). Attention control, memory updating, and emotion regulation temporarily reduce the capacity for executive control. *Journal of Experimental Psychology: General, 136*(2), 241–255. https://doi.org/10.1037/0096-3445.136.2.241

Schneider, S., Beege, M., Nebel, S., Schnaubert, L., & Rey, G. D. (2022). The Cognitive-Affective-Social Theory of Learning in digital Environments (CASTLE). *Educational Psychology Review, 34*(1), 1–18. https://doi.org/10.1007/s10648-021-09626-5

Schonert-Reichl, K. A. (2017). Social and emotional learning and teachers. *The Future of Children, 27*(1), 137–155. http://dx.doi.org/10.1353/foc.2017.0007

Schroeder, N. L., Nesbit, J. C., Anguiano, C. J., & Adesope, O. O. (2018). Studying and constructing concept maps: A meta-analysis. *Educational Psychology Review*, *30*(2), 431–455. https://doi.org/10.1007/s10648-017-9403-9

Schunk, D. H., & Zimmerman, B. J. (1997). Developing self-efficacious readers and writers: The role of social and self-regulatory processes. In J. T. Guthrie & A. Wigfield (Eds.), *Reading engagement: Motivating readers through integrated instruction* (pp. 34–50). Newark, DE: International Reading Association.

Seidel, T., Schnitzler, K., Kosel, C., Stürmer, K., & Holzberger, D. (2021). Student characteristics in the eyes of teachers: Differences between novice and expert teachers in judgment accuracy, observed behavioral cues, and gaze. *Educational Psychology Review*, *33*(1), 69–89. https://doi.org/10.1007/s10648-020-09532-2

Senko, C. (2016). Achievement goal theory: A story of early promises, eventual discords, and future possibilities. In K. Wentzel & D. B. Miele (Eds.), *Handbook of motivation at school* (2nd ed., pp. 75–95). New York: Routledge.

Shin, H. S., & Jeong, A. (2021). Modeling the relationship between students' prior knowledge, causal reasoning processes, and quality of causal maps. *Computers & Education*, *163*, Article 104113. https://doi.org/10.1016/j.compedu.2020.104113

Shin, S. H., Slater, C. L., & Backhoff, E. (2013). Principal perceptions and student achievement in reading in Korea, Mexico, and the United States: Educational leadership, school autonomy, and use of test results. *Educational Administration Quarterly*, *49*(3), 489–527.

Shuman, V., & Scherer, K. R. (2014). Concepts and structures of emotions. In R. Pekrun, & L. Linnenbrink-Garcia (Eds.), *International handbook of emotions in education* (pp. 13–35). New York: Routledge.

Siegler, R. S. (2002). Microgenetic studies of self-explanation. In N. Granott & J. Parziale (Eds.), *Microdevelopment: Transition processes in development and learning* (pp. 31–58). Cambridge, United Kingdom: Cambridge University Press.

Simms, J. A. (2016). *The critical concepts: English language arts, mathematics, and science*. Centennial, CO: Marzano Resources. Accessed at https://www.marzanoresources.com/the-critical-concepts.html on July 17, 2023.

Simonsmeier, B. A., Flaig, M., Deiglmayr, A., Schalk, L., & Schneider, M. (2022). Domain-specific prior knowledge and learning: A meta-analysis. *Educational Psychologist*, *57*(1), 31–54. https://doi.org/10.1080/00461520.2021.1939700

Sireci, S. G. (2021). NCME presidential address 2020: Valuing educational measurement. *Educational Measurement: Issues and Practice*, *40*(1), 7–16. https://doi.org/10.1111/emip.12415

Sklad, M., Diekstra, R., De Ritter, M., Ben, J., & Gravesteijn, C. (2012). Effectiveness of school-based universal social, emotional, and behavioral programs: Do they enhance students' development in the area of skill, behavior, and adjustment? *Psychology in the Schools*, *49*(9), 892–909. https://doi.org/10.1002/pits.21641

Skulmowski, A., & Rey, G. D. (2018). Embodied learning: Introducing a taxonomy based on bodily engagement and task integration. *Cognitive Research: Principles and Implications*, *3*(1), Article 6. https://doi.org/10.1186/s41235-018-0092-9

Slavin, R. E. (2020). How evidence-based reform will transform research and practice in education. *Educational Psychologist*, *55*(1), 21–31. https://doi.org/10.1080/00461520.2019.1611432

Slavin, R., & Smith, D. (2009). The relationship between sample sizes and effect sizes in systematic reviews in education. *Educational Evaluation and Policy Analysis*, *31*(4), 500–506. https://doi.org/10.3102/0162373709352369

Soncini, A., Visintin, E. P., Matteucci, M. C., Tomasetto, C., & Butera, F. (2022). Positive error climate promotes learning outcomes through students' adaptive reactions towards errors. *Learning and Instruction, 80*, Article 101627. https://doi.org/10.1016/j.learninstruc.2022.101627

Song, M., Zeiser, K., Atchison, D., & Brodziak de los Reyes, I. (2021). Early college, continued success: Longer-term impact of early college high schools. *Journal of Research on Educational Effectiveness, 14*(1), 116–142. https://doi.org/10.1080/19345747.2020.1862374

Sonnentag, S. (2001). Work, recovery activities, and individual well-being: A diary study. *Journal of Occupational Health Psychology, 6*(3), 196–210. https://doi.org/10.1037//1076-8998.6.3.196

Sonnentag, S., & Fritz, C. (2015). Recovery from job stress: The stressor-detachment model as an integrative framework. *Journal of Organizational Behavior, 36*(S1), S72–S103. https://doi.org/10.1002/job.1924

Sonnentag, S., & Kruel, U. (2006). Psychological detachment from work during off-job time: The role of job stressors, job involvement, and recovery-related self-efficacy. *European Journal of Work & Organizational Psychology, 15*(2), 197–217. https://doi.org/10.1080/13594320500513939

Sotola, L. K., & Crede, M. (2021). Regarding class quizzes: A meta-analytic synthesis of studies on the relationship between frequent low-stakes testing and class performance. *Educational Psychology Review, 33*(2), 407–426. https://doi.org/10.1007/s10648-020-09563-9

Spanjers, I. A. E., Könings, K. D., Leppink, J., Verstegen, D. M. L., de Jong, N., Czabanowska, K., et al. (2015). The promised land of blended learning: Quizzes as a moderator. *Educational Research Review, 15*, 59–74. https://doi.org/10.1016/j.edurev.2015.05.001

Spitzer, H. F. (1939). Studies in retention. *Journal of Educational Psychology, 30*(9), 641–656. Accessed at https://psycnet.apa.org/doi/10.1037/h0063404 on July 17, 2023.

SRI International. (2018, November). *Using technology to personalize learning in K–12 schools.* Menlo Park, CA: Author. Accessed at https://www.sri.com/wp-content/uploads/2021/12/using-technology-personalize-learning-k-12-schools.pdf on July 17, 2023.

Stahnke, R., & Blömeke, S. (2021). Novice and expert teachers' noticing of classroom management in whole-group and partner work activities: Evidence from teachers' gaze and identification of events. *Learning and Instruction, 74*, Article 101464. https://doi.org/10.1016/j.learninstruc.2021.101464

Stanovich, K. E. (2016). The comprehensive assessment of rational thinking. *Educational Psychologist, 51*(1), 23–34. https://doi.org/10.1080/00461520.2015.1125787

Starck, J. G., Riddle, T., Sinclair, S., & Warikoo, N. (2020). Teachers are people too: Examining the racial bias of teachers compared to other American adults. *Educational Researcher, 49*(4), 273–284. https://doi.org/10.3102/0013189X20912758

Steele, C. M., & Aronson, J. (1995). Stereotype threat and the intellectual test performance of African Americans. *Journal of Personality and Social Psychology, 69*(5), 797–811. https://doi.org/10.1037//0022-3514.69.5.797

Steenbergen-Hu, S., Makel, M. C., & Olszewski-Kubilius, P. (2016). What one hundred years of research says about the effects of ability grouping and acceleration on K–12 students' academic achievement: Findings of two second-order meta-analyses. *Review of Educational Research, 86*(4), 849–899. https://doi.org/10.3102/0034654316675417

Stringfield, S. (1995). Attempts to enhance students' learning: A search for valid programs and high-reliability implementation techniques. *School Effectiveness and School Improvement, 6*(1), 67–96.

Stringfield, S., Reynolds, D., & Schaffer, E. C. (2008). *Improving secondary students' academic achievement through a focus on reform reliability: Four- and nine-year findings from the High Reliability Schools project.* Berkshire, United Kingdom: CfBT Education Trust.

Stringfield, S., Reynolds, D., & Schaffer, E. (2012). Making best practice standard—and lasting. *Phi Delta Kappan, 94*(1), 45–50.

Stoll, L., Bolam, R., McMahon, A., Wallace, M., & Thomas, S. (2006). Professional learning communities: A review of the literature. *Journal of Educational Change, 7*(4), 221–258.

Studhalter, U. T., Leuchter, M., Tettenborn, A., Elmer, A., Edelsbrunner, P. A., & Saalbach, H. (2021). Early science learning: The effects of teacher talk. *Learning and Instruction, 71,* Article 101371. https://doi.org/10.1016/j.learninstruc.2020.101371

Sun, J., Anderson, R. C., Lin, T.-J., Morris, J. A., Miller, B. W., Ma, S., et al. (2022). Children's engagement during collaborative learning and direct instruction through the lens of participant structure. *Contemporary Educational Psychology, 69,* Article 102061. https://doi.org/10.1016/j.cedpsych.2022.102061

Sweller, J., & Levine, M. (1982). Effects of goal specificity on means-ends analysis and learning. *Journal of Experimental Psychology: Learning, Memory, and Cognition, 8*(5), 463–474. https://doi.org/10.1037/0278-7393.8.5.463

Sweller, J., van Merriënboer, J. J. G., & Paas, F. (1998). Cognitive architecture and instructional design. *Educational Psychology Review, 10*(3), 251–296. https://doi.org/10.1023/A:1022193728205

Sweller, J., van Merriënboer, J. J. G., & Paas, F. (2019). Cognitive architecture and instructional design: 20 years later. *Educational Psychology Review, 31*(2), 261–292. https://doi.org/10.1007/s10648-019-09465-5

Szumski, G., Smogorzewska, J., & Karwowski, M. (2017). Academic achievement of students without special educational needs in inclusive classrooms: A meta-analysis. *Educational Research Review, 21,* 33–54. https://doi.org/10.1016/j.edurev.2017.02.004

Tach, L. M., & Farkas, G. (2006). Learning-related behaviors, cognitive skills, and ability grouping when schooling begins. *Social Science Research, 35*(4), 1048–1079. https://doi.org/10.1016/j.ssresearch.2005.08.001

Tan, C. Y., Gao, L., & Shi, M. (2022). Second-order meta-analysis synthesizing the evidence on associations between school leadership and different school outcomes. *Educational Management Administration & Leadership, 50*(3), 469–490. https://doi.org/10.1177/1741143220935456

Taris, T. W. (2006). Is there a relationship between burnout and objective performance? A critical review of 16 studies. *Work & Stress, 20*(4), 316–334. https://doi.org/10.1080/02678370601065893

Taxer, J. L., & Frenzel, A. C. (2015). Facets of teachers' emotional lives: A quantitative investigation of teachers' genuine, faked, and hidden emotions. *Teaching and Teacher Education, 49,* 78–88. https://doi.org/10.1016/j.tate.2015.03.003

Taylor, V. J., & Walton, G. M. (2011). Stereotype threat undermines academic learning. *Personality and Social Psychology Bulletin, 37*(8), 1055–1067. https://doi.org/10.1177/0146167211406506

Tenenbaum, H. R., & Ruck, M. D. (2007). Are teachers' expectations different for racial minority than for European American students? A meta-analysis. *Journal of Educational Psychology, 99*(2), 253–273. https://doi.org/10.1037/0022-0663.99.2.253

Thiede, K. W., Wright, K. L., Hagenah, S., Wenner, J., Abbott, J., & Arechiga, A. (2022). Drawing to improve metacomprehension accuracy. *Learning and Instruction, 77,* Article 101541. https://doi.org/10.1016/j.learninstruc.2021.101541

Thorndike, E. L. (1906). *The principles of teaching based on psychology.* New York: A. G. Seiler.

Tian, J., Braithwaite, D. W., & Siegler, R. S. (2021). Distributions of textbook problems predict student learning: Data from decimal arithmetic. *Journal of Educational Psychology, 113*(3), 516–529. http://dx.doi.org/10.1037/edu0000618

Travers, C. J., Morisano, D., & Locke, E. A. (2015). Self-reflection, growth goals, and academic outcomes: A qualitative study. *British Journal of Educational Psychology, 85*(2), 224–241. https://doi.org/10.1111/bjep.12059

Trigwell, K. (2012). Relations between teachers' emotions in teaching and their approaches to teaching in higher education. *Instructional Science, 40*(3), 607–621. https://doi.org/10.1007/s11251-011-9192-3

Tulis, M., Steuer, G., & Dresel, M. (2016). Learning from errors: A model of individual processes. *Frontline Learning Research, 4*(2), 12–26.

Türktorun, Y. Z., Weiher, G. M., & Horz, H. (2020). Psychological detachment and work-related rumination in teachers: A systematic review. *Educational Research Review, 31,* Article 100354. https://doi.org/10.1016/j.edurev.2020.100354

Tyler, J. M., & Burns, K. C. (2008). After depletion: The replenishment of the self's regulatory resources. *Self and Identity, 7*(3), 305–321. https://doi.org/10.1080/15298860701799997

Tze, V. M. C., Daniels, L. M., & Klassen, R. M. (2016). Evaluating the relationship between boredom and academic outcomes: A meta-analysis. *Educational Psychology Review, 28*(1), 119–144. https://doi.org/10.1007/s10648-015-9301-y

Umansky, I. M., & Dumont, H. (2021). English learner labeling: How English learner classification in kindergarten shapes teacher perceptions of student skills and the moderating role of bilingual instructional settings. *American Educational Research Journal, 58*(5), 993–1031. https://doi.org/10.3102/0002831221997571

Urdan, T., & Kaplan, A. (2020). The origins, evolution, and future directions of achievement goal theory. *Contemporary Educational Psychology, 61,* Article 101862. https://doi.org/10.1016/j.cedpsych.2020.101862

Urhahne, D., & Wijnia, L. (2021). A review on the accuracy of teacher judgments. *Educational Research Review, 32,* Article 100374. https://doi.org/10.1016/j.edurev.2020.100374

U.S. Department of Education. (2010). *Transforming American education: Learning powered by technology.* Washington, DC: Office of Educational Technology. Accessed at http://www.ed.gov/sites/default/files/netp2010.pdf on July 17, 2023.

U.S. Department of Education. (2016). *Future ready learning: Reimagining the role of technology in education.* Washington, DC: Office of Educational Technology. Accessed at http://tech.ed.gov/files/2015/12/NETP16.pdf on July 17, 2023.

Uysal, S., & Sarier, Y. (2018). Meta-analysis of school leadership effects on student achievement in USA and Turkey. *Cypriot Journal of Educational Sciences, 13*(4), 590–603. https://doi.org/10.18844/cjes.v13i4.3539

Vandenberg, J., Zakaria, Z., Tsan, J., Iwanski, A., Lynch, C., Boyer, K. E., et al. (2021). Prompting collaborative and exploratory discourse: An epistemic network analysis study. *International Journal of Computer-Supported Collaborative Learning, 16*(3), 339–366. https://doi.org/10.1007/s11412-021-09349-3

van Gog, T., Hoogerheide, V., & van Harsel, M. (2020). The role of mental effort in fostering self-regulated learning with problem-solving tasks. *Educational Psychology Review, 32*(4), 1055–1072. https://doi.org/10.1007/s10648-020-09544-y

VanLehn, K., Siler, S., Murray, C., Yamauchi, T., & Baggett, W. (2003). Why do only some events cause learning during human tutoring? *Cognition and Instruction, 21*(3), 209–249. https://doi.org/10.1207/S1532690XCI2103_01

VanWeelden, K., & Whipple, J. (2007). Preservice music teachers' predictions, perceptions, and assessment of students with special needs: The need for training in student assessment. *Journal of Music Therapy, 44*(1), 74–84. https://doi.org/10.1093/jmt/44.1.74

Villena-Taranilla, R., Tirado-Olivares, S., Cózar-Gutiérrez, R., & González-Calero, J. A. (2022). Effects of virtual reality on learning outcomes in K–6 education: A meta-analysis. *Educational Research Review, 35,* Article 100434. https://doi.org/10.1016/j.edurev.2022.100434

Voelkel, R. H., & Chrispeels, J. H. (2017). Within-school differences in professional learning community effectiveness: Implications for leadership. *Journal of School Leadership, 27*(3), 424–451.

Volante, L., DeLuca, C., Adie, L., Baker, E., Harju-Luukkainen, H., Heritage, M., et al. (2020). Synergy and tension between large-scale and classroom assessment: International trends. *Educational Measurement: Issues and Practice, 39*(4), 21–29. https://doi.org/10.1111/emip.12382

Voss, T., Zachrich, L., Fauth, B., & Wittwer, J. (2022). The same yet different? Teaching quality differs across a teacher's classes, but teachers with higher knowledge make teaching quality more similar. *Learning and Instruction, 80,* Article 101614. https://doi.org/10.1016/j.learninstruc.2022.101614

Walraven, A., Brand-Gruwel, S., & Boshuizen, H. P. A. (2013). Fostering students' evaluation behaviour while searching the internet. *Instructional Science, 41*(1), 125–146.

Wang, B., Ginns, P., & Mockler, N. (2022). Sequencing tracing with imagination. *Educational Psychology Review, 34*(1), 421–449. https://doi.org/10.1007/s10648-021-09625-6

Wang, H., Hall, N. C., & Taxer, J. L. (2019). Antecedents and consequences of teachers' emotional labor: A systematic review and meta-analytic investigation. *Educational Psychology Review, 31*(3), 663–698. https://doi.org/10.1007/s10648-019-09475-3

Wang, X., Mayer, R. E., Zhou, P., & Lin, L. (2021). Benefits of interactive graphic organizers in online learning: Evidence for generative learning theory. *Journal of Educational Psychology, 113*(5), 1024–1037. http://dx.doi.org/10.1037/edu0000606

Watt, H. M. G., Butler, R., & Richardson, P. W. (2021). Antecedents and consequences of teachers' goal profiles in Australia and Israel. *Learning and Instruction, 76,* Article 101491. https://doi.org/10.1016/j.learninstruc.2021.101491

Webb, N. L. (1997). *Criteria for alignment of expectations and assessments in mathematics and science education* (Research Monograph No. 6). Washington, DC: Council of Chief State School Officers.

Webb, N. L. (2007). Issues related to judging the alignment of curriculum standards and assessments. *Applied Measurement in Education, 20*(1), 7–25.

Wedin, Å. (2010). A restricted curriculum for second language learners—A self-fulfilling teacher strategy? *Language and Education, 24*(3), 171–183. https://doi.org/10.1080/09500780903026352

Wegner, D. M. (1987). Transactive memory: A contemporary analysis of the group mind. In B. Mullen & G. R. Goethals (Eds.), *Theories of group behaviour* (pp.185–208). New York: Springer Verlag.

Weick, K. E., & Sutcliffe, K. M. (2007). *Managing the unexpected: Resilient performance in an age of uncertainty* (2nd ed.). San Francisco: Jossey-Bass.

Weick, K. E., Sutcliffe, K. M., & Obstfeld, D. (1999). Organizing for high reliability: Processes of collective mindfulness. *Research in Organizational Behavior, 1,* 81–123.

Weinstein, R. S. (2002). *Reaching higher: The power of expectations in schooling.* Cambridge, MA: Harvard University Press.

Weir, K. (2016, November). Inequality at school. *Monitor on Psychology, 47*(10), 42–47. Accessed at https://www.apa.org/monitor/2016/11/cover-inequality-school on July 17, 2023.

Welch, C. J., & Dunbar, S. B. (2020). Alignment and implications for test takers. *Educational Measurement: Issues and Practice, 39*(2), 8–17. https://doi.org/10.1111/emip.12332

Wen, C.-T., Liu, C.-C., Chang, H.-Y., Chang, C.-J., Chang, M.-H., Chiang, S.-H. F., et al. (2020). Students' guided inquiry with simulation and its relation to school science achievement and scientific literacy. *Computers & Education, 149*, Article 103830. https://doi.org/10.1016/j.compedu.2020.103830

Wendsche, J., & Lohmann-Haislah, A. (2017). A meta-analysis on antecedents and outcomes of detachment from work. *Frontiers in Psychology, 7.* https://doi.org/10.3389/fpsyg.2016.02072

West, M. R., Pier, L., Fricke, H., Hough, H., Loeb, S., Meyer, R. H., et al. (2020). Trends in student social-emotional learning: Evidence from the first large-scale panel student survey. *Educational Evaluation and Policy Analysis, 42*(2), 279–303. https://doi.org/10.3102/0162373720912236

Westermann, K., & Rummel, N. (2012). Delaying instruction: Evidence from a study in a university relearning setting. *Instructional Science, 40*(4), 673–689.

Westminster Public Schools. (2023). *Westminster instructional model.* Westminster, CO: Author.

Westphal, A., Becker, M., Vock, M., Maaz, K., Neumann, M., & McElvany, N. (2016). The link between teacher-assigned grades and classroom socioeconomic composition: The role of classroom behavior, motivation, and teacher characteristics. *Contemporary Educational Psychology, 46*, 218–227. https://doi.org/10.1016/j.cedpsych.2016.06.004

What Works Clearinghouse. (2017). *What Works Clearinghouse standards handbook version 4.0.* Washington, DC: Institute of Education Sciences, U.S. Department of Education.

White, R., Russell, G., Qualter, P., Owens, M., & Psychogiou, L. (2021). Do peer relationships mediate the association between children's facial emotion recognition ability and their academic attainment? Findings from the ALSPAC study. *Contemporary Educational Psychology, 64*, Article 101942. https://doi.org/10.1016/j.cedpsych.2021.101942

Widlund, A., Tuominen, H., & Korhonen, J. (2021). Development of school engagement and burnout across lower and upper secondary education: Trajectory profiles and educational outcomes. *Contemporary Educational Psychology, 66*, Article 101997. https://doi.org/10.1016/j.cedpsych.2021.101997

Wineburg, S., & McGrew, S. (2017). *Lateral reading: Reading less and learning more when evaluating digital information* (Working Paper No. 2017-A1). Stanford, CA: Stanford History Education Group. https://doi.org/10.2139/ssrn.3048994

Wing, J. (2006, March). Computational thinking. *Communications of the ACM, 49*(3), 33–35. https://doi.org/10.1145/1118178.1118215

Wing, J. (2011). Research notebook: Computational thinking—What and why? *The Link Magazine.* Accessed at https://www.cs.cmu.edu/link/research-notebook-computational-thinking-what-and-why on November 12, 2023.

Winne, P. H., & Hadwin, A. F. (1998). Studying as self-regulated learning. In D. J. Hacker, J. Dunlosky, & A. C. Graesser (Eds.), *Metacognition in educational theory and practice* (pp. 277–304). Hillsdale, NJ: Erlbaum.

Witziers, B., Bosker, R. J., & Krüger, M. L. (2003). Educational leadership and student achievement: The elusive search for an association. *Educational Administration Quarterly, 39*(3), 398–425. https://doi.org/10.1177/0013161X03253411

Wolf, R., Morrison, J., Inns, A., Slavin, R., & Risman, K. (2020). Average effect sizes in developer-commissioned and independent evaluations. *Journal of Research on Educational Effectiveness, 13*(2), 428–447. https://doi.org/10.1080/19345747.2020.1726537

Wolff, C. E., Jarodzka, H., & Boshuizen, H. P. A. (2021). Classroom management scripts: A theoretical model contrasting expert and novice teachers' knowledge and awareness of classroom events. *Educational Psychology Review, 33*(1), 131–148. https://doi.org/10.1007/s10648-020-09542-0

Wong, Z. Y., & Liem, G. A. D. (2022). Student engagement: Current state of the construct, conceptual refinement, and future research directions. *Educational Psychology Review, 34*(1), 107–138. https://doi.org/10.1007/s10648-021-09628-3

Wu, H., & Shen, J. (2022). The association between principal leadership and student achievement: A multivariate meta-meta-analysis. *Educational Research Review, 35*, Article 100423. https://doi.org/10.1016/j.edurev.2021.100423

Wyss, C., Rosenberger, K., & Bührer, W. (2021). Student teachers' and teacher educators' professional vision: Findings from an eye tracking study. *Educational Psychology Review, 33*(1), 91–107. https://doi.org/10.1007/s10648-020-09535-z

Xu, Z., Zhao, Y., Zhang, B., Liew, J., & Kogut, A. (2022). A meta-analysis of the efficacy of self-regulated learning interventions on academic achievement in online and blended environments in K–12 and higher education. *Behaviour and Information Technology*. https://doi.org/10.1080/0144929X.2022.2151935

Yeager, D. S., & Dweck, C. S. (2012). Mindsets that promote resilience: When students believe that personal characteristics can be developed. *Educational Psychologist, 47*(4), 302–314. https://doi.org/10.1080/00461520.2012.722805

Yin, H., Lee, J. C. K., Zhang, Z., & Jin, Y. (2013). Exploring the relationship among teachers' emotional intelligence, emotional labor strategies and teaching satisfaction. *Teaching and Teacher Education, 35*, 137–145. https://doi.org/10.1016/j.tate.2013.06.006

Yu, J., Kreijkes, P., & Salmela-Aro, K. (2022). Students' growth mindset: Relation to teacher beliefs, teaching practices, and school climate. *Learning and Instruction, 80*, Article 101616. https://doi.org/10.1016/j.learninstruc.2022.101616

Yurkofsky, M. M., Peterson, A. J., Mehta, J. D., Horwitz-Willis, R., & Frumin, K. M. (2020). Research on continuous improvement: Exploring the complexities of managing educational change. *Review of Research in Education, 44*(1), 403–433. https://doi.org/10.3102/0091732X20907363

Zavala, J., & Kuhn, D. (2017). Solitary discourse is a productive activity. *Psychological Science, 28*(5), 578–586. https://doi.org/10.1177/0956797616689248

Zembylas, M. (2002). Constructing genealogies of teachers' emotions in science teaching. *Journal of Research in Science Teaching, 39*(1), 79–103. https://doi.org/10.1002/tea.10010

Zhang, S., & Duke, N. K. (2011). The impact of instruction in the WWWDOT framework on students' disposition and ability to evaluate web sites as sources of information. *The Elementary School Journal, 112*(1), 132–154. https://doi.org/10.1086/660687

Zhao, L., Mao, H., Compton, B. J., Peng, J., Fu, G., Fang, F., et al. (2022). Academic dishonesty and its relations to peer cheating and culture: A meta-analysis of the perceived peer cheating effect. *Educational Research Review, 36*, Article 100455. https://doi.org/10.1016/j.edurev.2022.100455

Zheng, L. (2016). The effectiveness of self-regulated learning scaffolds on academic performance in computer-based learning environments: A meta-analysis. *Asia Pacific Education Review, 17*(2), 187–202. https://doi.org/10.1007/s12564-016-9426-9

Zimmerman, B. J. (2000). Attaining self-regulation: A social cognitive perspective. In M. Boekaerts, P. R. Pintrich, & M. Zeidner (Eds.), *Handbook of self-regulation* (pp. 13–39). San Diego, CA: Academic Press. http://dx.doi.org/10.1016/B978-012109890-2/50031-7

INDEX

The New Art and Science of Teaching Reading
Julia A. Simms and Robert J. Marzano
The New Art and Science of Teaching Reading presents a compelling model for reading development structured around five key topic areas. More than 100 reading-focused instructional strategies are laid out in detail to help teachers ensure every student becomes a proficient reader.
BKF811

Questioning Sequences in the Classroom
Robert J. Marzano and Julia A. Simms
Ask targeted questions to enhance students' reasoning skills and increase rigor in classrooms. You'll discover a four-phase questioning sequence that helps students make claims, build sound arguments, and provide evidence to support their points.
BKL018

The Handbook for the New Art and Science of Teaching
Robert J. Marzano
Rely on this comprehensive guide to help you implement the teaching methods of Robert J. Marzano's *The New Art and Science of Teaching* framework, with over 330 instructional strategies. Each chapter outlines actionable steps, tips, and examples to help you succeed with this powerful model in your classroom.
BKF844

Making Classroom Assessments Reliable and Valid
Robert J. Marzano
Classroom assessments (CAs) have key advantages over large-scale interim, end-of-course, and state assessments. This resource details why CAs should become the primary method for formally measuring student learning and outlines how to revamp your CAs to ensure validity and reliability.
BKF789

Motivating and Inspiring Students
Robert J. Marzano, Darrell Scott, Tina H. Boogren, and Ming Lee Newcomb
Bringing motivation and inspiration to the classroom is not easy. With this practical resource, you'll discover a results-driven framework—based on a six-level hierarchy of student needs and goals—that you can use to provide engaging instruction to students.
BKL025

MARZANO Resources

Visit MarzanoResources.com or call 888.849.0851 to order.